COMPUTER VISION FOR MICROSCOPY IMAGE ANALYSIS

Computer Vision and Pattern Recognition Series

Series Editors

Horst Bischof	Institute for Computer Graphics and Vision, Graz University of Technology, Austria
Kyoung Mu	Department of Electrical and Computer Engineering, Seoul National University, Republic of Korea
Sudeep Sarkar	Department of Computer Science and Engineering, University of South Florida, Tampa, United States

Also in the Series:

Lin and Zhang, Low-Rank Models in Visual Analysis: Theories, Algorithms and Applications, 2017, ISBN: 9780128127315

Zheng et al., Statistical Shape and Deformation Analysis: Methods, Implementation and Applications, 2017, ISBN: 9780128104934

De Marsico et al., Human Recognition in Unconstrained Environments: Using Computer Vision, Pattern Recognition and Machine Learning Methods for Biometrics, 2017, ISBN: 9780081007051

Saha et al., Skeletonization: Theory, Methods and Applications, 2017, ISBN: 9780081012918

Zheng et al., Statistical Shape and Deformation Analysis: Methods, Implementation and Applications, 2017, ISBN: 9780128104934

Murino et al., Group and Crowd Behavior for Computer Vision, 2017, ISBN: 9780128092767

Leo and Farinella, Computer Vision for Assistive Healthcare, 2018, ISBN: 9780128134450

Alameda-Pineda et al., Multimodal Behavior Analysis in the Wild, 2019, Advances and Challenges, ISBN: 9780128146019

Wang et al., Deep Learning Through Sparse and Low-Rank Modeling, 2019, ISBN: 9780128136591

Ying Yang, Multimodal Scene Understanding: Algorithms, Applications and Deep Learning, 2019, ISBN: 9780128173589

Hua et al., Spectral Geometry of Shapes: Principles and Applications, 2019, ISBN: 9780128138427

Computer Vision and Pattern Recognition

COMPUTER VISION FOR MICROSCOPY IMAGE ANALYSIS

Edited by

MEI CHEN

Principal Research Manager, Microsoft, Redmond, Washington, USA

Academic Press is an imprint of Elsevier
125 London Wall, London EC2Y 5AS, United Kingdom
525 B Street, Suite 1650, San Diego, CA 92101, United States
50 Hampshire Street, 5th Floor, Cambridge, MA 02139, United States
The Boulevard, Langford Lane, Kidlington, Oxford OX5 1GB, United Kingdom

Notices
Knowledge and best practice in this field are constantly changing. As new research and experience broaden our
understanding, changes in research methods, professional practices, or medical treatment may become necessary.

Practitioners and researchers must always rely on their own experience and knowledge in evaluating and using any
information, methods, compounds, or experiments described herein. In using such information or methods they
should be mindful of their own safety and the safety of others, including parties for whom they have a professional
responsibility.

To the fullest extent of the law, neither the Publisher nor the authors, contributors, or editors, assume any liability for
any injury and/or damage to persons or property as a matter of products liability, negligence or otherwise, or from
any use or operation of any methods, products, instructions, or ideas contained in the material herein.

Library of Congress Cataloging-in-Publication Data
A catalog record for this book is available from the Library of Congress

British Library Cataloguing-in-Publication Data
A catalogue record for this book is available from the British Library

ISBN 978-0-12-814972-0

For information on all Academic Press publications
visit our website at https://www.elsevier.com/books-and-journals

Publisher: Mara Conner
Acquisitions Editor: Tim Pitts
Editorial Project Manager: John Leonard
Production Project Manager: Kamesh Ramajogi
Cover Designer: Mark Rogers

Typeset by SPi Global, India

Contents

Dimitris Metaxas, Hui Qu, Gregory Riedlinger, Pengxiang Wu, Qiaoying Huang, Jingru Yi, and Subhajyoti De

Mei Chen

Contributors

Peter Bajcsy
Information Technology Laboratory, National Institute of Standards and Technology, Gaithersburg, MD, United States

Mary Brady
Information Technology Laboratory, National Institute of Standards and Technology, Gaithersburg, MD, United States

Weidong Cai
The University of Sydney, School of Computer Science, Darlington, NSW, Australia

Joe Chalfoun
Information Technology Laboratory, National Institute of Standards and Technology, Gaithersburg, MD, United States

Mei Chen
Microsoft, Redmond, WA, United States

Subhajyoti De
Rutgers Cancer Institute of New Jersey, New Brunswick, NJ, United States

Daniel J. Hoeppner
Astellas Research Institute of America, La Jolla Laboratory, San Diego, CA, United States

Qiaoying Huang
Rutgers University, Department of Computer Science, Piscataway, NJ, United States

Marcin Kociolek
Lodz University of Technology, Lodz, Poland

An-An Liu
Tianjin University, School of Electrical and Information Engineering, Tianjin, China

Yao Lu
Tianjin University, School of Electrical and Information Engineering, Tianjin, China

Dimitris Metaxas
Rutgers University, Department of Computer Science, Piscataway, NJ, United States

Hui Qu
Rutgers University, Department of Computer Science, Piscataway, NJ, United States

Nisha Ramesh
University of Utah, Scientific Computing and Imaging Institute, Salt Lake City, UT, United States

Gregory Riedlinger
Rutgers Cancer Institute of New Jersey, New Brunswick, NJ, United States

Mylene Simon
Information Technology Laboratory, National Institute of Standards and Technology, Gaithersburg, MD, United States

Yang Song
University of New South Wales, School of Computer Science and Engineering, Kensington, NSW, Australia

Hang Su
Tsinghua University, Department of Computer Science and Technology, Beijing, People's Republic of China

Yu-Ting Su
Tianjin University, School of Electrical and Information Engineering, Tianjin, China

Tolga Tasdizen
University of Utah, Scientific Computing and Imaging Institute, Salt Lake City, UT, United States

Pengxiang Wu
Rutgers University, Department of Computer Science, Piscataway, NJ, United States

Jingru Yi
Rutgers University, Department of Computer Science, Piscataway, NJ, United States

Zhaozheng Yin
Stony Brook University, Department of Biomedical Informatics and Department of Computer Science, Stony Brook, NY, United States

Preface

Advances in imaging technologies have enabled the acquisition of large volumes of microscopy images and made it possible to conduct large-scale, image-based experiments for biomedical discovery. Computer vision has huge potential in automating the analysis and understanding of such large data. In 2013, professors Takeo Kanade, Phil Campbell, Lee Weiss, and I cochaired the First International Workshop on Cell Tracking, hosted at Carnegie Mellon University's Robotics Institute. It was a 1.5 day by-invitation workshop that drew overwhelmingly positive feedback from the more than 50 attendees across academia, government, and industry. Encouraged by this success, in 2016 I chaired the First IEEE Workshop on Computer Vision for Microcopy Image Analysis (CVMI), held in conjunction with the high-impact IEEE Conference on Computer Vision and Pattern Recognition (CVPR). It was an immediate success despite being on the last afternoon of the last day of a 6-day conference. Since then, I have been able to grow CVMI into a full-day workshop at CVPR every year with sustained attendance of more than 120 participants.

It has taken a few years for all the contributors to accomplish this book project after Elsevier expressed interest at CVMI 2017, and I am proud to announce that it is both comprehensive in terms of the scope and easy to read in terms of the organization and writing. Since computer vision for microscopy image analysis is an interdisciplinary topic, we start the book with a chapter by Dr. Daniel Hoeppner presenting *A Biologist's Perspective on Computer Vision*, where he articulates the need for biologists and computer vision experts to collaborate to overcome the limits of human visual perception and enable quantitative, high-content analysis of phenotypic traits. The remaining chapters cover state-of-the-art techniques for researchers to tackle specific problems, with in-depth analysis of the pros and cons. The ordering of the chapters follows the flow of processing and analysis of microcopy images: from *Image Formation, Restoration, and Segmentation* by Drs. Zhaozheng Yin and Hang Su; to *Detection and Segmentation* by Dr. Tolga Tasdizen and team; then *Image Classification* by Drs. Yang Song and Weidong Cai; onto microscopy image sequence processing and analysis with *Cell Tracking* by me and *Mitosis Detection* by Dr. An-An Liu and team. The book concludes with *Numerical Evaluations* by Dr. Peter Bajcsy and team and an *Application to Imaging Genomics* by Dr. Dimitris Metaxas and team. Not included are traditional approaches (or the innumerable modifications of them) because they have been well covered in the literature.

It is a great honor to serve as the editor for this book, the first on this topic in more than a decade with up-to-date contemporary approaches. The contributors have made explicit efforts to emphasize how the latest state-of-the-art techniques in computer vision, especially *deep learning-based* techniques, apply to microscopy image analysis. I have learned a great deal from reading these chapters, and doing so increased my respect for and understanding of the larger challenges of employing computer vision for microscopy image analysis. I hope this book serves to attract, encourage, and enable more active researchers around the world to contribute to this exciting, promising, and challenging research topic.

I would like to express my gratitude to all the contributors and their teams, without whom the book would not have the depth and breadth it enjoys. I would also like to thank the editorial project managers at Elsevier for their guidance and patience during the process of this book project. I am confident that readers will find this book interesting, informative, actionable, and inspiring. As microscopy imaging data grow in quantity and diversity, their analysis and understanding can only grow in urgency and importance.

Happy reading.

Mei Chen
Microsoft, Redmond, WA, United States

CHAPTER 1

A biologist's perspective on computer vision

Daniel J. Hoeppner
Astellas Research Institute of America, La Jolla Laboratory, San Diego, CA, United States

Contents

1. Thesis

Biology, microscopy, and computer vision are part of a positive feedback ecosystem where progress in one provides opportunities and promotes advancement in the others. Unfortunately, development is normally responsive rather than coordinated.

2. Audience

As a computer vision-focused resource, I will assume that the reader is a student or professional practitioner of computer vision.

3. Aim

Inspire more interaction between biologists and computer vision professionals to create more impactful science.

Computer Vision for Microscopy Image Analysis
https://doi.org/10.1016/B978-0-12-814972-0.00001-1

1

4. Vision

Sydney Brenner, a major contributor to the field of developmental biology, gave a lecture at the NIH many years ago in which he both lamented and celebrated the decision of the publishers of the *Proceedings of the National Academy of Sciences* (PNAS) to end the practice of segregating papers into a separate section entitled "Biological Sciences: Developmental Biology." Using his characteristic combination of insight and humor, he argued that there was a period of time when developmental biologists would seek articles of interest in their specific field in this section. However, with time, the concepts and methodology previously unique to this niche discipline became more widely accepted and applied. Now people working in this area consider themselves biologists. Although sad to see the section disappear, Dr. Brenner actually saw this loss as a success—a graduation to the mainstream.

Practical integration of the biological subfields of developmental biology, cell biology, and molecular biology came from the power and robustness of the inventions that were reduced to practice, simplified, and transferred to related fields. It may seem far-fetched to seek parallels between this anecdotal example and the distant fields of microscopy and computer vision. However, the growing interdependence of these two disciplines predicts a union, like the subfields of biological sciences, in which future microscopists and computer vision experts identify themselves with the same job title. In 2002, Sydney Brenner, John Sulston, and Bob Horvitz received the Nobel Prize in Physiology or Medicine for their work in developmental biology of the nematode *Caenorhabditis elegans* [1–3]. This recognition was based on using a light microscope to manually trace the birth and migration of all 959 cells in living translucent normal worms (using pen and paper). The identification of genetic mutations that alter this stereotypical pattern of development was the key to their success. Tools that incorporate video recording of development with manual annotation established the robustness of these processes and enabled quantifying aberrations based on genetic mutation [4–6]. Combining the developmental biology of *C. elegans* with fluorescent reporters and computer vision, it is now possible to perform these analyses using full automation in real time [7, 8]. More recently, a landmark study using in toto analysis of early mouse development was enabled by a close collaboration of experts in biology, microscopy engineering, and computer vision [9].

5. Why biologists need computer vision experts

Prior to the advent of digital imaging and image processing, biologists recorded observations often in real time with manual event counters. In experimental systems that report a small number of discrete phenotypic (observational) classes, these measurements can be robust to replication by independent observers. However, most real-world examples have a significant gray zone that can suffer from subjective measurement.

A conceptual example is *cell passaging,* which means to count living cells when they are transferred to a fresh plate after multiplying exponentially for 3–5 days on a previous fresh plate. This procedure is performed nearly daily by most scientists who work with cell cultures. It is important to pass a specific number of living cells to the fresh plate, as the plating cell density is a critical variable affecting outcomes including cell viability, cell fate, and response to experimental variables like drugs or other perturbagens. However, the act of passaging using enzymes that cleave the connections between cells and their substrate, or other methods using low salt concentration solutions to create the same effect, kills some cells. To count the number of living and dead cells, biologists use trypan blue, an organic dye that stains dead cells dark blue but does not stain living cells. After brief staining, the cell suspension is injected into a small hematocrit chamber of known volume with the height of roughly one cell diameter, and then counted with a manual event counter. The resulting grid volume of cells displays a range of staining. Yet, when counting, the observer creates a personal intensity-based classifier in real time and counts the unstained putative viable cells. As the dead cells do not contribute to the next generation, they are excluded.

From personal experience, it is difficult to precisely replicate the counts of colleagues, as the personal definitions of "blue" are not identical. Person-to-person variability is usually not large and may or may not be impactful, but it is a common source of variability and is easy to eliminate with computer vision.

As the entrepreneurially minded reader might predict, commercial solutions have emerged that enable rapid and reproducible quantitation of cell viability using computer vision to segment objects and report the distribution of signal in each cell using a priori cutoffs for signal intensity and morphological parameters. Reduced variability results from a combination of removing observer bias, enabling measurement of far-larger numbers of cells, and employing the same classification algorithm for all measurements. These methods can readily be transferred to other research sites to standardize assessments and facilitate reproducibility.

The example of counting cells produces two dominant populations displaying high or low signals and a smaller population with intermediate signals. However, in practical terms, most biological experimental systems do not yield robustly binary events like head versus no head, but rather, they yield multiple classes or, more often, produce outputs that are best described with continuous variables. Some common examples include the assessment of cell morphology, cell size, cell contact (confluence), gene expression (fluorescence intensity, subcellular localization), and general cell vitality. This is where precise reproducible computer vision-based quantitation has the greatest benefit.

Biologists seriously consider the scale of studies during the experimental design phase, as measurement can be very time consuming. Before digital imaging became affordable, researchers might spend a full week in a dark microscopy room making measurements for a typical experiment. The idea of adding a time course with drug-dose response to the original study quickly becomes unreasonable simply because the measurement time is calculated to be a rate-limiting factor.

This author has seen the profoundly positive effect of enabling computer vision in the biology laboratory. When measurement time is no longer rate limiting, scientists begin to think less about simple experiments with a few replications, and more about arrays of experimental conditions, with subtle variations between each condition, knowing that computer vision can easily quantify the weak effect of these variations. Once reproducibility is established, they think about screening many hundreds or thousands of unknown compounds, seeking those rare compounds that repair an observable defect. The concept of phenotypic screening is addressed in this chapter, but it is important here to understand the significance of computer vision in enabling biologists to perform nonhypothesis-driven studies—you can screen a library of compounds for a specific phenotype of interest without knowing the mechanism of how to achieve this end point.

6. Why computer scientists need biologists

Computer scientists need biologists because they know which biological problems need solving. In addition, biologists can provide a greater context to a problem than simply accessing the data sets in a public repository without relevant background. As individual cellular processes are integrated into the complex biological machinery of the living cell, within living tissue, etc., with each element dependent upon context, there is a deep source of target material to work on if given prudent guidance.

More practically, biologists are the ones creating new large biological data sets. Currently, there is little guidance regarding publication of raw image data, and few journals are prepared to host the massive pixel data sets associated with these studies, so most image data sets remain outside the public domain. Ideally, biologists and computer vision experts can work together to strategically create new data sets that challenge the limitations of current biological knowledge, but they still are guided by consideration of the optimal imaging modality, contrast reagents, and other features that will optimize the ability to analyze these data using computer vision.

7. The limits of human visual perception from digital images

The visual display of digital images from medical applications such as X-ray and computed tomography (CT) has been widely studied in order to expand the visual detection limits for trained medical professionals. Both modeling of visual perception limits and direct measurement of visual discrimination limits in real-life environments have resulted in the definition of *Just Noticeable Difference (JND)*, the minimum signal difference that subjects are able to detect in 50% of trials [10–12]. The practical limit of JND, given an ideal lighting environment with a display calibrated to DICOM GSDF standards and the optimal viewing angle is only 700–900 shades of gray—less than the 1024 shades provided by a 10-bit output [13]. Despite access to monitors with high contrast and high bit-depth, some applications used by biologists to display digital images render data at 8 bits per channel, further limiting the practical perception of signal variation in biological samples.

In contrast, each of the 65,536 shades of gray in a single channel of a 16-bit image can be reproducibly quantified using computer vision. This ability to resolve signals across a narrow intensity range is particularly important for analyzing data from transmitted light modalities, including phase contrast optics and differential interference contrast optics.

8. Quantitative phenotypic traits, high-content analysis

D. Lansing Taylor coined the term *high content analysis* to represent the coordinated application of biological contrast agents, microscopy, application software, image acquisition, image processing, and informatics [14]. The convergence of these elements enabled large numbers of samples to be imaged using automation, and the images to be quantitatively assessed by a skilled operator for features including object shape, signal intensity, and signal location. Importantly, this convergence enabled subtle changes to be measured in response to exogenous variables such as dose of drug or addition of exogenous protein. With the development of genetic reagents, like small-interfering RNAs (siRNAs) that can specifically inactivate each gene in the genome, one at a time, and measure the quantitative effect on the resulting "knockdown" cells [15, 16]. Genetically encoded fluorescent reagents based on green fluorescent protein (GFP) from the jellyfish *Aequorea victoria* can be fused to endogenous genes to further enable the localization of specific fusion proteins in cells or animals [17–19]. An elegant early example study combined the technologies of siRNA knockdown, GFP, and automated time-lapse imaging in living human cells to characterize the defects in cell-cycle kinetics when genes known to affect cell division are disrupted [20]. This basic strategy is applied to further our understanding of the cellular response to drugs or to disease gene manipulation with evolving genetic technologies [21].

9. Different metrics for career advancement

There are major differences in expectations from a project in life sciences compared to one in computer vision. Naturally, scientific publication after peer review is the standard metric for productivity and career advancement. But that is where the similarity ends.

The difference in criteria and format of publication are explicit examples of contrast between these two fields. The SCIMAGO portal (https://www.scimagojr.com/) ranks journals by impact. The top-ranked journal in cell biology in 2018 (excluding method-focused and review journals), is *Nature Cell Biology* (https://www.nature.com/ncb/). In the notes to prospective authors, the publisher states that "*Nature Cell Biology* publishes papers of the highest quality from all areas of cell biology, encouraging those that shed light on the mechanisms underlying fundamental cell biological processes" (https://www.nature.com/ncb/about/aims). Here, the key word is *mechanism*. Biological manuscripts are often judged by how strongly their data support a mechanistic conclusion, referring to a tangible explanation of the process being studied. The second important expectation relates to novelty, or *shedding light* on a previous poorly understood concept. It is unusual to publish a comparison of methodological improvements (outside methodology journals) unless it is required for a dramatic enhancement of mechanistic biological understanding.

Biological research projects that culminate in a high-impact manuscript are often presented publicly at meetings prior to publication. However, the publication of a manuscript is normally a completely separate process from presenting data at a scientific conference; with a few exceptions, biological publications do not reflect conference proceedings. It is very unusual to expect a biologist to produce a manuscript based on the presentation at a conference. At most, biological abstracts will be archived and searchable, but these abstracts are not typically cited or used to support career advancement on an academic curriculum vitae. Consequently, attending and making presentations at a scientific conference have implicit value through the opportunity to discuss ideas with peers or experts and to receive feedback that could influence upcoming publications, but conference presentations have little explicit value per se.

In contrast, 8 of the 10 top-ranked 2018 journals in computer vision are conference proceedings. Regarding the acceptance of papers to prestigious conferences and journals, there is a clear expectation of methodologic improvement for speed or accuracy of performance. Unlike publications in biology, the more applied field of computer vision places less core emphasis on conceptual novelty.

10. The collaboration relationship

A good outcome from a collaborative relationship between a biologist and computer vision expert includes (1) a publication in a top-tier biological journal and (2) a conference paper at a top computer vision meeting, for which authors from both teams receive recognition emphasizing their complementary contributions in the formats that are most beneficial to each partner. This good outcome requires a significant investment of time to overcome the multiple barriers inhibiting the successful development of a working relationship, but the return is well worth the investment.

A few major barriers to initiating a successful collaboration include technical language, conceptual background, and understanding the goals of each field (all of which are almost completely different between the partners). With collaborators in one's own field of expertise, it may be possible to create a research proposal with just a few phone calls. However, new partnerships between biologists and computer vision experts need to spend far more time together developing an understanding of the problems with tangible examples, discussing the important biological features that need to be better understood, and determining the approach that would be most successful at shedding light on the most important biological mechanisms.

Minor barriers can be social, such as the fear of being perceived as ignorant of the other partner's field. This type of issue is best to just work through, as the other partner is almost surely as ignorant of your field as you are of theirs. Assume that fundamental intelligence and the self-selected willingness both to learn new concepts and to get the most out of a new scientific relationship based on the expected yield of complementary skills. The question then becomes: How do I best communicate complex ideas without using technical lingo? This author has enjoyed many of these experiences.

These collaborative barriers can be considered negative and inhibitory, but more optimistic readers will also view them as opportunities to develop skills and understanding beyond their area of expertise that will place them at significant advantage for future opportunities.

11. Biologists interacting with computer vision products

Most biologists will not learn a programming language as a prerequisite to running an image-processing algorithm. Therefore, it is prudent to consider the current software environment used in biology before launching a tool aimed at biologists as end users. By far, the most widely used image-processing tool for biologists is ImageJ, developed by Wayne Rasband at the NIH [22]. As Java has JREs for nearly every environment, a single distribution can be widely used. The ImageJ resource continues to evolve through community support of new plug-in development and core feature development that responds to the evolving needs of the microscopy community as FIJI [23]. The logical menus and modular tools enable sophisticated analysis without the requirement for command-line coding. Complex macros can be saved and transferred to colleagues. ImageJ/FIJI is also free—another nice advantage! For high-throughput image processing, another free distributable package named CellProfiler is widely used [24, 25].

Many companies produce packages for end users that include both sophisticated automated microscopy hardware and associated image-processing software. The early launches of these products in the mid-2000s required the end user to learn a new interface, and often a new programming language as well. This strategy was fine for core facilities that employ a dedicated programmer or system operator, but in standard biology labs, programming skills are hard to find. Over the past decade, instrumentation producers have recognized the importance of enabling the end-user biologist to interact easily with the product, assuming that this person has few if any programming skills. This evolution has facilitated the more widespread use of image processing by biologists and has also enabled the creation of a new market for smaller biology-laboratory-focused instrumentation. Similarly, for a research collaboration to have the widest impact, it would be prudent to be mindful of the user interface for any new tool.

12. Current needs in biology

Microscopy instrument developers continue to invent methods that redefine the limits of high resolution and sample size. Crossing the Nyquist limit with fluorescent light was a major achievement that relied heavily on novel optical concepts, fluorescent reagents, and computer vision to reconstruct imagery [26–28]. Superresolution microscopy enables the visualization of previously unresolved features, such as contacts between subcellular membrane-bound organelles, and provides the opportunity to analyze networks of discrete interacting objects with spectral imaging [29].

Further increasing resolution using electron microscopy (EM) requires reconstruction of serial sections to create useful maps of biological order. The application of automated EM serial section reconstruction recently enabled the representation of the entire *Drosophila* brain at synaptic resolution [30]. This is another important step toward the long-term goal of reconstructing the mammalian brain at synaptic resolution [31].

At the other end of the spectrum are tools that enable in toto imaging of small animal development or time-resolved imaging of organs in behaving animals. These include light sheet microscopy or SPIM [32], lattice light-sheet microscopy [33], and swept confocally aligned planar excitation (SCAPE) microscopy [34]. These major advances in imaging of biological specimens rely on fast data processing, as typical single experiments can create 10 TB of raw image data. Note that most biologists do not have a data management plan for large-scale image storage, such as those from the current generation of in toto imaging methods.

13. Conclusions and future perspectives

The fields of biology and computer vision provide many opportunities for interaction and mutual benefit. However, the coevolution of these fields requires effort to overcome the multiple scientific, conceptual, and social barriers separating the practitioners in each field. Publications such as this, aiming to bring these fields together, are an important part of the solution. Attending meetings of the other field allow both a broad survey of the field and the personal connections that are so important in facilitating any scientific relationship. Most of the major computer vision meetings have sessions or workshops in microscopy image analysis. I can envision graduate-level courses that aim to break through the field-specific barriers by training a generation of scientists to become skilled in both fields, like the basic science training and medical practice training currently provided by MD-PhD programs. Hopefully, we will experience the same sense of loss and satisfaction with microscopy and computer vision as Sydney Brenner did when his beloved developmental biology section became obsolete.

Of the many interesting open questions in biology, the relationship between the functional mind and the physical brain is a major driver of new microscopy hardware development and requisite software development. This field is very interesting, as it not only represents multiple problems of profound biological and computational complexity, but solutions to these problems will shed light on the physical structures that enable functional thought, where memories are stored and how are they retrieved, how emotions like love and hate are encoded in the mind-brain, and how these emotions affect other thought processes. These questions are deeply inspirational because they represent biological problems that extend into the philosophical domain.

Progress in understanding the mind-brain relationship will emerge from coordinated investments in microscopy tool development, neuroanatomical labeling technique development, functional labeling technique development, and computer vision development, such as those at the Janelia Farm campus of the Howard Hughes Medical Institute [35]. Imagine a future in which functional imaging of living systems in toto with the subnanometer resolution of cryo-EM is routine. The complexity of even a single synaptic connection between neurons may appear sufficiently great to preclude any comprehensive understanding of larger networks of nervous tissue [36]. However, through the coordinated development of computer vision that informs analytical systems with appropriate biological models [37], this will be the source of major discoveries for decades to come.

References

[1] S. Brenner, Nobel lecture. Nature's gift to science, Biosci. Rep. 23 (5-6) (2003) 225–237.

[2] H.R. Horvitz, Nobel lecture. Worms, life and death, Biosci. Rep. 23 (5–6) (2003) 239–303.

[3] J.E. Sulston, Caenorhabditis elegans: the cell lineage and beyond (Nobel lecture), Chembiochem 4 (8) (2003) 688–696.

[4] D.J. Hoeppner, M.O. Hengartner, R. Schnabel, Engulfment genes cooperate with ced-3 to promote cell death in Caenorhabditis elegans, Nature 412 (6843) (2001) 202–206.

[5] J.M. Kinchen, J. Cabello, D. Klingele, K. Wong, R. Feichtinger, H. Schnabel, R. Schnabel, M.O. Hengartner, Two pathways converge at CED-10 to mediate actin rearrangement and corpse removal in C. elegans, Nature 434 (7029) (2005) 93–99.

[6] R. Schnabel, H. Hutter, D. Moerman, H. Schnabel, Assessing normal embryogenesis in Caenorhabditis elegans using a 4D microscope: variability of development and regional specification, Dev. Biol. 184 (2) (1997) 234–265.

[7] C.L. Araya, T. Kawli, A. Kundaje, L. Jiang, B. Wu, D. Vafeados, R. Terrell, P. Weissdepp, L. Gevirtzman, D. Mace, W. Niu, A.P. Boyle, D. Xie, L. Ma, J.I. Murray, V. Reinke, R.H. Waterston, M. Snyder, Regulatory analysis of the C. elegans genome with spatiotemporal resolution, Nature 512 (7515) (2014) 400–405.

[8] D.L. Mace, P. Weisdepp, L. Gevirtzman, T. Boyle, R.H. Waterston, A high-fidelity cell lineage tracing method for obtaining systematic spatiotemporal gene expression patterns in Caenorhabditis elegans, G3 (Bethesda) 3 (5) (2013) 851–863.

[9] K. McDole, L. Guignard, F. Amat, A. Berger, G. Malandain, L.A. Royer, S.C. Turaga, K. Branson, P.J. Keller, In toto imaging and reconstruction of post-implantation mouse development at the single-cell level, Cell 175 (3) (2018) 859–876 e833.

[10] P.G.J. Barten, Physical model for the contrast sensitivity of the human eye, in: SPIE/IS&T 1992 Symposium on Electronic Imaging: Science and Technology, SPIE, 1992.

[11] W. Bialek, Physical limits to sensation and perception, Annu. Rev. Biophys. Biophys. Chem. 16 (1987) 455–478.

[12] S.J. Daly, Visible differences predictor: an algorithm for the assessment of image fidelity, in: SPIE/IS&T 1992 Symposium on Electronic Imaging: Science and Technology, SPIE, 1992.

[13] T. Kimpe, T. Tuytschaever, Increasing the number of gray shades in medical display systems—how much is enough? J. Digit. Imaging 20 (4) (2007) 422–432.

[14] D.L. Taylor, J.R. Haskins, K.A. Giuliano, High content screening: a powerful approach to systems cell biology and drug discovery, Humana Press, Totowa, NJ, 2007.

[15] A.Z. Fire, Gene silencing by double-stranded RNA (Nobel lecture), Angew. Chem. Int. Ed. Eng. 46 (37) (2007) 6966–6984.

[16] C.C. Mello, Return to the RNAi world: rethinking gene expression and evolution (Nobel lecture), Angew. Chem. Int. Ed. Eng. 46 (37) (2007) 6985–6994.

[17] M. Chalfie, GFP: lighting up life (Nobel Lecture), Angew. Chem. Int. Ed. Eng. 48 (31) (2009) 5603–5611.

[18] O. Shimomura, Discovery of green fluorescent protein (GFP) (Nobel Lecture), Angew. Chem. Int. Ed. Eng. 48 (31) (2009) 5590–5602.

[19] R.Y. Tsien, Constructing and exploiting the fluorescent protein paintbox (Nobel lecture), Angew. Chem. Int. Ed. Eng. 48 (31) (2009) 5612–5626.

[20] B. Neumann, M. Held, U. Liebel, H. Erfle, P. Rogers, R. Pepperkok, J. Ellenberg, High-throughput RNAi screening by time-lapse imaging of live human cells, Nat. Methods 3 (5) (2006) 385–390.

[21] G. Pegoraro, T. Misteli, High-throughput imaging for the discovery of cellular mechanisms of disease, Trends Genet. 33 (9) (2017) 604–615.

[22] C.A. Schneider, W.S. Rasband, K.W. Eliceiri, NIH image to ImageJ: 25 years of image analysis, Nat. Methods 9 (7) (2012) 671–675.

[23] J. Schindelin, C.T. Rueden, M.C. Hiner, K.W. Eliceiri, The ImageJ ecosystem: an open platform for biomedical image analysis, Mol. Reprod. Dev. 82 (7-8) (2015) 518–529.

[24] A.E. Carpenter, T.R. Jones, M.R. Lamprecht, C. Clarke, I.H. Kang, O. Friman, D.A. Guertin, J.H. Chang, R.A. Lindquist, J. Moffat, P. Golland, D.M. Sabatini, CellProfiler: image analysis software for identifying and quantifying cell phenotypes, Genome Biol. 7 (10) (2006) R100.

[25] C. McQuin, A. Goodman, V. Chernyshev, L. Kamentsky, B.A. Cimini, K.W. Karhohs, M. Doan, L. Ding, S.M. Rafelski, D. Thirstrup, W. Wiegraebe, S. Singh, T. Becker, J.C. Caicedo, A. E. Carpenter, CellProfiler 3.0: next-generation image processing for biology, PLoS Biol. 16 (7) (2018). e2005970.

[26] E. Betzig, Single molecules, cells, and super-resolution optics (Nobel lecture), Angew. Chem. Int. Ed. Eng. 54 (28) (2015) 8034–8053.

[27] S.W. Hell, Nanoscopy with focused light (Nobel lecture), Angew. Chem. Int. Ed. Eng. 54 (28) (2015) 8054–8066.

[28] W.E. Moerner, Single-molecule spectroscopy, imaging, and photocontrol: foundations for super-resolution microscopy (Nobel lecture), Angew. Chem. Int. Ed. Eng. 54 (28) (2015) 8067–8093.

[29] A.M. Valm, S. Cohen, W.R. Legant, J. Melunis, U. Hershberg, E. Wait, A.R. Cohen, M.W. Davidson, E. Betzig, J. Lippincott-Schwartz, Applying systems-level spectral imaging and analysis to reveal the organelle interactome, Nature 546 (7656) (2017) 162–167.

[30] Z. Zheng, J.S. Lauritzen, E. Perlman, C.G. Robinson, M. Nichols, D. Milkie, O. Torrens, J. Price, C.B. Fisher, N. Sharifi, S.A. Calle-Schuler, L. Kmecova, I.J. Ali, B. Karsh, E.T. Trautman, J.A. Bogovic, P. Hanslovsky, G. Jefferis, M. Kazhdan, K. Khairy, S. Saalfeld, R.D. Fetter, D.D. Bock, A complete electron microscopy volume of the brain of adult drosophila melanogaster, Cell 174 (3) (2018) 730–743.e722.

[31] N. Kasthuri, K.J. Hayworth, D.R. Berger, R.L. Schalek, J.A. Conchello, S. Knowles-Barley, D. Lee, A. Vazquez-Reina, V. Kaynig, T.R. Jones, M. Roberts, J.L. Morgan, J. C. Tapia, H.S. Seung, W.G. Roncal, J.T. Vogelstein, R. Burns, D.L. Sussman, C. E. Priebe, H. Pfister, J.W. Lichtman, Saturated reconstruction of a volume of neocortex, Cell 162 (3) (2015) 648–661.

[32] R. Tomer, K. Khairy, F. Amat, P.J. Keller, Quantitative high-speed imaging of entire developing embryos with simultaneous multiview light-sheet microscopy, Nat. Methods 9 (7) (2012) 755–763.

[33] B.C. Chen, W.R. Legant, K. Wang, L. Shao, D.E. Milkie, M.W. Davidson, C. Janetopoulos, X.S. Wu, J.A. Hammer, Z.L. 3rd, B.P. English, Y. Mimori-Kiyosue, D.P. Romero, A.T. Ritter, J. Lippincott-Schwartz, L. Fritz-Laylin, R.D. Mullins, D.M. Mitchell, J.N. Bembenek, A.C. Reymann, R. Bohme, S.W. Grill, J.T. Wang, G. Seydoux, U.S. Tulu, D.P. Kiehart, E. Betzig, Lattice light-sheet microscopy: imaging molecules to embryos at high spatio-temporal resolution, Science 346 (6208) (2014), 1257998.

[34] M.B. Bouchard, V. Voleti, C.S. Mendes, C. Lacefield, W.B. Grueber, R.S. Mann, R.M. Bruno, E.M. Hillman, Swept confocally-aligned planar excitation (SCAPE) microscopy for high speed volumetric imaging of behaving organisms, Nat. Photonics 9 (2) (2015) 113–119.

[35] I. Amato, HHMI's biggest experiment, ACS Cent. Sci. 1 (1) (2015) 8–10.

[36] N.A. O'Rourke, N.C. Weiler, K.D. Micheva, S.J. Smith, Deep molecular diversity of mammalian synapses: why it matters and how to measure it, Nat. Rev. Neurosci. 13 (6) (2012) 365–379.

[37] E. Jonas, K.P. Kording, Could a neuroscientist understand a microprocessor? PLoS Comput. Biol. 13 (1) (2017), e1005268.

CHAPTER 2

Microscopy image formation, restoration, and segmentation

Zhaozheng Yin* and Hang Su[†]
[*]Stony Brook University, Department of Biomedical Informatics and Department of Computer Science, Stony Brook, NY, United States
[†]Tsinghua University, Department of Computer Science and Technology, Beijing, People's Republic of China

Contents

1. Introduction

The demand of visualizing transparent cells without altering the specimen itself motivated microscopists to develop several successful microscopy techniques in the 20th century. Based on the observation that cells change the phase of incident wave-fronts due to their thickness and refractive index differing from the surrounding medium, Phase contrast and differential interference contrast (DIC) microscopy techniques were invented to convert the minute phase variations to intensity changes for human observation ([5], Chapters 7 and 10). These two noninvasive optical microscopy techniques allow cell observation without exogenous fixing or staining, and thus enable long-term monitoring of the behavior of live cells by recording time-lapse microscopy images, such as cell migration, cell cycle, and cell differentiation.

As shown in Fig. 2.1A, when imaged by positive phase contrast optics, cells appear darker than the surrounding medium. When imaged by a DIC microscope, cells have

Computer Vision for Microscopy Image Analysis
https://doi.org/10.1016/B978-0-12-814972-0.00002-3

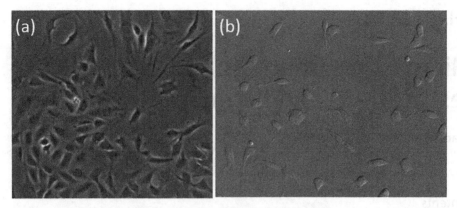

Fig. 2.1 Samples of phase contrast microscopy (A) and DIC (B) images.

3D-like topographical appearance (Fig. 2.1B). However, several inherent artifacts can be observed in these microscopy images. There are bright halos around cell membranes in the phase contrast image (Fig. 2.1A); thus, the observed pixel intensities around halo regions do not directly reflect the specimen properties. There is a pseudo-3D shading effect in the DIC image (Fig. 2.1B), where regions with an increasing optical path difference appear brighter than those with a decreasing optical path difference. This shadow-cast effect only indicates the sign and slope orientation of optical path gradients, and it does not indicate the actual topographical structures of cells.

These artifacts have hindered the process of automated microscopy image analysis, such as cell segmentation, which is a critical element of automated cell tracking systems [3]. Most of the previous microscopy image segmentation methods do not consider the image formation process of microscopy images and treat them in the same manner as natural images. However, there are apparent differences between natural images and DIC/phase contrast microscopy images, such as the halo and shadow-case effects. In this chapter, we derive computational imaging models corresponding to the microscopy imaging optics and formulate image restoration problems to restore microscopy images without halo or shadow-cast effects. With artifacts removed, high-quality segmentation can be achieved on the restored images.

2. Image formation

Compared to the common bright-field microscope, phase contrast and DIC microscopes have specially designed optical components to convert the minute phase differences to visible intensities. For example, phase contrast microscopes add a conjugate pair of a condenser annulus and a phase plate into their optical system (Fig. 2.2); DIC microscopes have four specially designed optical components along its optical pipeline (Fig. 2.3): a polarizer, a conjugate pair of prisms, and an analyzer. In this section, we derive the computational imaging model for each microscopy imaging modality.

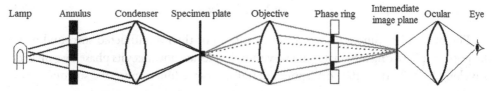

Fig. 2.2 Phase contrast microscopy optics.

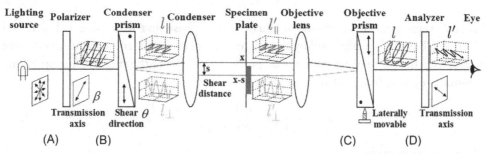

Fig. 2.3 DIC microscopy optics.

2.1 Phase contrast microscopy image formation model

Following the optical principle of the phase contrast microscope (Fig. 2.2), we derive its computational imaging model in this subsection. We assume that the illuminating waves arrive at the specimen plate with the same amplitude and phase, and denote them as

$$l(\mathbf{x}) = Ae^{i\beta} \tag{2.1}$$

where $\mathbf{x} = \{(\mathbf{x}_j^r, \mathbf{x}_j^c), \quad j = 1, \ldots, J\}$ denotes 2D locations (row and column) of the total J image pixels on the specimen plate; $i^2 = -1$; and A and β are the illuminating wave's amplitude and phase before hitting the specimen plate.

After illuminating waves pass through the specimen plate, they divide into two components: the unaltered surround wave $l_S(\mathbf{x})$ and the diffracted wave $l_D(\mathbf{x})$, which is attenuated and retarded by the specimen:

$$l_S(\mathbf{x}) = l(\mathbf{x}) = Ae^{i\beta} \tag{2.2}$$

$$l_D(\mathbf{x}) = \zeta_c e^{-if(\mathbf{x})} l(\mathbf{x}) = \zeta_c A e^{i(\beta - f(\mathbf{x}))} \tag{2.3}$$

where ζ_c is the amplitude attenuation factor and $f(\mathbf{x})$ represents phase shift caused by the specimen at location $\mathbf{x}$. Our goal is to restore $f(\mathbf{x})$, the "authentic" phase contrast image corresponding to the specimen's optical path length without artifacts.

A thin lens with a large aperture essentially performs a spatial Fourier transform ($\mathcal{F}$) on the waves from its front focal plane to its rear focal plane. Thus, after the surround and diffracted waves pass the objective lens, the waves in front of the phase plate are

$$L_S(\mathbf{w}) = \mathcal{F}(l_S(\mathbf{x})) \tag{2.4}$$

$$L_D(\mathbf{w}) = \mathcal{F}(l_D(\mathbf{x})) \tag{2.5}$$

The phase plate functions as a bandpass filter. For the nondiffracted surround wave, the positive phase ring attenuates the wave amplitude and advances its phase by a quarter-wavelength ($\pi/2$); thus, the corresponding transmittance function for the surround wave is

$$T_S(\mathbf{w}) = \zeta_p e^{i\frac{\pi}{2}} = i\zeta_p \tag{2.6}$$

where ζ_p represents the amplitude attenuation by a phase ring with outer radius R and width W (R and W are provided by the microscope manufacturers). The diffracted wave spreads over the phase plate, with a small portion leaking into the ring. Its corresponding transmittance function is a bandpass filter:

$$T_D(\mathbf{w}) = \begin{cases} i\zeta_p & \text{if } R - W \leq w_r \leq R \\ 1 & \text{otherwise} \end{cases} \tag{2.7}$$

which can be rewritten as

$$T_D(\mathbf{w}) = 1 + \left(i\zeta_p - 1\right) \left[\text{cyl}\left(\frac{w_r}{R}\right) - \text{cyl}\left(\frac{w_r}{R - W}\right) \right] \tag{2.8}$$

where $w_r = \sqrt{w_u^2 + w_v^2}$ is the radial frequency and $\text{cyl}(\cdot)$ is a 2D cylinder function:

$$\text{cyl}(w) = \begin{cases} 1 & \text{if } 0 \leq w \leq 1 \\ 0 & \text{otherwise} \end{cases} \tag{2.9}$$

After the bandpass filtering, we have the waves after the phase plate as

$$\widetilde{L}_S(\mathbf{w}) = L_S(\mathbf{w}) T_S(\mathbf{w}) \tag{2.10}$$

$$\widetilde{L}_D(\mathbf{w}) = L_D(\mathbf{w}) T_D(\mathbf{w}) \tag{2.11}$$

The ocular lens performs another Fourier transform. Mathematically, the forward and inverse Fourier transforms are identical except for a minus sign, and thus, applying the Fourier transform on $\widetilde{L}_S(\mathbf{w})$ and $\widetilde{L}_D(\mathbf{w})$ is equivalent to applying an inverse Fourier transform on them with a minus sign on the input variable of the resultant function.

The waves after the ocular lens are

$$\widetilde{l}_S(\mathbf{x}) = l_S(\mathbf{x})^* t_S(\mathbf{x}) \tag{2.12}$$

$$\widetilde{l}_D(\mathbf{x}) = l_D(\mathbf{x})^* t_D(\mathbf{x}) \tag{2.13}$$

where * denotes the convolution operator. $t_S(\cdot)$ and $t_D(\cdot)$ denote the inverse Fourier transforms of $T_S(\cdot)$ and $T_D(\cdot)$, respectively. The inverse Fourier transform of $T_S(\cdot)$ (Eq. 2.6) is

$$t_S(\mathbf{x}) = i\zeta_p \delta(\mathbf{x}) \tag{2.14}$$

where $\delta(\cdot)$ is a Dirac delta function. The inverse Fourier transform of $T_D(\cdot)$ (Eq. 2.8) is

$$t_D(\mathbf{x}) = \delta(\mathbf{r}) + \left(i\zeta_p - 1\right)\text{airy}(\mathbf{r}) \tag{2.15}$$

where airy($\mathbf{r}$) is an obscured Airy pattern where a bright region in the center is surrounded by a series of concentric, alternating bright/dark rings.

Substituting l_S, t_S, l_D, and t_D into $\widetilde{l}_S$ and $\widetilde{l}_D$ in Eqs. (2.12), (2.13), we get

$$\widetilde{l}_S(\mathbf{x}) = i\zeta_p A e^{i\beta} \tag{2.16}$$

$$\widetilde{l}_D(\mathbf{x}) = \zeta_c A e^{i(\beta - f(\mathbf{x}))} + \left(i\zeta_p - 1\right)\zeta_c A e^{i(\beta - f(\mathbf{x}))} * \text{airy}(\mathbf{r}) \tag{2.17}$$

The first term in Eq. (2.17) is the primary component of the diffracted wave that destructively interferes with the nondiffracted surround wave and generates the contrast for human observation. The second term in Eq. (2.17) comes from the diffracted wave leaking into the phase ring, which causes the halo and shade-off artifacts. The intensity of the final observed image is computed as [10]

$$g(\mathbf{x}) \propto (\delta(\mathbf{r}) - \text{airy}(\mathbf{r})) * f(\mathbf{x}) + C \tag{2.18}$$

where C is a constant. The convolution kernel in Eq. (2.18) represents the point spread function (PSF) of the phase contrast microscope:

$$\text{PSF}_{Phase\,contrast}(u, v) = \delta(u, v) - \text{airy}\left(\sqrt{u^2 + v^2}\right) \tag{2.19}$$

which is a linear operator. Note that in the positive phase contrast microscope, cells appear darker than the surrounding medium. However, in negative phase contrast microscope (surround wave is retarded instead of being advanced), cells appear brighter than the surrounding medium. The corresponding PSF for the negative phase contrast is

$$\text{PSF}_{Phase\,contrast}(u, v) = \text{airy}\left(\sqrt{u^2 + v^2}\right) - \delta(u, v) \tag{2.20}$$

In our restoration framework, we use Eq. (2.20) for both positive and negative phase contrast microscopes, such that in restored images, cells are bright while the background is dark.

2.2 DIC microscopy image formation model

In contrast to phase contrast microscopy, the DIC microscope does not obstruct the condenser or objective lens, thus enabling a full aperture during imaging, and it can observe relatively thick specimens without halo artifacts. Compared to a traditional bright-field microscope, the DIC microscope has four specially designed optical components along its optical pipeline (Fig. 2.3): a polarizer, a conjugate pair of prisms, and an analyzer.

The polarizer, placed after the lighting source, screens the incoming light waves that vibrate in all directions and outputs a plane-polarized light wave vibrating only along the polarizer's transmission axis (direction β in Fig. 2.3(a)). The condenser prism, placed at the front focal plane of the condenser, consists of two quartz wedges with perpendicular optical axis orientations. It splits the incoming plane-polarized wave into two closely spaced components that have the same amplitude and vibrate in orthogonal directions. The condenser prism's *shear direction* (θ in Fig. 2.3(b)) is defined by the optical axis of the first quartz wedge, and it is usually oriented 45 degrees away from the polarizer's transmission axis. The minute *shear distance* (s in Fig. 2.3) between the two component waves is smaller than the microscope's lateral resolution. The shear direction and shear distance are constant for all paired waves passing through the condenser prism, regardless of the incident point on the prism; thus, every point on the specimen plate is uniformly sampled by a pair of closely spaced waves.

We denote the paired waves before the specimen plate as

$$l_{\parallel}(\mathbf{x}) = A e^{i\phi} \tag{2.21}$$

$$l_{\perp}(\mathbf{x}) = A e^{i\phi} \tag{2.22}$$

where $\mathbf{x}$ is a location on the specimen plate, $\parallel$ and $\perp$ represent the vibration directions of the paried waves, and A and ϕ are the amplitude and phase of the waves. Note that the two component waves have the same amplitude, but they vibrate in orthogonal directions.

After the paired waves pass through two adjacent locations on the specimen plane, with their optical path length (OPL) difference caused either by the cell periphery or by the inner cell structures, the relative phase relation between the two waves is changed. We denote the two waves after the specimen plane as

$$l'_{\parallel}(\mathbf{x}) = l_{\parallel}(\mathbf{x}) e^{-if(\mathbf{x})} \tag{2.23}$$

$$l'_{\perp}(\mathbf{x}) = l_{\perp}(\mathbf{x}) e^{-if(\mathbf{x}-\mathbf{s})} \tag{2.24}$$

where $f(\mathbf{x})$ and $f(\mathbf{x}-\mathbf{s})$ denote the phase shifts at locations $\mathbf{x}$ and $\mathbf{x}$–$\mathbf{s}$, respectively; and $\mathbf{s} = (s\cos\theta, s\sin\theta)$ is a vector in the shear direction θ, with the shear distance s. Note that the condenser prism itself also introduces a phase shift into the two component waves, but this phase shift will be compensated by the conjugate objective prism later, so we do not include it in the derivation.

The objective prism, placed at the rear focal plane of the objective lens, has a shear axis orthogonal to that of the condenser prism. Thus, it recombines the two split waves into a single elliptically polarized wave (Fig. 2.3(c)). Different from the fixed condenser prism in Fig. 2.3(b), the objective prism is laterally movable along the direction perpendicular to the optical pipeline. The movable objective prism introduces a relative *phase bias* to the paired waves and causes the pseudo-3D effect.

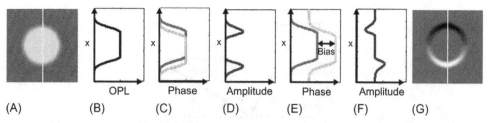

Fig. 2.4 Toy example to illustrate the phase bias and the cause of the pseudo-3D artifact. (A) A specimen on a plate; (B) the OPL of the specimen's central column (*white line* in (A)); (C) the phases of paired illumination waves are shifted by the specimen; (D) the amplitude of recombined wave corresponding to (C); (E) the phases of paired illumination waves are shifted by the specimen, with the phase bias added; (F) the amplitude of the recombined wave corresponding to (E); and (G) The observed DIC image with the pseudo-3D effect. Here, (F) is the central profile of (G).

We use a synthesized example (Fig. 2.4) to illustrate the cause of artifact. Fig. 2.4A shows a specimen on the plate with its central column's OPL profile as shown in Fig. 2.4B. The paired waves travel through the specimen with their phases shifted as shown in Fig. 2.4C (phase shift is proportional to OPL). When there is no phase bias added (i.e., the center of the objective prism is on the optical pipeline), the amplitude of recombined wave shows peaks on cell boundaries (Fig. 2.4D). If phase bias is added (Fig. 2.4E) by moving the objective prism, after recombination, the wave amplitude has both peak and valley values (Fig. 2.4F), which generate the pseudo-3D effect in DIC images (Fig. 2.4G). The pseudo-3D effect helps biologists observe specimens, but image intensities in Fig. 2.4F are no longer created by linear mapping of the specimen's OPL in Fig. 2.4B.

We denote the recombined wave after the objective prism as

$$l(\mathbf{x}) = l'_{\|}(\mathbf{x}) + l'_{\perp}(\mathbf{x})e^{-ib} \tag{2.25}$$

where b is the relative phase bias added to the paired waves. Note that b is assumed to be $\pi/4$ in [2], but this assumption is not true for general DIC microscope settings.

The analyzer, placed after the objective prism, has a transmission axis orthogonal to that of the polarizer. The incoming elliptically polarized wave is decomposed into two components on the coordinates defined by the transmission axes of the polarizer and analyzer. Only the component along the analyzer's transmission axis can pass through the analyzer. Thus, the wave after the analyzer is computed as

$$
\begin{aligned}
l'(\mathbf{x}) &= \text{proj}_a\big(l(\mathbf{x})\big) \\
&= \text{proj}_a\Big(l'_{\|}(\mathbf{x})\Big) + \text{proj}_a\Big(l'_{\perp}(\mathbf{x})e^{-ib}\Big) \\
&= l'_{\|}(\mathbf{x})\cos(\theta - \beta) + l'_{\perp}(\mathbf{x})e^{-ib}\sin(\theta - \beta)
\end{aligned} \tag{2.26}
$$

where $\text{proj}_a(l(\cdot))$ projects wave l onto the analyzer's transmission axis (i.e., the two terms in Eq. 2.25 are decomposed to the analyzer's transmission axis). Fig. 2.5 illustrates the projection angles between vectors.

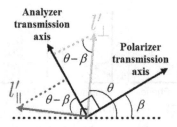

Fig. 2.5 Decomposing the paired waves ($I_{\parallel}{}'$ and $I_{\perp}{}'$) onto the coordinates defined by the transmission axes of the polarizer and analyzer.

When the paired waves pass through locations on the specimen plate with equal optical path lengths (e.g., background regions), they will be recombined by the objective prism into a plane-polarized wave rather than an elliptically polarized wave caused by specimens. The recombined, plane-polarized wave has the same vibration axis as the wave before the condenser prism, (i.e., for adjacent locations with equal OPL, the wave-splitting function of the condenser prism is counteracted by the wave recombination of the objective prism). Because the plane-polarized wave vibrates in a plane orthogonal to the analyzer's transmission axis, it is totally blocked by the analyzer (called *extinction*). Hence, at the eyepiece, the observed contrast between the specimen and the extincted background is

$$g(\mathbf{x}) = |I'(\mathbf{x}) - 0|^2 = |I'(\mathbf{x})|^2 \approx k\nabla_{\theta}f(\mathbf{x}) + c \qquad (2.27)$$

where $\nabla_{\theta}f(\mathbf{x})$ is the first derivative of f along the shear direction θ, and $k = sA^2 \sin(2\theta - 2\beta)\sin b$ and $c = A^2(1 + \sin(2\theta - 2\beta)\cos b)$ are constants defined by DIC optics. The derivative kernel in Eq. (2.27), which can be approximated by a steerable first derivative of Gaussian, represents the PSF of the DIC microscope:

$$PSF_{DIC}(u, v) = -ue^{\frac{u^2 + v^2}{\sigma^2}}\cos(\theta) - ve^{\frac{u^2 + v^2}{\sigma^2}}\sin(\theta) \qquad (2.28)$$

3. Optics-based image restoration

Based on the understanding of microscopy imaging optics, we first propose an image restoration method using a simplified linear imaging model. Then we derive a dictionary learning-based method to extract optics-oriented feature maps to facilitate cell image analysis. Furthermore, considering the complete image acquisition pipeline (microscope optics plus a camera system), we investigate a virtual cell-sensitive imaging solution to visualize specimens clearly using multiple exposures.

3.1 Image restoration using a linear imaging model

We can define a simplified linear imaging model between $\mathbf{g}$ (a vectorized observed microscopy image) and $\mathbf{f}$ (a vectorized, artifact-free microscopy image to be restored) as

$$\mathbf{g} \approx \mathbf{Hf} + C \qquad (2.29)$$

where $\mathbf{H}$ is defined by the PSF (Eq. 2.19 for phase contrast microscopy and Eq. 2.28 for DIC microscopy, as illustrated in Fig. 2.6). In practice, we discretize the PSF kernel as a $(2M+1) \times (2M+1)$ matrix (e.g., $M = 5$) and the $\mathbf{H}$ matrix is defined by

$$\left(\mathbf{Hf} \right)_j = \sum_{u=1}^{2M+1} \sum_{v=1}^{2M+1} \mathrm{PSF}(u, v) \mathbf{f} \left(\mathbf{x}_j^r + u - M, \mathbf{x}_j^c + v - M \right) \qquad (2.30)$$

Eq. (2.30) indicates that the jth element of multiplying $\mathbf{f}$ by $\mathbf{H}$ is defined by the convolution of the PSF kernel on image $\mathbf{f}$ around pixel location $(\mathbf{x}_j^r, \mathbf{x}_j^c)$. Each row of $\mathbf{H}$ has only $(2M+1) \times (2M+1)$ nonzero elements corresponding to the PSF kernel; thus, $\mathbf{H}$ is a $J \times J$ symmetric sparse matrix.

The first step is to remove the background C from $\mathbf{g}$ in Eq. (2.29). Ideally, the background C should be a constant for every pixel location. However, that is not true in reality due to the lens aberration. We model $\mathbf{C}$ by a second-order polynomial surface. Given an observed image, we compute the background as $\mathbf{C} = \mathbf{Ak}^*$ and remove it from the observed image (i.e., $\mathbf{g} \leftarrow \mathbf{g} - \mathbf{C}$). Thus, the new imaging model is

$$\mathbf{g} = \mathbf{Hf} \qquad (2.31)$$

The second and major step is to solve $\mathbf{f}$ from Eq. (2.31). An attempt to solve it by simply inversing $\mathbf{H}$ is known to be highly noise prone. Instead, we formulate the following constrained quadratic function to restore $\mathbf{f}$:

$$\mathbf{O}(\mathbf{f}) = \|\mathbf{Hf} - \mathbf{g}\|_2^2 + \omega_S \mathbf{f}^T \mathbf{Lf} + \omega_r \|\mathbf{\Lambda f}\|_1 \qquad (2.32)$$

where $\mathbf{L}$ is a Laplacian matrix defining the similarity between spatial pixel neighbors. $\mathbf{L} = \mathbf{D} - \mathbf{W}$, where $\mathbf{W}$ is a symmetric matrix whose off-diagonal elements are defined

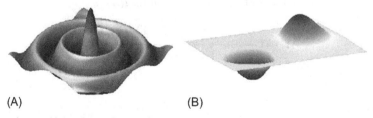

(A)   (B)

Fig. 2.6 Convolutional kernels used in our linear imaging model. (A) Obscured airy kernel in the phase contrast imaging; (B) difference-of-Gaussian kernel in the DIC imaging.

as $\mathbf{W}(i,j) = e^{-(\mathbf{g}_i - \mathbf{g}_j)^2/\sigma^2}$, where σ^2 can be computed as the mean of all instances of $(\mathbf{g}_i - \mathbf{g}_j)^2$. $\mathbf{D}$ is a diagonal degree matrix in which $\mathbf{D}(i,i) = \sum_j \mathbf{W}(\mathbf{i},\mathbf{j})$. $\mathbf{\Lambda}$ is a positive diagonal matrix defining the elementwise weight on pixels by the l_1-norm sparseness regularization. The balance coefficients on various regularization terms (ω_s and ω_r) are to be learned by grid-searching.

If given an observed sequence of N images, $\{\mathbf{g}^{(t)}\}_{t=1, \ldots, N}$, we restore the artifact-free sequence, $\{\mathbf{f}^{(t)}\}_{t=1, \ldots, N}$, by considering the temporal consistency between consecutive images [9]. The objective function is[1]

$$\mathbf{O}(\mathbf{f}) = \|\mathbf{Hf} - \mathbf{g}\|_2^2 + \omega_s \mathbf{f}^T \mathbf{Lf} + \omega_r \|\mathbf{\Lambda f}\|_1 + \omega_t \left(\mathbf{f} - \mathbf{f}^{(t)}\right)^T \sum \left(\mathbf{f} - \mathbf{f}^{(t)}\right) \qquad (2.33)$$

where $\mathbf{\Sigma}$ is a matrix defining the similarity between temporal pixel neighbors and ω_t is the weighting factor on the temporal consistency regularization.

There is no closed-form solution to $\mathbf{f}$ in Eq. (2.33), and only numerical approximation is achievable. We constrain the restored $\mathbf{f}$ to have nonnegative values and convert Eq. (2.33) to the following optimization problem:

$$\mathbf{O}(\mathbf{f}) = \mathbf{f}^T \mathbf{Qf} + 2\mathbf{b}^T \mathbf{f} + c \quad s.t. \quad \mathbf{f} \geq 0 \qquad (2.34)$$

where

$$\mathbf{Q} = \mathbf{H}^T \mathbf{H} + \omega_S \mathbf{L} + \omega_t \mathbf{\Sigma} \qquad (2.35)$$

$$\mathbf{b} = -\mathbf{H}^T \mathbf{g} - \omega_t \mathbf{\Sigma}^T \mathbf{f}^{(t)} + \omega_r \operatorname{diag}(\mathbf{\Lambda})/2 \qquad (2.36)$$

We propose an iterative algorithm to solve $\mathbf{f}$ in Eq. (2.34) by nonnegative multiplicative updating (Eq. 2.37), given in Algorithm 1. Reweighting Eq. (2.38) is an option to accelerate the convergence process.

Algorithm 1: Restoring artifact-free microscopy images

Initialize $\mathbf{f} = \mathbf{f}^{init}$ and $\mathbf{\Lambda} = \mathbf{\Lambda}^{init}$.

Repeat the following steps for all pixel j:

$$\mathbf{b} = -\mathbf{H}^T \mathbf{g} - \omega_t \mathbf{\Sigma}^T \mathbf{f}^{(t)} + \omega_r \operatorname{diag}(\mathbf{\Lambda})/2$$

$$\mathbf{f}_j \leftarrow \mathbf{f}_j \frac{-b_j + \sqrt{b_j^2 + 4(\mathbf{Q}+\mathbf{f})_j(\mathbf{Q}-\mathbf{f})_j}}{2(\mathbf{Q}+\mathbf{f})_j} \qquad (2.37)$$

$$\mathbf{\Lambda}_{jj} \leftarrow \frac{\mathbf{\Lambda}_{jj}^{init}}{f_j + \varepsilon} \qquad (2.38)$$

Until convergence.

---

[1] To simplify notation, we denote $\mathbf{f}$ as the image to be restored at time $t+1$, $\mathbf{g}$ as the image observed at time $t+1$, and $\mathbf{f}^{(t)}$ as the restored image at time t.

Phase contrast image, CMU   Phase contrast image, DNP Corp.   Phase contrast image, JHU

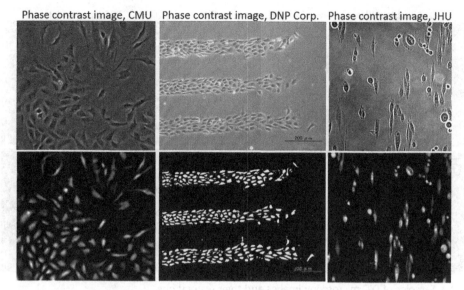

Fig. 2.7 Samples of phase contract microscopy images and their restorations.

where ε is a small constant to avoid dividing by zero and diag(Λ) denotes the diagonal vector of matrix Λ, and

$$\mathbf{Q}_{uv}^{+} = \begin{cases} \mathbf{Q}_{uv} & \text{if } \mathbf{Q}_{uv} > 0 \\ 0 & \text{otherwise} \end{cases} \quad \text{and} \quad \mathbf{Q}_{uv}^{-} = \begin{cases} |\mathbf{Q}_{uv}| & \text{if } \mathbf{Q}_{uv} < 0 \\ 0 & \text{otherwise} \end{cases} \quad (2.39)$$

Here, Λ^{init} can be an identity matrix (uniform weights on all pixels) or nonuniform weights on pixels defined by input image properties [10]; and $\mathbf{f}^{init}$ is the initialization on the image to be restored, which can be a constant initialization or obtained from a lookup table [10]. Note that when restoring a single phase contrast image, we drop the terms related to temporal consistency in $\mathbf{Q}$ and $\mathbf{b}$.

Figs. 2.7 and 2.8 show restoration examples on phase contrast and DIC microscopy images, respectively. Although the images are captured from different laboratories with different microscope configurations, the proposed method can restore artifact-free images in order to facilitate cell image analysis tasks such as cell segmentation.

3.2 Dictionary-based restoration

Although the aforementioned linear imaging model is demonstrated to remove the artifacts effectively, it usually fails to segment bright cells in phase contrast microscopy images (e.g., mitotic or apoptotic cells) because the model assumes that the phase retardation caused by cells is small, which is not valid when cells become thick during their mitotic or apoptotic stages and thus appear bright in phase contrast microscopy. To address this issue, we derive a method to restore microscopy imaging based on sparse coding. Specifically, we first construct a dictionary by considering the diffraction patterns with various

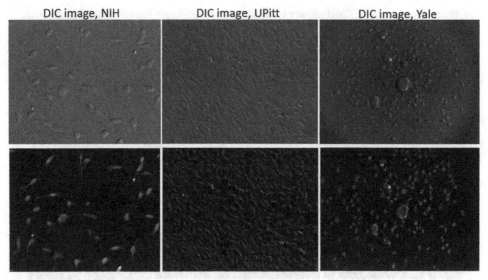

Fig. 2.8 Samples of DIC microscopy images and their restorations.

phase retardations. Afterward, we model a phase contrast microscopy image by sparse representation of diffraction patterns (i.e., a linear combination of a few bases corresponding to different diffraction patterns selected from the dictionary).

As mentioned previously, phase contrast microscopy employs interference optics to convert phase differences of light induced by transparent specimens and background media into visible intensity variations. The particle wave l_P is then calculated as

$$
\begin{aligned}
l_P &= l_S + l_D \\
&= Ae^{i\beta}\left(i\zeta_p + \zeta_c e^{i\theta(\mathbf{x})} + \left(i\zeta_p - 1\right)\zeta_c e^{i\theta(\mathbf{x})} \cdot \text{airy}(r)\right)
\end{aligned}
\tag{2.40}
$$

Therefore, the intensity of an observed image $\mathbf{g}$ is calculated as

$$
\begin{aligned}
\mathbf{g} &= \left\|l_p\right\|^2 \\
&= (l_S + l_D)(l_S + l_D)^* \\
&= A^2 \left\{
\begin{array}{l}
\zeta_p^2 + \zeta_c^2 - 2\zeta_c^2 \cdot \text{airy}(r) + \left(\zeta_p^2 + 1\right)\zeta_c^2 \cdot (\text{airy}(r))^2 + \\
i\zeta_p\zeta_c\left(e^{-i\theta(\mathbf{x})} - e^{i\theta(\mathbf{x})}\right) + \zeta_p\zeta_c\left(\left(\zeta_p - i\right)e^{-i\theta(\mathbf{x})} + \left(\zeta_p + i\right)e^{i\theta(\mathbf{x})}\right) \cdot \text{airy}(r)
\end{array}
\right\}
\end{aligned}
\tag{2.41}
$$

During the linear imaging model derivation, the exponential terms in Eq. (2.41) are approximated using $e^{i\theta(x)} \approx 1 + i\theta(x)$. Note that this approximation is valid only when the phase retardation $\theta(x)$ is close to zero. The assumption is apparently not applicable to general cases because $\theta(x)$, which is a function of the refractive indices and the thickness of cells, often varies along with cell types and stages; more formally, the phase retardation θ can be calculated as

$$\theta = \frac{2\pi}{\lambda}(n_1 - n_2)t \tag{2.42}$$

where λ denotes the wavelength of the incident light; t is the thickness of the cell; and n_1 and n_2 denote the refractive indices of the cell and medium, respectively.

In this section, we propose a generalized imaging model by approximating the term $e^{i\theta(x)}$ in Eq. (2.41) using a linear combination of $\{e^{i\theta_m}\}$ as

$$e^{i\theta(x)} \approx \sum_{m=0}^{M-1} \psi_m(x)e^{i\theta_m}, \quad s.t. \quad \psi_m(x) \geq 0 \tag{2.43}$$

where $\{\theta_m\} = \left\{0, \frac{2\pi}{M}, ..., \frac{2m\pi}{M}, ..., \frac{2(M-1)\pi}{M}\right\}$ We impose the nonnegative constraint because the solution would not be unique without it, as $\psi_m(x)e^{i\theta_m} = -\psi_m(x)e^{i(\theta_m+\pi)}$. Moreover, the nonnegative constraint removes the absolute operator of the ℓ_1 norm, allowing the problem to be solved in a standard manner.

Substituting the exponential terms in Eq. (2.41) by Eq. (2.43) yields a linear representation of the observed image as

$$\mathbf{g} = A^2 \left\{ \begin{array}{l} \zeta_p^2 + \zeta_c^2 - 2\zeta_c^2 \cdot \mathrm{airy}(r) + \left(\zeta_p^2 + 1\right)\zeta_c^2 \cdot (\mathrm{airy}(r))^2 + \\ \sum_{m=0}^{M-1} \psi_m(\mathbf{x})\left(2\zeta_p\zeta_c \sin\theta_m \cdot \delta(r) + 2\zeta_p\zeta_c\left(\zeta_p\cos\theta_m - \sin\theta_m\right) \cdot \mathrm{airy}(r)\right) \end{array} \right\} \tag{2.44}$$

$$= C_1 + C_2 \sum_{m=0}^{M-1} \psi_m(\mathbf{x})\left(\sin\theta_m\delta(r) + \left(\zeta_p\cos\theta_m - \sin\theta_m\right)\mathrm{airy}(r)\right)$$

where $\delta(\cdot)$ is a Dirac delta function, C_1 is a constant that indicates the items unrelated to the feature vector $\psi_m(\mathbf{x})$, and C_2 is another constant.

The constant C_1 can be eliminated by flat-field correction [10]; that is, $\mathbf{g} \leftarrow (\mathbf{g} - C_1)$. Hence,

$$\mathbf{g} \quad \infty \quad \sum_{m=0}^{M-1} \psi_m(\mathbf{x})\left(\sin\theta_m\delta(r) + \left(\zeta_p\cos\theta_m - \sin\theta_m\right)\mathrm{airy}(r)\right)$$

$$\triangleq \sum_{m=0}^{M-1} \psi_\mathrm{m}(\mathbf{x})\mathrm{DPK}(\theta_\mathrm{m}) \tag{2.45}$$

where $DPK(\theta_m)$ denotes the diffraction pattern kernel with phase retardation θ_m. In our experiments, ζ_p was set between 0.4 and 0.5 based on the characteristics of the microscope that we used. Fig. 2.9 shows samples of the obscured Airy pattern and diffraction pattern kernels with different retarded phases.

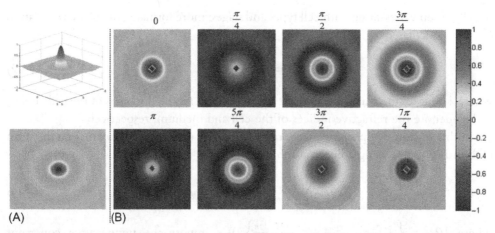

Fig. 2.9 Airy pattern and diffraction patterns (best viewed in color). (A) airy(r), obscured Airy pattern with 3D surface view and 2D top view; (B) *DPK* (θ_m), the diffraction pattern kernels with different phase retardations.

After discretizing the $DPK(\theta_m)$ as a $(2T+1) \times (2T+1)$ kernel, the imaging model in Eq. (2.45) is rewritten as

$$\mathbf{g}(x^r, x^c) = \sum_{m=0}^{M-1} \sum_{u=0}^{2T} \sum_{v=0}^{2T} \psi_m(x^r + u - T, x^c + v - T) DPK(u, v, \theta_m) \qquad (2.46)$$

where x^r and x^c denote a 2D location (row and column) on the specimen plate.

According to Eq. (2.46), each pixel at position $\mathbf{x}$ has a feature vector $\boldsymbol{\Psi}(\mathbf{x}) = \{\Psi_0(\mathbf{x}), -\ldots, \Psi_m(\mathbf{x}), \ldots, \Psi_{M-1}(\mathbf{x})\}$ to describe it. By vectorizing the diffraction pattern $DPK(\theta_m)$ at different positions in the observed image $\mathbf{g}$ (an image with P pixels), we construct a dictionary $\{\mathbf{H}_m\}_{m=0}^{M-1}$ ($P \times P$ matrices), where $\mathbf{H}_m$ is a basis of diffraction pattern with phase retardation θ_m. The p_{th} row of $\mathbf{H}_m$ is corresponding to the vectorized kernel function $DPK(\theta_m)$ around pixel location $\mathbf{x}_p$, which has only $(2T+1) \times (2T+1)$ nonzero elements. Thus, the convolution in Eq. (2.46) can be represented by a matrix-vector multiplication between a large sparse matrix $\mathbf{H}_m$ and the vectorized phase retardation feature as

$$(\mathbf{H}_m \boldsymbol{\psi}_m)_p = \sum_{u=0}^{2T} \sum_{v=0}^{2T} DPK(u, v, \theta_m) \psi_m \left(x_p^r + u - T, \ x_p^c + v - T \right) \qquad (2.47)$$

where $\mathbf{x}_p = (x_p^r, x_p^c)$ denotes location (x_p^r, x_p^c) on the 2D specimen plate and the p_{th} pixel in the vectorized image, and $\boldsymbol{\psi}_m(P \times 1)$ is the vectorized representation of the coefficients $\psi_m(\mathbf{x})$ for each pixel corresponding to the retarded phase θ_m.

Therefore, we have a dictionary-based imaging model:

$$\mathbf{g} = \sum_{m=0}^{M-1} \mathbf{H}_m \boldsymbol{\psi}_m, \quad s.t. \quad \boldsymbol{\psi}_m \geq 0 \tag{2.48}$$

where $\mathbf{g}$ is the vectorized observed image.

Next, we propose an iterative optimization algorithm to solve this $min\text{-}\ell_1$ optimization problem because it is known that there is no closed-form solution for such a problem. We first search the best-matching N bases in the dictionary $\{H_m\}$ with the matching pursuit algorithm [6], and then utilize a nonnegative multiplicative updating method [7] to obtain the nonnegative feature vectors $\{\boldsymbol{\psi}_{mk}\}$. The procedure is described in Algorithm 2.

Algorithm 2: Optimization algorithm for calculating the phase retardation feature

> **for** $k = 0 \rightarrow N-1$ **do**
>> **for** $m = 0 \rightarrow M-1$ **do**
>>> Compute inner product as $\rho_m(i) = \langle H_m(:,i), R_g^k \rangle$.
>>> **if** m is equal to zero, **then**
>>> $\rho_k \leftarrow \rho_m, H_{m_k} \leftarrow H_m$.
>>> **else if** $\|\rho_m\|_0 > \|\rho_k\|_0$ **then**
>>> $\rho_k \leftarrow \rho_m, H_{m_k} \leftarrow H_m$.
>>> **end if**
>> **end for**
>> $g'(i) = 0$ if $\rho_k(i) \leq th$.
>> $g'(i) \leftarrow R_g^k(i)$ if $\rho_k(i) > th$.
>> Formulate a subproblem as
>> $\min \left\| \Psi_{m_k} \right\|_1 + w_s \Psi_{m_k}{}^T \mathbf{L} \Psi_{m_k} \quad s.t. \quad \left\| g' - H_{m_k} \Psi_{m_k} \right\|_2 < \varepsilon \ and \ \Psi_{m_k} \geq 0$.
>> Obtain the feature vector Ψ_{m_k} by solving this problem with the method
>> $R_g^{k+1} \leftarrow R_g^k - H_{m_k} \Psi_{m_k}$.
> **end for**

Fig. 2.10 shows some sample results of restoration based on sparse representation. For better illustration, we use a color-coded method to demonstrate the results. More specifically, we map the top three principal elements of the phase retardation feature vectors $[\Psi_0, \Psi_1, \Psi_2]$ corresponding to each pixel (i.e., the coefficients for bases with the top three representative scores to R, G, and B values of a color image, respectively).

Fig. 2.10A is the original phase contrast microscopy image. Column (c) shows the zoomed-in color-coded images for discrimination-oriented sparse representation. From this result, we can observe that pixels belonging to different clusters have distinguishable

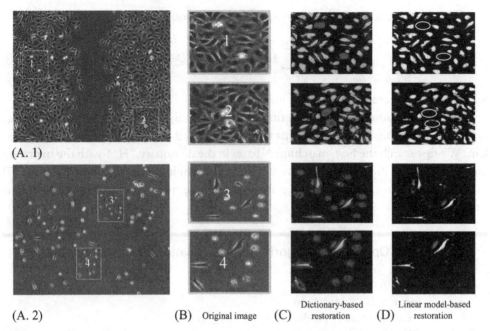

Fig. 2.10 Color-coded representation of restoration results for different approaches (best viewed in color). (A) Original phase contrast microscopy images; (B) zoomed-in phase contrast microscopy images; (C) restoration based on sparse representation, where phase-related coefficients corresponding bases with the top three representative scores are mapped onto R, G, and B values, respectively; (D) linear imaging model, which utilizes a grayscale image to demonstrate the results.

phase retardation features based on our sparse representation algorithm (i.e., bright cells are well represented by ψ_0 while dark cells are represented by ψ_1). Column (d) shows the restoration based on the linear imaging model [10], which fails to detect the bright cells because the phase retardation caused by the bright cells is relative large, which voids the assumption.

3.3 Cell-sensitive microscopy imaging

The complete pipeline of phase contrast microscopy image formation is summarized in Fig. 2.11, which consists of a phase contrast microscope and a digital camera to record time-lapse microscopy images on cells to analyze their properties. Starting from the beginning of the pipeline, the illuminance (L) passes through a petri dish culturing cells and phase contrast microscope optics, and generates the irradiance (E) observable by the naked human eye or a digital camera. The camera captures the irradiance (E) within an exposure duration (Δt) and transforms the accumulated irradiance (X, $X = E\Delta t$) into pixel values (I) in digital images by a CCD camera whose sensor response function is f (i.e., the pixel value in a microscopy image is a function of irradiance and exposure time: $I = f(E\Delta t)$).

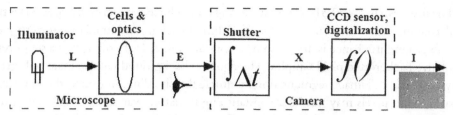

Fig. 2.11 Phase contrast microscopy imaging consists of two components: the microscope optics and a digital camera. The illuminance L from an illuminator passes through a petri dish culturing cells and the optics of phase contrast microscope, forming an irradiance E, which is visible to human eyes and digital cameras. The camera records the irradiance (E) within an exposure duration (Δt) into an accumulated irradiance ($X, X = E\Delta t$). Then, irradiance $\boldsymbol{X}$ is transformed into pixel values (I) in digital images by a CCD camera whose sensor response function is f (i.e., $I = f(E\Delta t)$).

3.3.1 Estimate the cell-sensitive camera response function

Let E_i be the irradiance at the i_{th} pixel location in a cell dish I_{ij}. The intensity of the i_{th} pixel in the j_{th} image with exposure duration Δt_j, is computed by

$$I_{ij} = f\left(E_i \Delta t_j\right) \tag{2.49}$$

where f is the camera response function and f is assumed to be the same for all pixel locations on the camera sensor. Without any exception, we assume that our camera response function is also monotonic and invertible. Because a camera's response function may vary significantly from an analytic format, we do not assume any parametric model in our estimation of camera response function. Computing the inverse function of Eq. (2.49) and taking the logarithm on both sides, we have

$$\log f^{-1}\left(I_{ij}\right) = \log E_i + \log \Delta t_j \tag{2.50}$$

Here, we formulate a constrained least-square minimization problem to solve the unknown camera response function and irradiance signal:

$$O(g, E) = \sum_{i=1}^{N}\sum_{j=1}^{P}\left\{\omega\left(I_{ij}\right)\left[g\left(I_{ij}\right) - \log E_i - \log \Delta t_j\right]\right\}^2$$
$$+ \alpha \sum_{i \in [1,\,N],\, i \in \psi} \left(\log E_i\right)^2 \tag{2.51}$$
$$+ \beta \sum_{I=I_{min}+1}^{I_{max}-1} \left[\omega(I)g''(I)\right]^2$$

where $g = \log f^{-1}$. Note that we only need to estimate a lookup table for the function g because its input domain is the pixel value range. For a 12-bit TIFF image, the lookup table's length is 4096 with the minimum pixel value $I_{min} = 0$ and the maximum $I_{max} = 4095$. N and P denote the number of pixel samples and exposed images, respectively.

The first term in Eq. (2.51) is the data-fitting cost. The second term in Eq. (2.51) is the regularization cost, which enforces the logarithm of background irradiance to zero (i.e., the background irradiance is driven to be a constant value, 1). Further, ψ is a set of representative background pixel samples. The constant background will facilitate cell image analysis, such as cell image segmentation by simple thresholding. In reality, the irradiance of background pixels may not be a constant due to natural variations. The goal of this constraint is to recover a camera response function similar to Fig. 2.12. Given a wide range of background pixel intensities, their corresponding irradiance values are recovered into a small range around zero. This regularization is still applicable when there is a slow irradiance gradient across the image. If the value range of the background irradiance is different from the cell irradiance, we can still segment cells out of the background. In fact, the irradiance from the background is different from the irradiance from cells in the phase contrast microscope. Otherwise, we cannot visualize cells through the ocular lens using human eyes.

The third term in Eq. (2.51) is a smooth term avoiding overfit on the data, which is defined by the second-order derivative:

$$g''(I) = g(I-1) - 2g(I) + g(I+1) \tag{2.52}$$

The second derivative measures the discontinuity of the curve function. When the second derivative is high, the curve has a sharp curvature. Therefore, minimizing the second derivative can ensure the smoothness during curve fitting. A common camera response function has a steep slope at the end of the camera response curve due to oversaturation or underexposure. In phase contrast microscopy images, the objects of interest (cells) are either dark or bright, while the background pixels have a broad value range in the middle. To visualize the cells better, we can introduce a weight function $\omega(I)$ to

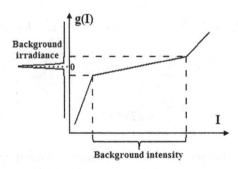

Fig. 2.12 An estimated camera response function such that the logarithm of irradiance values ($g(I)$) of background pixels are recovered to a small range close to zero, while the irradiance details of cell pixels are well recovered by the two ends of the camera response function.

emphasize the smoothness of the two ends of the camera response function. For example, a simple inverted hat function is a good choice for $\omega(I)$:

$$\omega(I) = \left| I - \frac{I_{min} + I_{max}}{2} \right| \tag{2.53}$$

The inverted hat function puts more emphasis on the two ends of the camera response curve (i.e., sensitive to cells) and less in the middle (i.e., to have a flat background region).

In Eq. (2.51), α and β are coefficients that balance the three cost terms. In our experiments, we choose fixed coefficients with $\alpha = 1000$ and $\beta = 1000$.

Because the objective function in Eq. (2.51) is quadratic, taking its derivatives related to g and E and setting them to zero create an overdetermined system of linear equations, ($\mathbf{Ax} = \mathbf{b}$), which can be solved using the pseudo-inverse or singular value decomposition method. The unknown variable in the linear equation system is $\mathbf{x} = [g(I_{min}), \ldots, g(I_{max}), -\log E_1, \ldots, \log E_N]$, whose first part ($[g(I_{min}), \ldots, g(I_{max})]$) is the cell-sensitive camera response function, a lookup table. Given N pixels from P multiexposed images, we have $(I_{max} - I_{min} + 1) + N$ unknown variables in $\mathbf{x}$. To avoid rank deficiency in the linear equation system, we require the number of data–fitting equations $NP > (I_{max} - I_{min} + 1) + N$. For our experiments, $P = 6$, $I_{min} = 0$, and $I_{max} = 4095$. We choose $N = 1000$ to satisfy this requirement.

3.3.2 Restoring the irradiance signal

After the cell-sensitive camera response function is estimated from the first set of multiexposed images, for any other sets in the time–lapse image sequence, we can easily restore their relative irradiance signals from image pixel values by

$$\log E_i = \frac{\sum_{j=1}^{P} w(I_{ij})(g(I_{ij}) - \Delta t_j)}{\sum_{j=1}^{P} w(I_{ij})} \tag{2.54}$$

where all the exposures are used to restore the irradiance signal robustly.

Fig. 2.13A shows one of a set of multiexposed phase contrast microscopy images. Fig. 2.13B is the restored irradiance signal map, which clearly demonstrates that the non-cell background region has a uniform background and the contrast between cells and background in the restored irradiance signal map is high. We sort the irradiance values in ascending order (Fig. 2.13C). The majority of the 1.4 million pixels of a 1040×1388 signal map has $E = 1$ (i.e., $\log E = 0$, which is the goal of the second regularization term in Eq. 2.51). The restored irradiance signal can facilitate the cell image segmentation tasks. For example, by selecting two thresholds T_H and T_L, the microscopy image can be easily thresholded to detect the cells and halo regions (Fig. 2.13D).

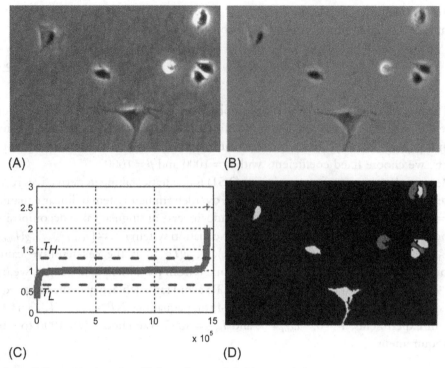

Fig. 2.13 Cell-sensitive imaging. (A) One of a set of multiexposed phase contrast microscopy images; (B) restored irradiance signal map with constant irradiance values on the background and high signal contrast; (C) the sorted irradiance signal values; (D) segmentation by thresholding the irradiance signals.

4. Cell segmentation

The restoration of microscopy images facilitates the subsequential segmentation of cells. In this section, we present various methods to implement cell segmentation, which utilizes a small number of labeled atoms, together with large amounts of unlabeled atoms, to build a better classifier. The scheme requires less human effort and leads to a better result.

4.1 Generation of phase-homogeneous superpixel

Rather than using the pixel grid, we adopt a method to partition a microscopy image into superpixels and utilize them as elements for cell segmentation. Aggregating pixels into superpixels eliminates the local redundancy of an image, which preserves local structures but avoids oversegmented, noisy clips. The computational cost is also significantly reduced without sacrificing the final cell segmentation accuracy, because the partition greatly reduces the number of instances for classification. Moreover, it allows for measuring an atom's statistical characteristics (e.g., distribution of phase retardation features) rather than a pixel's individual characteristics (e.g., intensity).

Compared with conventional superpixels based on image intensities [1], superpixels in this section are generated by clustering neighboring pixels with their pairwise similarity of phase retardation features. Therefore, phase retardation is statistically homogeneous within a superpixel, which is called a *phase-homogeneous superpixel*. Given two feature vectors at positions $\mathbf{x}_i$ and $\mathbf{x}_j$, the dissimilarity between $\boldsymbol{\Psi}(\mathbf{x}_i)$ and $\boldsymbol{\Psi}(\mathbf{x}_j)$ is defined as

$$d_p = \left\| \boldsymbol{\Psi}(\mathbf{x}_i) - \boldsymbol{\Psi}(\mathbf{x}_j) \right\|_2 \le \left\| \boldsymbol{\Psi}(\mathbf{x}_i) \right\|_2 + \left\| \boldsymbol{\Psi}(\mathbf{x}_j) \right\|_2 \le 2\sqrt{K} \tag{2.55}$$

Considering the spatial proximity, the spatial distance between $\mathbf{x}_i$ and $\mathbf{x}_j$, which are expected to be within the same superpixels, is

$$d_s = \left\| \mathbf{x}_i - \mathbf{x}_j \right\|_2 \le S \tag{2.56}$$

where $S = P/N$ denotes the approximate size of each superpixel, with P being the number of image pixels and N being a user-specified number of superpixels.

The partition of superpixels $\{\mathcal{A}_n\}_{n-1}^{N}$ is determined by minimizing the normalized distortion of phase retardation features and spatial positions as

$$\min \sum_{n=1}^{N} \sum_{\mathbf{x} \in \mathcal{A}_n} \left(\frac{1}{4K} \left\| \boldsymbol{\Psi}(\mathbf{x}) - \boldsymbol{\mu}_p^{(n)} \right\|_2^2 + \frac{\omega_s}{S^2} \left\| \mathbf{x} - \boldsymbol{\mu}_s^{(n)} \right\|_2^2 \right) \tag{2.57}$$

where $\mathbf{x}$ is the spatial coordinate; $\boldsymbol{\Psi}(\mathbf{x})$ is the corresponding phase retardation feature; and $\boldsymbol{\mu}_p^{(n)}$ and $\boldsymbol{\mu}_s^{(n)}$ are the prototype and mean of phase retardation features and spatial coordinates for superpixel $\mathcal{A}_n$, respectively. Further, ω_s is a balance variable to adjust the weight between the phase and spatial proximities. The minimization problem can be solved by associating each pixel to its nearest seed iteratively.

Fig. 2.14 shows an example of the atom generation based on phase retardation features, compared with superpixels by image intensities. The phase-homogeneous atoms

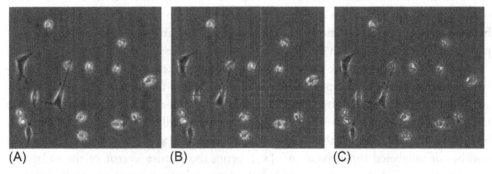

Fig. 2.14 Superpixel generation (best viewed in color). (A) Original phase contrast microscopy image; (B) phase-homogeneous superpixels; (C) intensity-homogeneous superpixels.

preserve the local structure of cell images (i.e., cell regions and halos are segmented into separated atoms, which is consistent with biophysical content of cell images). Nevertheless, the intensity-homogeneous atoms are more likely to produce oversegmented, noisy clips because cell intensities within cells often vary among subcellular structures.

In this case, cell segmentation can be performed by classifying the phase-homogeneous superpixels into several clusters (e.g., bright and dark cells, halos, background). We model the characteristic of feature vectors $\{\boldsymbol{\Psi}(\mathbf{x})\}$ within a specific superpixel $\mathcal{A}_n$, using a multivariate Gaussian distribution with mean vector $\boldsymbol{\mu}_n$ and covariance matrix $\boldsymbol{\Sigma}_n$, as

$$\boldsymbol{\mu}_n = \frac{1}{\zeta_n} \sum_{i=1}^{\zeta_n} \boldsymbol{\Psi}(\mathbf{x}_i), \quad \sum_n = \frac{1}{\zeta_n - 1} \sum_{i=1}^{\zeta_n} (\boldsymbol{\Psi}(\mathbf{x}_i) - \boldsymbol{\mu}_n)(\boldsymbol{\Psi}(\mathbf{x}_i) - \boldsymbol{\mu}_n)^T \tag{2.58}$$

where ζ_n is the number of pixels in superpixel $\mathcal{A}_n$.

In revealing the identity of a superpixel, its neighborhood information plays an important role, in addition to the characteristics of itself. For example, without neighboring information, halos and bright cells may not be distinguishable from each other based on phase retardation features within a superpixel. Specifically, both halos and bright cells are represented by similar distributions of phase retardations. In such a case, neighborhood information helps to distinguish them because most halos are around dark cell regions, while bright cells are surrounded by background.

To explore the relation of a superpixel $\mathcal{A}_n$ with its neighboring superpixel $\mathcal{A}_m$, we define the *neighborhood feature* of $\mathcal{A}_n$ as its most distinctive neighboring superpixel, which is measured with the pairwise Kullback-Leibler divergence to measure the dissimilarity between any pair of superpixels. By combining the feature within a superpixel and the most distinctive one, we obtain the descriptor $\mathbf{f}_n$ for a superpixel $\mathcal{A}_n$.

4.2 Semisupervised cell segmentation

In this section, we introduce a semisupervised classification approach to segment cells out of the background by classifying the partitioned superpixels into specific clusters. Based on a few phase-homogeneous superpixels annotated in each image, identities of the unlabeled superpixels are determined by propagating the labels from the user-specified superpixels. Cell segmentation can be attained based on the classification results.

Mathematically, we define the set of annotated superpixels as $\mathcal{L} \triangleq \{\mathbf{x}_l, \mathbf{y}_l\}_{l=1}^{N_l}$, where N_l is the number of annotated superpixels; $\mathbf{x}_l$ is a feature vector that describes the visual characteristics of the lth labeled superpixel; and $\mathbf{y}_l$ is a binary indicator corresponding to the identity of the lth superpixel—that is, $\mathbf{y}_l(k) = 1$ means that the lth superpixel is labeled as belonging to the kth class. In the same way, we define $\mathcal{U} \triangleq \{\mathbf{x}_u, \mathbf{y}_u\}_{u=1}^{N_u}$, with N_u being the number of unlabeled superpixels and $\{\mathbf{x}_u\}$ being the feature vector of the unlabeled superpixels. The label vectors of unlabeled superpixels $\{\mathbf{y}_u\}$ are going to be inferred via the label propagation procedure.

First, we construct an $\in$-nearest neighboring graph to characterize the pairwise similarity between superpixels. The adjacency matrix of the weight graph is denoted as $\mathbf{W} = [w_{ij}]$, which is an $N \times N$ nonnegative and symmetric matrix, with $N = N_l + N_u$ being the number of total superpixels. To implement label propagation, the Laplacian matrix $\mathbf{L}$ that corresponds to $\mathbf{W}$ (i.e., $\mathbf{L} = \mathbf{D} - \mathbf{W}$, with $\mathbf{D}$ being the diagonal degree matrix) is rearranged by splitting it into labeled and unlabeled submatrices:

$$\mathbf{L} \leftarrow \begin{bmatrix} \mathbf{L}_{ll} & \mathbf{L}_{lu} \\ \mathbf{L}_{ul} & \mathbf{L}_{uu} \end{bmatrix} \tag{2.59}$$

where $\mathbf{L}_{ll}$ is the Laplacian submatrix that characterizes the relationship between labeled superpixels; $\mathbf{L}_{uu}$ denotes the submatrix corresponding to the unlabeled superpixels; $\mathbf{L}_{lu}$ is a submatrix that interrelates the labeled and unlabeled superpixels; and $\mathbf{L}_{ul} = \mathbf{L}_{lu}^T$. Then, the problem of label propagation is formulated in a matrix form [8] as

$$\mathbf{Y}_u^* = \underset{\mathbf{Y}_u}{\arg\min} \ \mathrm{tr}\left([\mathbf{Y}_l; \mathbf{Y}_u]^T \begin{bmatrix} \mathbf{L}_{ll} & \mathbf{L}_{lu} \\ \mathbf{L}_{ul} & \mathbf{L}_{uu} \end{bmatrix} [\mathbf{Y}_l; \mathbf{Y}_u] \right) \tag{2.60}$$

where tr is the trace operator and $\mathbf{Y}_l$ and $\mathbf{Y}_u$ are binary indicator matrices corresponding to the labeled and unlabeled superpixels, respectively. Specifically, the indicator matrices $\mathbf{Y}_l$ and $\mathbf{Y}_u$ are constructed by stacking up the binary row indicators $\{\mathbf{y}_n\}_{n=1}^N$ in corresponding rows; namely, for the labeled superpixels $\mathbf{Y}_l = [\mathbf{y}_1; \cdots; \mathbf{y}_{N_l}]$, and for the unlabeled superpixels $\mathbf{Y}_u = [\mathbf{y}_{N_l+1}; \cdots; \mathbf{y}_u; \cdots; \mathbf{y}_{N_l+Nu}]$.

Based on the work by Zhu et al. [11], label propagation is solved by Gaussian fields harmonic functions (GFHFs), and the solution is given by a hypothesis $\mathcal{H}$ as

$$\mathcal{H} : \mathbf{Y}_u^* = -(\mathbf{D}_{uu} - \mathbf{W}_{uu})^{-1} \mathbf{L}_{ul} \mathbf{Y}_l$$
$$= -\mathbf{L}_{uu}^{-1} \mathbf{L}_{ul} \mathbf{Y}_l \tag{2.61}$$

where $\mathbf{D}_{uu}$ is a diagonal degree matrix with $\mathbf{D}_{uu}(i, i) = \sum_{j=1}^{N_l + N_u} \mathbf{W}(i, j)$. Note that the elements of $\mathbf{Y}_u^*$ are not binary numbers, but are real; thus, $\mathbf{Y}_u^*$ can be considered as soft-label results. The hard-label vector can be obtained simply by converting the maximum value in each $\mathbf{y}_u^*$ into 1 and the others into 0. Finally, cell segmentation is conducted by grouping the neighboring superpixels with the same labels.

Fig. 2.15 shows some sample results of image segmentation with label propagation, which demonstrates that high-quality cell segmentation is realized with only a small amount of human annotations. We first partition the phase contrast microscopy images into phase-homogeneous superpixels by aggregating the neighboring pixels with similar phase retardation features, as is shown in Fig. 2.15C. Consequentially, the superpixels are utilized as elements for image segmentation. The superpixels marked as *gray*, *light gray*, and *black* are annotated as bright cells, dark cells, and background regions. Fig. 2.15D shows the soft segmentation results based on label propagation, in which the *gray*, *light*

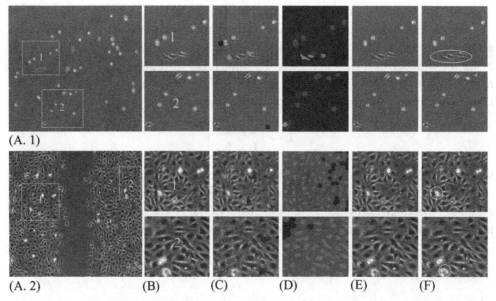

Fig. 2.15 Sample results of cell segmentation. (A) Input phase contrast microscopy images. (B) Zoom-in subimages. (C) Sample selection and annotation over the phase-homogeneous superpixels, where the *gray*, *light gray*, and *black* annotations indicate the corresponding superpixels are annotated as bright cells, dark cells, and background, respectively. (D) Soft classification results based on label propagation with human annotations. The *gray*, *light gray*, and *black* channel values in the soft classification results indicate the likelihoods of the superpixels belonging to bright cell, dark cell, and background regions, respectively. (E) Cell segmentation by finding the labels with the maximum likelihood, and grouping the neighboring superpixels with the same labels. (F) Cell segmentation based on linear imaging models as comparison.

gray, and *black* channel values in the soft segmentation indicate the likelihoods of the superpixels belonging to bright cell, dark cell, and background regions, respectively. Each soft segmentation result was converted into a hard segmentation result by finding the label with the maximum likelihood, and grouping the neighboring superpixels with the same labels, as shown in Fig. 2.15E. For comparison, we also implemented cell segmentation based on the linear imaging model, as is shown in Fig. 2.15F. The results demonstrate that there are false cell detections for some challenging cases, as marked with white circles. Halos are recognized as cell regions in the first row, when cells form as clusters, and some bright cells with low contrast to the background are also missed in the second row.

4.3 Online correction of cell segmentation

Although the previous approach of cell segmentation has been shown to be effective, but it still is not error-free. A classifier learned from initial labeling tends to result in more and more misclassifications when the data sets expand over time, with more and more unseen data. Therefore, it is worth considering how to incorporate human guidance further to achieve better results—in other words, how to propagate the human corrections to unlabeled samples in order to fix analogous errors. However, it is expensive to rebuild a classifier from scratch using newly collected training data because it requires a lot of human annotations. It would be nice to reuse the previous labeled data and then incorporate subsequent human verifications or corrections.

Once the reliability of segmentation is below a given threshold or obvious erroneous segmentations are detected, the system queries for active verification actively. Then, the user will examine the results, and correct misclassifications by clicking the corresponding regions with a mouse. Human correction will be propagated to the unlabeled samples to fix analogous misclassifications. The simplest way to conduct this task would be to rebuild or modify the affinity matrix in Eq. (2.59) and reperform label propagation. However, this scheme is too inefficient for the verification to be interactive because the inverse of the Laplacian matrix in Eq. (2.61) needs to be recalculated.

Instead, we propose a verification propagation scheme by extending the augmented graph method introduced by Zhu et al. [12] to handle a batch of samples at each round for more effective and efficient interaction. We build an augmented graph by adding auxiliary nodes, which are called *virtual supervisors* and denoted by $S = \{\mathbf{y}_s\}_{s=1}^{N_s}$, with N_s being the number of virtual supervisors and $\mathbf{y}_s$ being the human label given on the sth sample, and connect them to the corrected samples with weight w, such that $w \rightarrow +\infty$, as shown in Fig. 2.16. Then the adjacency matrix of the augmented graph can be built by adding rows and columns to the original adjacency matrix as follows:

$$\mathbf{W}^+ \leftarrow \begin{bmatrix} \mathbf{W}_{ll} & \mathbf{W}_{lu} & \mathbf{O}_{ls} \\ \mathbf{W}_{ul} & \mathbf{W}_{uu} & \mathbf{W}_{us} \\ \mathbf{O}_{sl} & \mathbf{W}_{su} & \mathbf{O}_{ss} \end{bmatrix} \tag{2.62}$$

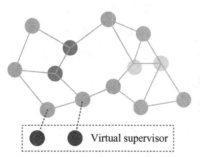

Virtual supervisor

Fig. 2.16 An augmented graph example where *dark gray* and *light gray* nodes indicate differently labeled samples, and *gray* nodes are unlabeled samples. Human labels are given on the most confusing samples by adding auxiliary nodes named *virtual supervisors* and connecting them to the samples with an infinite weight.

where $\mathbf{O}_{ls}$, $\mathbf{O}_{sl}$, and $\mathbf{O}_{ss}$ are zero submatrices with appropriate sizes, and $\mathbf{W}_{us} = w\mathbf{Z}_{us}$ and $\mathbf{W}_{us} = w\mathbf{Z}_{su} = w\mathbf{Z}_{us}^T$, where $\mathbf{Z}_{us}$ and $\mathbf{Z}_{su}$ are binary indicator matrices indicating which virtual supervisor is connected to which unlabeled sample.

The label propagation over this augmented graph can be obtained by minimizing the following objective function [4]:

$$f(\mathbf{Y}_u) = \mathrm{tr}\left([\mathbf{Y}_l; \mathbf{Y}_u; \mathbf{Y}_s]^T \mathbf{L}^+ \begin{bmatrix} \mathbf{Y}_l \\ \mathbf{Y}_u \\ \mathbf{Y}_s \end{bmatrix} \right) \tag{2.63}$$

where $\mathbf{L}^+$ is the Laplacian matrix of $\mathbf{W}^+$ and $\mathbf{Y}_s$ is the label matrix of virtual supervisors. Minimizing this objective yields a closed-form solution:

$$\begin{aligned} \mathbf{Y}_u^+ &= -\left(\mathbf{L}_{uu}^+\right)^{-1} [\mathbf{L}_{ul} \mathbf{L}_{us}] \begin{bmatrix} \mathbf{Y}_l \\ \mathbf{Y}_s \end{bmatrix} \\ &= -\boldsymbol{\Gamma}_{uu}^+ (\mathbf{L}_{ul}\mathbf{Y}_l - w\mathbf{Z}_{us}\mathbf{Y}_s) \end{aligned} \tag{2.64}$$

where $\mathbf{L}_{uu}^+$ denotes the Laplacian submatrix of the augmented graph corresponding to the unlabeled samples; $\boldsymbol{\Gamma}_{uu}^+$ is its inverse; and $\mathbf{L}_{us} = -\mathbf{W}_{us} = -w\mathbf{Z}_{us}$.

In the rest of this section, we will show how to efficiently compute $\boldsymbol{\Gamma}_{uu}^+$ and $\mathbf{Y}_u^+$. The diagonal submatrix of the augmented graph corresponding to the unlabeled samples $\mathbf{D}_{uu}^+$ is computed as

$$\begin{aligned} \mathbf{D}_{uu}^+(i, i) &= \sum_{j=1}^{N_t} \mathbf{W}_{ul}(i,j) + \sum_{j=1}^{N_u} \mathbf{W}_{uu}(i,j) + \sum_{j=1}^{N_s} \mathbf{W}_{us}(i,j) \\ &= \mathbf{D}_{uu}(i, i) + w(\mathbf{Z}_{us}\mathbf{Z}_{su})(i, i) \end{aligned} \tag{2.65}$$

We can easily prove that $\sum_{j=1}^{N_s} \mathbf{Z}_{us}(i,j) = (\mathbf{Z}_{us}\mathbf{Z}_{su})(i,i)$ with the fact that $\mathbf{Z}_{us}$ is a binary indicator matrix. Note that $\mathbf{Z}_{us}\mathbf{Z}_{su}$ is a diagonal matrix. Then, $\mathbf{L}_{uu}^+$ can be computed as

$$\begin{aligned} \mathbf{L}_{uu}^+ &= \mathbf{D}_{uu}^+ - \mathbf{W}_{uu}^+ \\ &= \mathbf{L}_{uu} + w\mathbf{Z}_{us}\mathbf{Z}_{su} \end{aligned} \tag{2.66}$$

and accordingly, $\boldsymbol{\Gamma}_{uu}^+$ can be calculated using the binomial inverse theorem:

$$\begin{aligned} \boldsymbol{\Gamma}_{uu}^+ &= \left(\mathbf{L}_{uu}^+\right)^{-1} \\ &= \left(\mathbf{L}_{uu} + w\mathbf{Z}_{us}\mathbf{Z}_{su}\right)^{-1} \\ &= \mathbf{L}_{uu}^{-1} - w\mathbf{L}_{uu}^{-1}\mathbf{Z}_{us}\left(\mathbf{I}_{N_s} + w\mathbf{Z}_{su}\mathbf{L}_{uu}^{-1}\mathbf{Z}_{us}\right)^{-1}\mathbf{Z}_{su}\mathbf{L}_{uu}^{-1} \\ &= \boldsymbol{\Gamma}_{uu} - \boldsymbol{\Gamma}_{uk}\left(\mathbf{I}_{N_s}/w + \boldsymbol{\Gamma}_{kk}\right)^{-1}\boldsymbol{\Gamma}_{ku} \end{aligned} \tag{2.67}$$

where $\mathbf{I}_{N_s}$ is an $N_s \times N_s$ identity matrix and $\boldsymbol{\Gamma}_{uk}$, $\boldsymbol{\Gamma}_{kk}$, and $\boldsymbol{\Gamma}_{ku}$ are submatrices of $\boldsymbol{\Gamma}_{uu}$ such that $\boldsymbol{\Gamma}_{uk} = \boldsymbol{\Gamma}_{uu}\mathbf{Z}_{us} = [\boldsymbol{\Gamma}_{uu}(i,j)], \forall i \in \mathcal{U}, j \in \mathcal{K}; \boldsymbol{\Gamma}_{kk} = [\boldsymbol{\Gamma}_{uu}(i,j)], \forall i \in \mathcal{K}, j \in \mathcal{K}$; and $\boldsymbol{\Gamma}_{ku} = \mathbf{Z}_{su}\boldsymbol{\Gamma}_{uu} = [\boldsymbol{\Gamma}_{uu}(i,j)], \forall i \in \mathcal{K}, j \in \mathcal{U}$, where $\mathcal{K}$ is a set of selected samples among $\mathcal{U}$ for human verification.

By substituting Eq. (2.67) into Eq. (2.64), we obtain

$$\mathbf{Y}_u^+ = -\mathbf{\Gamma}_{uu}^+(\mathbf{L}_{ul}\mathbf{Y}_l - w\mathbf{Z}_{us}\mathbf{Y}_s)$$
$$= -\left(\mathbf{\Gamma}_{uu} - \mathbf{\Gamma}_{uk}(\mathbf{I}_{N_s}/w + \mathbf{\Gamma}_{kk})^{-1}\mathbf{\Gamma}_{ku}\right)\mathbf{L}_{ul}\mathbf{Y}_l + w\left(\mathbf{\Gamma}_{uu} - \mathbf{\Gamma}_{uk}(\mathbf{I}_{N_s}/w + \mathbf{\Gamma}_{kk})^{-1}\mathbf{\Gamma}_{ku}\right)\mathbf{Z}_{us}\mathbf{Y}_s$$

$$(2.68)$$

Let $w \to +\infty$; then, we can obtain

$$\mathbf{Y}_u^+ = \mathbf{Y}_u - \mathbf{\Gamma}_{uk}\mathbf{\Gamma}_{kk}^{-1}\mathbf{Y}_k + \mathbf{\Gamma}_{uk}\mathbf{\Gamma}_{kk}^{-1}\mathbf{Y}_s$$
$$= \mathbf{Y}_u + \mathbf{\Gamma}_{uk}\mathbf{\Gamma}_{kk}^{-1}\left(\mathbf{Y}_s - \mathbf{Y}_k\right)$$

$$(2.69)$$

where $\mathbf{Y}_k$ is a submatix of $\mathbf{Y}_u$ that is constructed by stacking the rows of $\mathbf{Y}_u$ that correspond to queried samples.

We denote $\mathbf{\Gamma}_{uk}\mathbf{\Gamma}_{kk}^{-1}$ as the *verification propagation matrix*. By propagating the human verification information through this matrix, the segmentation results can be incrementally improved. Note that we compute the inverse of $\mathbf{\Gamma}_{kk}$, which is an $N_s \times N_s$ matrix; rather than $\mathbf{L}_{uu}^+$, which is an $N_u \times N_u$ matrix. As a result, verification propagation can be efficiently performed, leading to efficient interactive segmentation.

Examples of the cell segmentation results for the subsequential frames are shown in Fig. 2.17. In Fig. 2.17C and D, we demonstrate the soft and hard segmentation results based on label propagation of the initial human annotation from the first image. As can be

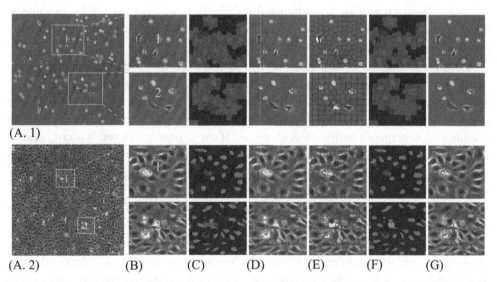

Fig. 2.17 Erroneous segmentation fixing examples with verification propagation on three images from Seq1 (top), Seq2 (middle), and Seq3 (bottom). (A) Input phase contrast microscopy images. (B) Zoom-in subimages. (C) Soft segmentation based on label propagation using annotation acquired in the first frame. (D) Hard segmentation based on the corresponding soft segmentation. (E) Actively selected superpixels for verification marked by *white*. (F) Improved soft segmentation after verification propagation. (G) Improved hard segmentation based on the improved soft segmentation.

seen in Fig. 2.17D, the segmentation result contains several errors (i.e., some dark cells are missed and bright halos are misclassified into cells). These errors are ascribed to inadequate or unbalanced human labels because the phase retardation features of some cells are different from the first frame in the sequence. Some of the superpixels containing errors were automatically selected by our algorithm to be verified and corrected by humans, as is shown in Fig. 2.17E. In Fig. 2.17F and G, we demonstrate the improved soft and hard segmentation results after human correction and its propagation. As shown in Fig. 2.17G, in addition to the errors of superpixels selected by superpixel selection, similar errors of other superpixels are effectively fixed as well.

5. Conclusion

As the amount of data increases in the long-term, high-throughput biological experiments, cell detection and segmentation are recognized as fundamental components in both fundamental biology research and clinical applications. In this chapter, we have presented numerous works on microscopy image analysis by considering the particular imaging mechanism. We introduced work on the understanding of phase contrast microscopy imaging and differential interference contrast microscopy, and then presented the imaging models based on the optics of microscopes. Specifically, the linear imaging models can approximate the imaging formation process, which removes artifacts and segments cells with effortless thresholding. The dictionary-based restoration further boosts the performance by considering the diffraction patterns caused by specimens. Phase retardation features of each cell can be effectively restored by solving a quadratic cost function with a sparse regularization.

With the microscopy image properly restored, we further proposed to segment cells out of the background with a few human annotations. The microscopy images can be partitioned into several superpixels by clustering the neighboring pixels with similar phase retardation features. Cell segmentation is consequently performed by grouping neighboring superpixels with similar identities. If the segmentation result is not reliable, we seek to select a batch of error-prone superpixels to query for verification. Once errors are detected and corrected, the information is systematically propagated over an augmented affinity graph to the unlabeled superpixels. This step is efficiently conducted by introducing a verification correction propagation matrix rather than reperforming the label propagation from the beginning.

Nowadays, deep learning has dramatically improved the state-of-the-art performance of computational models in many domains by learning representations of data with multiple levels of abstraction. The large volumes of image data captured from the long-term, high-throughput biological experiments make it possible to develop a deep architecture model. It is believable that a deep neural network such as CNNs would promote the progress of microscopy image analysis. Nevertheless, the performance of CNN would be improved if we could take the particular imaging mechanism into account.

Acknowledgments

National Key Research and Development Program of China (No.2020AAA0104304), NSFC Project 62076147. This project was supported by NSF CAREER Award IIS-2019967.

References

[1] R. Achanta, A. Shaji, K. Smith, A. Lucchi, P. Fua, S. Sustrunk, SLIC superpixels compared to state-of-the-art superpixel methods, IEEE Transactions on Pattern Analysis and Machine Intelligence 34 (2012) 2274–2282.

[2] K. Li, T. Kanade, Nonnegative mixed-norm preconditioning for microscopy image segmentation, in: Proc. International Conference on Information Processing in Medical Imaging, 2009, pp. 362–373.

[3] K. Li, E.D. Miller, M. Chen, T. Kanade, L.E. Weiss, P.G. Campbell, Cell population tracking and lineage construction with spatiotemporal context, Med. Image Anal. 12 (2008) 546–566.

[4] W. Liu, S.F. Chang, Robust multi-class transductive learning with graphs, in: IEEE Conference on Computer Vision and Pattern Recognition, 2009, pp. 381–388.

[5] D. Murphy, Phase contrast microscopy and dark-field micorscopy, in: Fundamentals of Light Microscopy and Electronic Imaging, Wiley, 2001, pp. 97–116.

[6] D. Needell, R. Vershynin, Signal recovery from incomplete and inaccurate measurements via regularized orthogonal matching pursuit, IEEE J. Sel. Top. Signal Process. 4 (2010) 310–316.

[7] F. Sha, Y. Lin, L.K. Saul, D.D. Lee, Multiplicative updates for nonnegative quadratic programming, Neural Comput. 19 (2007) 2004–2031.

[8] H. Su, Z. Yin, S. Huh, T. Kanade, Cell segmentation in phase contrast microscopy images via semi-supervised classification over optics-related features, Med. Image Anal. 17 (2013) 746–765.

[9] Z. Yin, T. Kanade, Restoring artifact-free microscopy image sequences, in: IEEE International Symposium on Biomedical Imaging: From Nano to Macro, 2011, pp. 909–913.

[10] Z. Yin, T. Kanade, M. Chen, Understanding the phase contrast optics to restore artifact-free microscopy images for segmentation, Med. Image Anal. 16 (2012) 1047–1062.

[11] X. Zhu, Z. Ghahramani, J. Lafferty, Semi-supervised learning using gaussian fields and harmonic functions, in: Twentieth International Conference on Machine Learning (ICML), 2003, pp. 912–919.

[12] X. Zhu, J. Lafferty, Z. Ghahramani, Combining active learning and semi-supervised learning using gaussian fields and harmonic functions, in: ICML 2003 workshop on The Continuum from Labeled to Unlabeled Data in Machine Learning and Data Mining, 2003, pp. 58–65.

CHAPTER 3

Detection and segmentation in microscopy images

Nisha Ramesh and Tolga Tasdizen
University of Utah, Scientific Computing and Imaging Institute, Salt Lake City, UT, United States

Contents

1. Introduction

Detection and segmentation of objects of interest play a critical role in the analysis of anatomical structures for various biomedical applications. Detection is generally considered to be a precursor for solving higher-level problems, such as segmentation, tracking, and morphological analysis. There are multiple challenges seen in microscopy images for detection of objects of interest, such as low signal-to-noise ratio, low contrast, overlapping objects, low resolution, and variation in appearance. A significant challenge in biomedical image segmentation is the variability in the appearance of objects, such as contrast and texture, due to different imaging conditions and settings. Typical approaches used for detection and segmentation are based on one of a number of categories, such as feature thresholding, region-based clustering, deformable models, and supervised learning approaches. The various supervised learning techniques that we focus on include hierarchical methods and deep learning approaches using convolutional neural networks (CNNs) for detection and segmentation in optical and electron microscopy images.

Computer Vision for Microscopy Image Analysis
https://doi.org/10.1016/B978-0-12-814972-0.00003-5

Hierarchical methods encompass segmentations of an image at various detail levels and thresholds, the higher-level regions can be obtained from a combination of regions from segmentations at lower levels [5, 10, 26, 27, 30, 51, 52, 79, 90]. Hierarchical methods have been used to solve both detection and segmentation problems in microscopy images. Hierarchical methods preserve the spatial and neighboring information among segmented regions. A number of methods, such as the watershed transform [14], an ultrametric contour map (UCM) [8], Felzenszwalb's method [25], and an MSER detector [55], can be used to generate superpixels in hierarchical approaches. *Superpixels* are a group of pixels in spatial proximity that have similar intensity and texture, thereby preserving the boundaries' features [1, 81].

CNNs provide state-of-the-art solutions for various computer vision applications [31, 42, 53, 65] and have been used extensively to solve various classification problems. However, in many biomedical imaging applications, the desired output requires pixelwise predictions (i.e., a class label is predicted for each pixel). A patch-based approach was introduced to address problems such as segmentation of neural membranes and mitosis detection using CNNs, where the pixels are classified based on the neighborhood region [19, 20]. The patch-based classification relies on the size of the patch to determine the localization accuracy and contextual information. Even though CNNs have been the method of choice for object recognition and classification tasks, their performance on dense output prediction problems for biomedical applications needs to be improved. Recently, fully convolutional networks (FCNs) that can be trained in an end-to-end manner have been used for semantic labeling tasks, where a class label is assigned to each pixel [53]. Based on the FCN, U-Net architecture was introduced for biomedical image segmentation. U-Net architecture has been the preferred network for various applications in the field of medical imaging. In Fakhry et al. [24], residual connections were introduced between the encoder and decoder parts of a network to segment neurons in electron microscopy images. CNNs and FCNs have also been used to detect cell centers [88] and count cells by predicting cell density [84] in microscopy images.

There are two significant challenges that limit the performance of CNNs in biomedical applications: (1) large-labeled training data sets with thousands of training images that are well distributed to capture the potential variability of the data, (2) and the training data distribution needs to be representative of the images that the model is used to make predictions for. It is tedious and expensive to acquire fine-grained, pixel-level manual annotations to learn models to predict segmentation labels. There may be discrepancies between the training and testing distributions when the learned model is deployed to make predictions for images collected with different settings, illumination, contrast, and varying image acquisition techniques. In this chapter, we focus on two distinct applications in biomedical imaging: (1) detection and segmentation of cells in optical microscopy images; and (2) and segmentation of neuronal structures in electron microscopy images.

1.1 Cell detection and segmentation in optical microscopy images

A cell is considered to be the fundamental, structural, and functional building unit of all living organisms. Cells have the ability to divide and replicate and are responsible for the evolution of an organism. Studying the underlying principles related to cell theory is critical to help gain perspective on cellular mechanics. Due to the advancement in the field of microscopic imaging techniques, it is feasible to acquire very large numbers of images in a short span of time. The abundance and complexity in the data generated using modern equipment drives us to pursue computerized techniques for cellular image analysis. Automated image segmentation for cell analysis is a challenging problem due to the large variability (different microscopes, stains, cell types, and cell densities) and complexity of the data (time-lapse, large numbers of cells). Accurately detecting a large number of cells in dense images is difficult due to multiple problems, such as occlusion from overlapping of several objects in the depth direction and spatially overlapping cells. Therefore, it is important to develop robust generic algorithms that can be used on a variety of cells from different modalities. Next, we discuss the current contributions in the field of cellular image analysis and extrapolate possible improvements.

1.1.1 Intensity thresholding and filtering

Intensity thresholding based on the distribution of pixel values is considered to be one of the earliest approaches used for cell segmentation [56, 83]. A global or adaptive threshold is chosen to distinguish cell regions from its background, which is feasible only if the cells have homogeneous intensities, have a high contrast with background, and are distinctly separable. Generally, intensity thresholding is used as a preliminary step in algorithms to eliminate background clutter. The intensity images can also be transformed to represent some derived features such as edges and blobs using filtering operations. Edge detection is used to delineate cell contours [17, 54] and is often used in the initial stages of various segmentation algorithms as a feature detector [4, 16]. Morphological filtering is used frequently as a preprocessing or postprocessing step in cell detection and segmentation [7, 22, 62]. Detection and segmentation based on local image information can be erroneous because they can be associated with imaging artifacts or noise.

1.1.2 Region-based segmentation

Region-based segmentation, in which pixels that belong to a cell are grouped, is a popular approach for cell segmentation. Typically, region-growing algorithms start from selected seed points and grow regions by augmenting more connected points that have properties similar to the seed points, such as specific ranges of intensity or color, to form a labeled image [2]. Region-based segmentation approaches also use clustering algorithms with no seed points, where similar image pixels are aggregated in an unsupervised framework. Gaussian mixture models were used to cluster pixels using color and texture features [11]. The watershed transform is one of the more popular region accumulation methods; it requires an edge-enhanced image to segment an image into multiple regions and catchment basins. In most scenarios, this method produces oversegmentation and requires further processing. Hence, several algorithms use the watershed transform as an initial step in their segmentation pipeline.

Hierarchical image segmentation has been demonstrated to be an effective method for cell detection and segmentation [5, 10, 26, 27, 30, 51, 52, 78, 79, 90]. A hierarchical representation for the segmentation is constructed using the cell candidates, such that higher-level regions are built by merging regions at lower levels. Supervised algorithms with handcrafted features are used to train classifiers to merge the regions in the hierarchical representation [26, 28, 50, 51, 76]. Alternatively, learning algorithms can also be used to predict probability scores for the cell candidates [26, 64, 79]. Dynamic programming or integer linear programming is used to find a nonoverlapping set of candidates from a hierarchical representation. It is challenging to choose a good feature set to discriminate target cells from the background because feature selection relies on prior knowledge about the data.

Images can also be represented using a graphical representation, where pixels are the nodes and the edge weights are based on the similarity with neighbors [70, 92]. The segmentation problem is then solved as a graph-partitioning problem. To reduce the computational load, the graphical representation has also been constructed using superpixels. In Zhang et al. [92], a region adjacency graph is constructed using superpixels, and then the segmentation is inferred by partitioning the graph using correlation clustering.

1.1.3 Deformable models

Cell contours can be represented using deformable models. Among these methods, variational image segmentation with level sets has been a well-known choice due to attractive properties such as adaptive topology, which can naturally change during evolution [15, 61]. Level sets evolve by minimizing an energy functional that is chosen to distinguish the foreground from the background. An application of level sets to segment cells is seen in Nath et al. [58]. However, due to the nonparametric nature of level sets, level-set propagation always has to include a regularization term, such as a penalty on curve length, surface area, or curvature [21]. Implicit parametric shape models (namely, disjunctive normal shape models) are used to accurately learn cell boundaries in Ramesh et al. [63]. Implicit parametric models have the advantage of being able to easily learn statistics and naturally change topology during its evolution. Evolving the boundaries for individual cells can get computationally expensive because the time complexity increases with the density of cells in the images.

1.1.4 Convolutional neural networks

CNNs have been used recently for semantic labeling tasks, where a class label is assigned to each pixel. A FCN [53] was proposed for semantic segmentation that can be trained in an end-to-end manner. FCNs avoid redundant computations; however, this comes at the cost of localization accuracy. Based on the FCN, U–Net architecture was introduced to segment cells in biomedical images [66]. The architecture uses skip connections between the encoder and decoder parts of the network to enable precise localization. The U–Net architecture relies on strong data augmentation strategies. It is difficult to obtain pixel-level annotations to train a CNN to segment cells in microscopy images, and training a network with limited labeled data makes the task challenging. To enhance the performance of CNNs, specialized feature maps like eigenvalue of Hessian and wavelet-filtered images have been used with raw intensity images for training [67]. In Akram et al. [3], two networks are used—one for predicting cell proposals trained using the ground truth bounding boxes, and the other for generating cell segmentation masks for the proposed candidates trained using pixel-level labels.

Conventionally, CNNs have been used for solving classification and segmentation problems. CNNs can also be used to solve cell detection problems [48, 84–88]. Cell detection is a critical problem in biomedical image analysis, which is often a prerequisite for segmentation. It is difficult to detect cells when there is a high degree of overlap between them. A good subset of cell proposals generated with different parameters are used to train a CNN to learn to predict its probability of being a cell [48]. In Xie et al. [85], a CNN was modified to represent a regression model on a structured proximity space for cell detection. A FCN-based framework trained end on end on image patches was introduced by Xie et al. [84] for predicting a spatial density map of target cells, and the number of cells is estimated by integration over the learned density map. A similar approach is seen in Xue et al. [88], where the global cell count is cast as a regression problem using CNNs. A CNN-based regression network was used to predict the compressed vectors that encode the output pixel space indicating cell centers from the input pixels [87]. In Sirinukunwattana et al. [71], a spatially constrained CNN (SC-CNN) regresses the likelihood of a pixel being the center of a nucleus to detect nuclei and uses a locality sensitive CNN for classification. A structured regression model based on a fully residual CNN was used for efficient cell detection [86].

1.2 Neuronal segmentation in electron microscopy images

The study of neural circuit reconstruction (i.e., connectomics) remains one of the most challenging problems in neuroscience. Image analysis techniques are used to study the connectivity of nervous systems. Electron microscopy (EM) images have been used for neural circuit reconstruction because they provide high resolution of the intracellular structures, synapses, and gap junctions. Automated and semiautomated 3D reconstruction of neurites in EM stacks can be tremendously helpful for accelerating connectomics research [9]. The main goal in this problem is to identify neurons that span multiple adjacent image slices and reconstruct them. Conventionally, the 3D reconstruction problem can be broken into two tasks: (1) 2D prediction task, where each image slice is segmented independently; and (2) a postprocessing step on segmented slices to reconstruct the 3D neurites by linking similar segments across the entire image stack. Supervised algorithms with handcrafted features are used to learn classifiers for the postprocessing step to link similar segments together across the entire image stack. The classifiers incorporate prior knowledge and understanding of the data; hence, classifiers trained on a particular data set may not perform well when tested on data sets acquired in a different scenario. Alternatively, there are methods that seek to achieve 2D segmentation and 3D reconstruction at the same time. Next, we discuss the current contributions in the field of neural circuit reconstruction and extrapolate possible improvements.

1.2.1 Traditional filtering approaches

There have been numerous unsupervised algorithms that have been proposed to segment 2D neurons [38, 44, 74]. Anisotropic directional filtering was used to enhance the contrast and continuity of cell membranes [38, 74]. These filtering approaches do not remove intracellular structures, reducing the accuracy for membrane segmentation. In Kumar et al. [44], radon-like features were introduced to aggregate desired information derived from images and suppress undesirable intracellular structures.

1.2.2 Supervised learning

Supervised learning methods have been used extensively for segmenting membranes and neurons in 2D. These include single-layer networks [57], cascades of classifiers [37, 68], and hierarchical contextual models [69]. A single-layer artificial neural network (ANN) with Hessian eigenspace features was used for segmentation [57]. A cascade of ANNs were used [37]. Several ANNs are used in series; each ANN uses the classification context provided by the previous network to improve detection accuracy [37]. The model in Seyedhosseini [68] uses contextual information along with radon-like features to learn about a series of discriminative models. The multiscale model representation of the context image was used to give the subsequent classifiers access to a larger contextual area for better detection of neuron membranes in EM images. In Seyedhosseini and Tasdizen [69], a multiclass, multiscale contextual model was introduced that exploits both input image features and contextual information with a logistic disjunctive normal network classifier to detect membranes. Region-based methods are used to transform the membrane probability maps into cell segments; they are required for improving the segmentation accuracy from membrane detections in EM images [9].

A hierarchical merge tree structure was built to represent multiple region hypotheses, and the merge tree was resolved with consistency constraints to acquire final intrasection segmentation [50]. The sections were linked to reconstruct the intersection neurons using supervised learning. In Hu et al. [34], unsupervised learning and signal-processing techniques are used to obtain high depth-resolution EM images computationally without sacrificing throughput. Several methods have been used to link similar neuron sections across the image stack. A graph-cut framework was proposed to trace 2D contours in 3D [89]. In Vitaladevuni and Basri [82], the neuron segments are jointly clustered based on their likelihood of belonging to the same neuron. The 3D linking was formulated as a quadratic optimization problem by coclustering each pair of adjacent segments. An automatic processing pipeline was introduced that combines the probabilistic output of a random forest classifier with geometrical consistency constraints to optimize the 3D affinity matrix [40]. In Laptev [45], global dense correspondences between the sections was established using a SIFT-Flow [49] algorithm in order to evaluate the features of the corresponding pixels and use them to perform the segmentation.

Alternatively, there are a set of methods that perform 2D segmentation and 3D reconstruction simultaneously. A reinforcement learning framework was proposed to merge supervoxels into segmentations [36]. A supervoxel merging method was proposed for segmenting neurons, all merging decisions were coupled in a graphical model that incorporates both supervoxel face and boundary curve information [6]. The use of supervoxels allows the extraction of expressive geometric features that are used by the higher-order potentials in the graphical model. Multiple 2D segmentation hypotheses were generated for each section in the stack, and segments were fused to provide the most globally consistent segmentation of the stack in a Markov random field framework [80]. In a similar manner, 2D segmentation hypotheses were generated as a tree structure, and then the 2D segmentation and 3D reconstruction were formulated as an integer linear program with constraints [29]. A reinforcement learning framework was used to learn a merging policy for superpixel agglomeration [60]. There are also other semiautomatic methods that utilize user input to improve the segmentation of neurons. Neurons are oversegmented into 2D and 3D regions, and the regions that belong to one neuron are manually merged [18]. Skeleton reconstructions of neurons are combined with automated volume segmentations [13]. To be able to segment image volumes in 3D requires the data to be mostly isotropic. There are limitations to the image volume size that can be generated with isotropic resolution. Direct 3D segmentation approaches may not be feasible for anisotropic data sets.

1.2.3 Convolutional neural networks

Even though deep networks give state-of-the-art solutions for object recognition and classification tasks, their performance on dense output prediction problems has room for improvement, especially in neural circuit reconstruction applications using high-resolution EM images [23, 35, 46, 73, 77]. A convolutional network was trained to classify pixels as membrane or nonmembrane [35]. Patch-based approaches for dense output prediction problems have the conflicting goals of full-resolution prediction and incorporation of sufficient contextual information [41]. A deconvolution network was introduced [59] for semantic segmentation. Residual deconvolutional networks (RDNs) were proposed to balance the tradeoff between increasing contextual information to exploit the multiscale features and the ability to preserve the pixel-level resolution and accuracy expected for dense output prediction [24]. Multiple residual shortcut paths were added to a fully deconvolutional network with minimum additional computations and the final pixel-level predictions incorporate features from both pathways. To achieve human-level performance, Zeng et al. [91] employ a combination of novel boundary map generation methods, with optimized model ensembles using CNNs to address the challenges of segmenting anisotropic image EM stacks. Their deep network for 3D neurite boundary detection deals with anisotropy and misalignment problems that are commonly seen in 3D EM data. A variant of 3D U-Net architecture was proposed [47] to learn two tasks. The primary task predicts affinities between nearest-neighbor voxels, and the auxiliary task predicts long-range affinities. The learned network is used to generate oversegmented supervoxels, which are greedily agglomerated based on mean affinity. Data augmentation is used to address challenges such as misalignments, missing sections, and out-of-focus sections in EM images.

2. Cell detection and segmentation in optical microscopy images

In this section, we focus on methods for detection and segmentation of cells in optical microscopy images. Because detection is a preliminary step for classification, we also review an approach for nucleus detection and classification.

2.1 Learning to detect cells using nonoverlapping extremal regions

A generic learning-based method was introduced for detecting cells across different microscopy modalities [10]. A highly efficient MSER detector [55] was used to generate cell candidate regions. Let $R_1, R_2, \ldots R_N$ be the set of N cell candidate regions in an image. A feature vector $\mathbf{f_i}$ was computed for every cell candidate region R_i. A classifier with weight vector $\mathbf{w}$ was learned to predict V_i, the probability of the region belonging to the class of cells of interest. The classifier model was learned in a structured SVM framework from dot-annotated training data to score each candidate region for the detection task. A subset of cell candidates was picked such that the sum of scores of the picked regions was maximized while satisfying the nonoverlap constraint (i.e., the chosen regions did not overlap). Binary indicator variables $\mathbf{y} = \{y_1, y_2, \ldots, y_N\}$ are used to identify the regions that are picked. Let † be a set of those region subsets that do not overlap; that is, $\dagger = \{\mathbf{y} \mid \forall i, j : (i \neq j) \wedge (y_i = 1) \wedge (y_j = 1) \Rightarrow R_i \cap R_j = \oslash\}$. The optimization problem was formulated as

$$F(\mathbf{y}) = \max_{\mathbf{y} \in \dagger} \sum_{i=1}^{N} \gamma_i V_i \tag{3.1}$$

The nestedness property of the extremal regions was exploited to obtain an exact solution of Eq. (3.1) via dynamic programming. They assume a set of M training images $\mathcal{I}^1, \mathcal{I}^2, \dots \mathcal{I}^M$, where each training image $\mathcal{I}^j$ has a set of N^j MSER regions $(R_1^j, R_2^j, \dots R_{N^j}^j)$. The training images are annotated such that n_i^j denotes the number of user-placed dots (annotations) inside the region R_i^j. For each of these regions R_i^j, a feature vector $\mathbf{f}_i^j$ was computed. The goal of learning, then, is to find a weight vector $\mathbf{w}$ so that the regions with $n_i^j = 1$ are selected, and also to ensure that for each dot, a region is selected that contains it. A structured SVM was used to optimize the performance of the inference procedure on the training data. The configuration $\mathbf{y}^j \in \dagger^j$ is the set of nonoverlapping regions for the image $\mathcal{I}^j$. The researchers introduced a loss function associated with $\mathbf{y}^j$ to measure the deviation from the one-to-one correspondence between the user-placed dots and the picked regions:

$$L(\mathbf{y}^j) = \sum_{i=1}^{N^j} \gamma_i^j |n_i^j - 1| + U^j(\mathbf{y}^j) \tag{3.2}$$

where $U^j(\mathbf{y}^j)$ denotes the number of user-placed dots that have no correspondences and are not covered by any region R_j^i with $y_j^i = 1$. The ground truth configurations $\bar{\mathbf{y}}^j = \left\{ \bar{\gamma}_1^j, \bar{\gamma}_2^j, \dots, \gamma_{N_j}^j \right\} \in \dagger$ is determined for every training image, such that an unique extremal region is assigned to every dot annotation. The optimal weight vector $\mathbf{w}$ was found by minimizing the following convex objective:

$$L(\mathbf{w}) = \frac{1}{2} |\mathbf{w}|^2 + \frac{C}{M} \sum_{y=1}^{M} \max_{\mathbf{y}^j \in \gamma^j} \left(\sum_{i=1}^{N^j} \left(\mathbf{w} \cdot \mathbf{f}_i^j \right) \gamma_i^j - \sum_{i=1}^{N^j} \left(\mathbf{w} \cdot \mathbf{f}_i^j \right) \bar{\gamma}_i^j + L(\mathbf{y}^j) \right) \tag{3.3}$$

where the first term is a regularizer on the weights $\mathbf{w}$, C is a scalar regularization parameter, and the maximum inside the sum represents a convex upper bound on the loss defined in Eq. (3.2).

They evaluate their method on three data sets for cell detection: (1) ICPR 2010 histopathology images of stained breast cancer tissue [32], (2) fluorescence microscopy images of human embryonic kidney (HEK) cells [12], and (3) phase-contrast images of cervical cancer cell colonies of the HeLa cell line (Fig. 3.1). Each of the data sets imposes a different challenge for detection. In the histopathology images, it is difficult to identify the lymphocyte nuclei from the breast cancer nuclei due to their similar appearance. The detection task in the HEK cells is challenging due to the significant intensity variations among cells across the image, fading boundaries, and frequent cell clumping. The phase-contrast HeLa cells present a high variability in cell shapes and sizes.

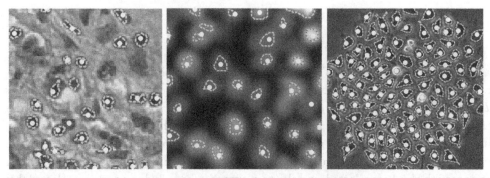

Fig. 3.1 Example images from the data sets used for cell detection. Left: Histopathology image of breast cancer tissue, fluorescence microscopy image of human embryonic kidney cells. Right: Phase-contrast HeLa cells. *(C. Arteta, V. Lempitsky, J.A. Noble, A. Zisserman, Learning to detect cells using non-overlapping extremal regions, in: Medical Image Computing and Computer-Assisted Intervention—MICCAI: 15th International Conference, Nice, France, October 1–5, 2012, Proceedings, Part I, Springer Berlin Heidelberg, 2012, pp. 348–356, Figure 3. Reprinted with permission.)*

They evaluate the performance of the algorithm for detecting cell centroids using precision, recall, and F-measure. The precision and recall metrics are indicators for the number of false positives and false negatives, respectively. For the histopathology images [32], two additional metrics were calculated: (1) mean and standard deviation of the Euclidean distance between detected dots and ground truth dots, and (2) absolute difference between the number of cells found and the ground truth number of cells. Three variations of their method was evaluated in their experiments: (1) direct classification (DC) using a learned binary classifier with a **w** vector to evaluate all MSERs to choose the region with the highest score in every set of overlapping regions with positive scores; (2) binary SVM + inference (B + I), where the inference is based on the weight vector learned through binary classification; and (3) structured SVM + inference (S + I), which uses inference with the weight vector learned by the structured SVM. Fig. 3.2 shows the precision-recall curves for the various evaluations. From their experiments, it can be observed that enforcing the nonoverlap constraint increases the accuracy when **w** is learned within the structured SVM framework. Table 3.1 compares the quantitative experimental results on the histopathology data set. One of the disadvantages is that the research relies heavily on a robust region detector, and thus the application of the results is limited. Also, the researchers use handcrafted features to train the classifier, which may not capture the variability in the classes.

2.2 U-Net: Convolutional networks for biomedical image segmentation

The U-Net architecture [66] is based on the FCN [53]; it encompasses an encoder to capture context and a symmetric decoder to enable precise localization (Fig. 3.3). The encoder is supplemented with successive layers, where pooling operators are replaced

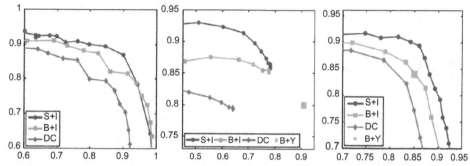

Fig. 3.2 Precision (vertical) versus recall (horizontal) curves for the three data sets for the three variations of their approach and Ref. [12] (denoted as B+Y, where available). Significant improvements brought by the nonoverlap constraint (B+I) and the structured SVM (S+I) can be observed. *(C. Arteta, V. Lempitsky, J.A. Noble, A. Zisserman, Learning to detect cells using non-overlapping extremal regions, in: Medical Image Computing and Computer-Assisted Intervention—MICCAI: 15th International Conference, Nice, France, October 1–5, 2012, Proceedings, Part I, Springer Berlin Heidelberg, 2012, pp. 348–356, Figure 4. Reprinted with permission.)*

Table 3.1 Detection results for the ICPR 2010 histopathology images [32].

Method	Precision	Recall	F-score	$\mu_d + \sigma_d$	$\mu_n + \sigma_n$
Arteta et al. [10]	86.99	90.03	88.48	1.68 ± 2.55	2.90 ± 2.13
Bernardis [12]	–	–	–	3.13 ± 3.08	12.7 ± 8.70

by upsampling operators to increase the resolution of the output. For localization, high-resolution features from the encoder are concatenated with the upsampled output. Every layer of the encoder has two 3×3 convolutions, followed by a rectified linear unit (ReLu) and a 2×2 max pooling with stride 2 for downsampling. The number of feature channels is doubled after every downsampling. Similarly, in the decoder, each layer consists of an upsampling of the feature map, followed by an upconvolution of 2×2 and then two 3×3 convolutions with a ReLu layer. The number of feature channels is halved after every upsampling. Skip connections between the encoder and decoder are established by concatenating the layers with the same number of feature channels to introduce high-resolution features to the decoder, enabling precise localization. A pixelwise, softmax layer was used over the final feature map, combined with the cross-entropy loss function to learn segmentation. Thus, the last layer for the segmentation task uses a 1×1 convolution to reduce the number of output channels to the number of labels. The softmax layer is defined as $p_k(x) = \exp(a_k(x))/(\sum_{k'=1}^{K} \exp(a_{k'}(x)))$, where $a_k(x)$ denotes the activation in feature channel k at the pixel position $x \in \Omega$ with $\Omega \subset Z^2$ and K is the number of classes. The cross-entropy then penalizes at each position the deviation of $p_{l(x)}$ from 1 using

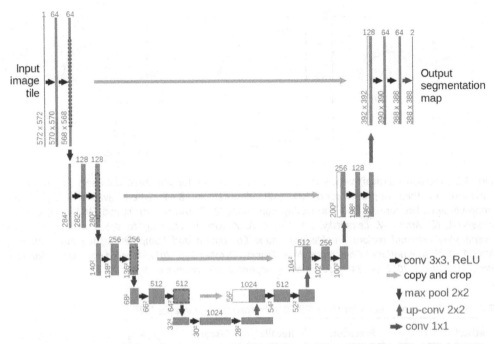

Fig. 3.3 The U-Net architecture (example for 32 × 32 pixels in the lowest resolution). Each *dark box* corresponds to a multichannel feature map. The number of channels is denoted on top of the box. The *x-y*-size is provided at the lower-left edge of the box. *White boxes* represent copied feature maps. The *arrows* denote the various operations. (*O. Ronneberger, P. Fischer, T. Brox, U-net: convolutional networks for biomedical image segmentation, in: Medical Image Computing and Computer-Assisted Intervention—MICCAI 2015: 18th International Conference, Munich, Germany, October 5–9, 2015, Proceedings, Part III, 2015, pp. 234–241, Figure 1. Reprinted with permission.*)

$$E = \sum_{x \in \Omega} w(x) \log \left(p_{l(x)} \right) \tag{3.4}$$

where $l : \Omega \rightarrow 1, \ldots, K$ is the true label of each pixel and $w : \Omega \rightarrow R$ is a weight map used to give importance to the edge pixels. They address the challenge of separating touching cells by using a weighted loss function such that the separating background labels between the touching cells take on a large weight in the loss function. The weight map is precomputed; it forces the network to learn the small separation borders that is introduced between touching cells using morphological operations. The weight map was computed as

$$w(x) = w_c(x) + w_0 \cdot \exp \left(-\frac{(d_1(x) + d_2(x))^2}{2\sigma^2} \right) \tag{3.5}$$

where $w_c : \Omega \rightarrow R$ is the weight map to balance the class frequencies, $d_1 : \Omega \rightarrow R$ denotes the distance to the border of the nearest cell, and $d_2 : \Omega \rightarrow R$ is the distance to the border of

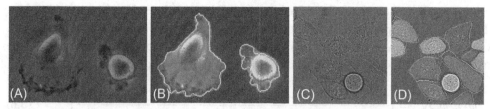

Fig. 3.4 The results of the ISBI cell-tracking challenge. (A) Part of an input image of the PhC-U373 data set. (B) Segmentation result *(highlighted region)* with manual ground truth *(region boundary)*. (C) Input image of the DIC-HeLa data set. (D) Segmentation result *(highlighted regions)* with manual ground truth *(yellow border)*. *(O. Ronneberger, P. Fischer, T. Brox, U-net: convolutional networks for biomedical image segmentation, in: Medical Image Computing and Computer-Assisted Intervention—MICCAI 2015: 18th International Conference, Munich, Germany, October 5–9, 2015, Proceedings, Part III, 2015, pp. 234–241, Figure 4. Reprinted with permission.)*

the second-nearest cell. Data augmentation was used to compensate for the limited training data in biomedical segmentation problems. The network learns invariances to elastic deformations, without the need to see the transformations in the annotated images. The U–Net architecture can be trained in an end-to-end manner.

The U–Net architecture was evaluated for segmentation of neuronal membranes from the EM segmentation challenge [9] and cell segmentation from the ISBI cell-tracking challenge [72] in light microscopic images. The segmentations were evaluated for the PhC-U373 and DIC-HeLa data sets from the cell-tracking challenge. Visual results for the cell segmentation is shown in Fig. 3.4. The U–Net architecture has been used for several biomedical segmentation applications; it requires very few annotated images because it incorporates data augmentation with elastic deformations. The U–Net architecture achieves a warping error of 0.0003529 and a rand error of 0.0382 for the EM segmentation challenge [9], and these results are significantly better than the sliding-window convolutional neural network approach [19], which has a warping error of 0.000420 and a rand error of 0.0504. The U–Net architecture relies on strong data augmentation strategies. Also, the architecture is not robust to variability in the appearance of objects such as contrast and texture due to different imaging settings.

2.3 Improving the robustness of convolutional networks to appearance variability in biomedical images

A neighborhood similarity layer (NSL) [75] was introduced as an additional layer in CNNs to overcome problems posed by variability due to changes in the appearance of objects such as contrast and texture. Data augmentation methods cannot adapt to variations that are not well represented in the training data, whereas the NSL can adapt to unforeseen appearance changes that are not present in the training data set. NSL computes the normalized inner products of feature vectors of the previous layer between a central pixel that acts as a frame of reference and the spatial neighborhood of that pixel. The NSL is an appearance invariance-inducing transformation on image feature maps. Given an n-dimensional feature map $\phi : \Omega \to \mathbb{R}^n$ and a neighborhood structure $\mathcal{N}$, the NSL $\psi : \Omega \to \mathbb{R}^m$ is the vector map of normalized inner products:

$$\psi(\mathbf{x}, \phi, \mathcal{N}) = \left[\frac{\langle \phi(\mathbf{x}+\mathbf{v}) - \overline{\phi}, \phi(\mathbf{x}) - \overline{\phi} \rangle}{\left(\langle \phi(\mathbf{x}+\mathbf{v}) - \overline{\phi}, \phi(\mathbf{x}+\mathbf{v}) - \overline{\phi} \rangle \langle \phi(\mathbf{x}) - \overline{\phi}, \phi(\mathbf{x}) - \overline{\phi} \rangle \right)^{1/2}} \right]_{\mathbf{v} \in \mathcal{N}} \quad (3.6)$$

where $\overline{\phi} = (1/|\Omega|) \sum_{\mathbf{x} \in \Omega} \phi(\mathbf{x})$ is the mean feature vector over Ω.

These are some of the favorable properties of the NSL: (1) it is a parameter-free layer, and hence independent of training data; (2) it is not a convolution, but a spatially varying operation that uses the feature vectors at each pixel as a frame of reference; (3) the output feature map ψ has the same dimensionality as the number of pixels in $\mathcal{N}$ and (4) when $\mathcal{N}$ is a square patch, the vector $\psi(\mathbf{x})$ corresponds to a square patch of similarities around and excluding $\mathbf{x}$.

An NSL can be placed after any feature map-producing layer in a network, as shown in Fig. 3.5. Note that a convolutional layer following an NSL operates on a map of feature vectors that correspond to square patches of similarity vectors.

NSL improves the accuracy of regular training and domain adaptation scenarios for cell detection and eye vasculature segmentation. The Fluo-N2DH-GOWT1 and Fluo-N2DL-HeLa data sets used in the experiments are from the cell-tracking challenge [72]. The detection performance was evaluated using the U-Net architecture as a baseline [66] and a modified U-Net architecture with NSL (9×9 $\mathcal{N}$) after the first convolution layer. Cells were detected as locations of the local maxima of the output of the U-Net. Visual results for cell detection on both data sets are displayed in Fig. 3.6. With the addition of

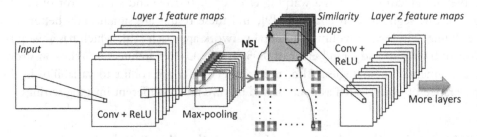

Fig. 3.5 An NSL placed between two layers of a network. At any location **x** (the top-left corner is shown), the NSL computes a neighborhood of similarities to $\phi(\mathbf{x})$. This creates an image of two-dimensional neighborhood similarities that are flattened into one-dimensional vectors, creating the output of the NSL. The relationship between a 3×3 $\mathcal{N}$ and eight similarity maps are shown with the color coding. (T. Tasdizen, M. Sajjadi, M. Javanmardi, N. Ramesh, Improving the robustness of convolutional networks to appearance variability in biomedical images, in: 2018 IEEE 15th International Symposium on Biomedical Imaging (ISBI 2018), 2018, pp. 549–553, Figure 1. Reprinted with permission.)

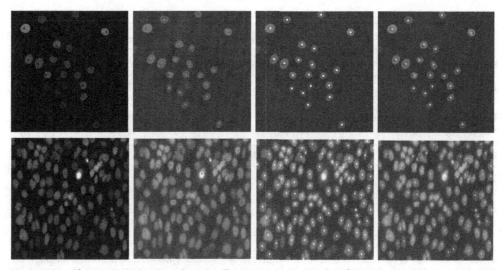

Fig. 3.6 Top: Fluo-N2DH-GOWT1-1. Bottom: Fluo-N2DL-HeLa-2 [72]. Left to right: Test image, predicted centroids without and with NSL, and ground-truth centroids overlaid onto contrast-enhanced images (for display only). *(T. Tasdizen, M. Sajjadi, M. Javanmardi, N. Ramesh, Improving the robustness of convolutional networks to appearance variability in biomedical images, in: 2018 IEEE 15th International Symposium on Biomedical Imaging (ISBI 2018), 2018, pp. 549–553, Figure 2. Reprinted with permission.)*

NSL, low contrast cells in the Fluo–N2DH–GOWT1 data set is identified better. In the case of the Fluo–N2DL–HeLa data set, clumped cells are individually identified with the NSL. For quantitative evaluation, the Hungarian algorithm [43] was used to match ground-truth dot annotations with local maxima of the network output. Precision, recall, and F-score were the metrics used to evaluate the detection performance. All the experiments used a single NSL after the first convolutional layer of networks as an appearance invariance-inducing transformation. The detection performance was also compared with that found in Türetken et al. [78] and the U–Net architecture without NSL using contrast-enhanced images. The quantitative results from the evaluations are reported in Table 3.2. The improvement with NSL significantly exceeds the improvement obtained with contrast enhancement of the input images in terms of F-score. The experiments do not use the target data for learning, which facilitates the use of pretrained models with NSL without retraining for domain adaption scenarios. Inclusion of NSL is helpful for discarding the variability seen in cell images.

2.4 Locality sensitive deep learning for detection and classification of nuclei in routine colon cancer histology images

A spatially constrained convolutional neural network (SC-CNN) was introduced to detect nuclei in routine hematoxylin and eosin-stained histopathology images of colorectal

Table 3.2 Cell-detection testing precision, recall, and F-scores.

	Precision	Recall	F-score
Data set	**Fluo-N2DH-GOWT1-1**		
ECLIP [78]	100.0	31.0	47.33
U–Net	94.91	82.71	88.39
U–Net + contrast-enhanced	94.66	86.16	90.21
U–Net + 9 × 9 NSL	96.95	94.59	95.75
Data set	**Fluo-N2DL-HeLa-2**		
ECLIP [78]	78.0	86.0	81.80
U–Net	85.74	69.94	77.03
U–Net + contrast-enhanced	85.86	71.97	78.30
U–Net + 9 × NSL	89.60	79.49	84.24

Source: T. Tasdizen, M. Sajjadi, M. Javanmardi, N. Ramesh, Improving the robustness of convolutional networks to appearance variability in biomedical images, in: 2018 IEEE 15th International Symposium on Biomedical Imaging (ISBI 2018), 2018, pp. 549–553, Table 1. Reprinted with permission.

adenocarcinoma [71]. The SC-CNN was trained as a spatial regression network that reduces the likelihood of a pixel being the nucleus center. The network utilizes the distance from the center of an object (the nucleus, in this case) to calculate a probability map for detecting that object. SC-CNN contains a layer that was specifically designed to predict the centroid locations of nuclei, as well as the confidence of the locations whether or not they correspond to true centroids. The spatial constraints were used to assign high probability values to pixels in the vicinity of the centers of nuclei. A neighboring ensemble predictor (NEP) was used with the SC-CNN to predict the class label of the detected cell nuclei. A weighted ensemble of local predictors leverages all relevant patch-based predictions in the local neighborhood of the nucleus to yield an accurate classification. Their approach does not require segmentation of the nuclei; rather, they use a sliding window to train the networks on small patches instead of the whole image.

The network is trained on image patches and probability maps representing the nuclei centers. The probability map that is defined has a high peak in the vicinity of the center of each nucleus and is flat elsewhere. The architecture used in SC-CNN is inspired by the results of Ciresan et al. and Krizhevsky et al. [19, 42]. The network consists of conventional layers such as input, convolution, spatial max-pooling, and fully connected layers. The last three layers of the SC-CNN are a fully connected layer F, a parameter estimation layer S1, and a spatially constrained layer S2. Parameters such as the center of the nucleus and the height of the probability mask are estimated in the S1 layer. The predicted output probability is generated from the spatially constrained layer S2 of the network using the estimated parameters for the nucleus. An example of the training patch, the training output patch, and the last three layers of the SC-CNN is shown in Fig. 3.7. The weight vectors and biases was learned by solving the following loss function:

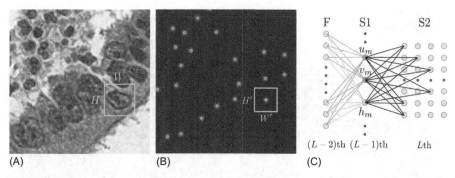

Fig. 3.7 An illustration of the spatially constrained CNN. (A) An input patch. (B) A training output patch **y** from a probability map showing the probability of being the centers of nuclei. (C) Last three layers of the spatially constraint CNN, F is the fully connected layer, S1 is the new parameter estimation layer, S2 is the spatially constrained layer, and L is the total number of layers in the network. *(K. Sirinukunwattana, et al., Locality sensitive deep learning for detection and classification of nuclei in routine colon cancer histology images, IEEE Trans. Med. Imaging 35 (5) (2016) 1196–1206, Figure 2. Reprinted with permission.)*

$$l(\mathbf{y}, \hat{\mathbf{y}}) = \sum_j (y_j + \in) H\left(y_j, \hat{y}_j\right) \tag{3.7}$$

where $H\left(y_j, \hat{y}_j\right)$ is the cross entropy loss and $\hat{y}_j$ and y are the predicted and training output, respectively.

Classification of nuclei is the next step after detection. A CNN was trained using a softmax layer to produce an output $\hat{\mathbf{y}}(x) \in R^C$, such that

$$c = \arg \max_j \hat{y}_j(x) \tag{3.8}$$

where $y_j(x)$ denotes the jth element of $\hat{\mathbf{y}}(x)$ and C is the number of classes. A single patch was used to make predictions for classifying the nuclei (SSPP). Alternatively, a NEP was introduced, which computes the weighted sum of predictions from all neighboring patches to predict the class for an individual patch. Both predictors are shown in Fig. 3.8. NEP takes into account the uncertainty in the detection of center locations, as well as variability in the appearance of nuclei. The class predicted for an input patch **x** with corresponding network output $\hat{\mathbf{y}}(\mathbf{x})$ is as follows:

$$\hat{c} = \arg \max_j \sum_{\mathbf{x}^{(i)} \in B(\mathbf{x})} w\left(\mathbf{z}\left(\mathbf{x}^{(j)}\right)\right) p_j\left(\hat{\mathbf{y}}\left(\mathbf{x}^{(i)}\right)\right) \tag{3.9}$$

where w is a function that assigns weight to an input patch $\mathbf{x}^{(i)}$ based on its center position $\mathbf{z}(\mathbf{x}^{(i)})$, $B(\mathbf{x})$ is the set of neighboring patches, and $p_j\left(\hat{\mathbf{y}}\left(\mathbf{x}^{(i)}\right)\right)$ is the output of the softmax function.

The experiments were performed on 100 stained histology images of colorectal adenocarcinomas. The qualitative results for the detection are shown in Fig. 3.9. SC-CNN

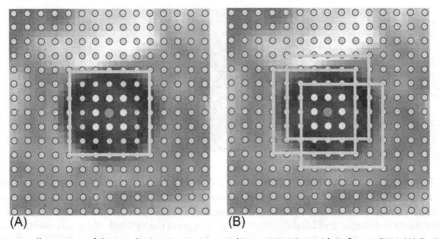

Fig. 3.8 An illustration of the prediction strategies used in conjunction with softmax CNN: (A) Standard single-patch predictor and (B) neighboring ensemble predictor. The *large dot* at the center represents the center of the detected nucleus. The center of the neighboring patches are represented using the 8-connected dots surrounding the central dot. *(K. Sirinukunwattana, et al., Locality sensitive deep learning for detection and classification of nuclei in routine colon cancer histology images, IEEE Trans. Med. Imaging 35 (5) (2016) 1196–1206, Figure 3. Reprinted with permission.)*

simplifies the learning process of CNN by imposing the output functional form of the network. The spatial constraint in SC-CNN forces a narrower spread of pixels with high probability values. Thus, SC-CNN yields a lower value of median distance between the detected points and their nearest ground-truth centers. The performance of SC-CNN is compared with that of SR-CNN [85]. Both SC-CNN and SR-CNN use spatial regression, and SR-CNN directly learns the structure from the training output data; hence, SR-CNN is more flexible in general. The F1-score for the combined detection and classification is calculated separately for each class label.

The overall performance is calculated using a weighted average F1 score, where the weight term for each nucleus class is defined by the number of data samples in that class. The combined performance for nucleus detection and classification was evaluated for different permutations of SC-CNN ($M = 1$ and $M = 2$) with NEP and SSPP and compared with SR-CNN with NEP, where M refers to maximum number of predicted nuclei in an output patch (see Fig. 3.10 and Table 3.3). The comparison favors the spatially constrained CNN for nucleus detection and the softmax CNN with the NEP for nucleus classification. An appropriate size of the patch needs to be chosen for classification to determine the localization accuracy. For many biomedical applications, it may not be feasible to extract patches with just one or two objects, and so this approach may not address the problem of detecting overlapping objects.

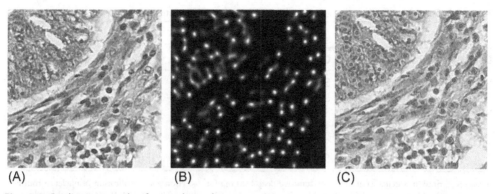

(A)   (B)   (C)

Fig. 3.9 Qualitative results for nucleus detection. (A) An example image. (b) Probability maps generated by SC-CNN. The probability value in the probability map indicates the likelihood of a pixel being the center of a nucleus. (C) Detection results of SC-CNN. The detected centers of the nuclei are indicated as *dots*, and the ground-truth areas are shown as *highlighted regions*. *(K. Sirinukunwattana, et al., Locality sensitive deep learning for detection and classification of nuclei in routine colon cancer histology images, IEEE Trans. Med. Imaging 35 (5) (2016) 1196–1206, Figure 6. Reprinted with permission.)*

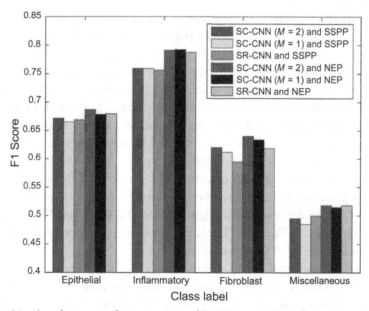

Fig. 3.10 Combined performance of permutations of SC-CNN on nucleus detection and classification stratified according to class label. *(K. Sirinukunwattana, et al., Locality sensitive deep learning for detection and classification of nuclei in routine colon cancer histology images, IEEE Trans. Med. Imaging 35 (5) (2016) 1196–1206, Figure 8. Reprinted with permission.)*

Table 3.3 Combined performance on nucleus detection and classification.

Method		Weighted average F1-score
Detection	**Classification**	
SC-CNN ($M=1$)	Softmax CNN + SSPP	0.664
	Softmax CNN + NEP	0.688
SC-CNN ($M=2$)	Softmax CNN + SSPP	0.670
	Softmax CNN + NEP	0.692
SR-CNN [85]	Softmax CNN + SSPP	0.662
	Softmax CNN + NEP	0.683

Source: K. Sirinukunwattana, et al., Locality sensitive deep learning for detection and classification of nuclei in routine colon cancer histology images, IEEE Trans. Med. Imaging 35 (5) (2016) 1196–1206, Table 4. Reprinted with permission.

3. Segmentation of neuronal structures in EM images

In this section, we discuss a hierarchical method and a deep-learning approach using CNNs for membrane detection and segmentation of neuronal structures in EM images.

3.1 Multiclass, multiscale series contextual model for image segmentation

A multiclass, multiscale (MCMS) series contextual model [69] was introduced, which uses contextual information from multiple objects at various scales for learning discriminative models in a supervised setting. A scale-space representation was generated by applying a series of simple linear filters to the context image consecutively, which enables the classifiers to access samples of the scale space. The coarser representations are more robust to small variations in the location of features and noise. The rich contextual information from the image enables the later stage classifiers to improve the performance of the early stage classifiers. The multiclass series architecture allows the classifier for each object type to access the contextual information from the previous stage. The framework captures dependencies among multiple objects along with local contextual information, thus combining cross-object and interobject information into one probabilistic framework. The MCMS model was used for segmentation of EM images. The multiscale contextual model is shown in Fig. 3.11. The scale-space representation of the context image is generated using a series of Gaussian filters.

The multiclass contextual model is illustrated in Fig. 3.12. The multiclass model has multiple binary classifiers, and each classifier is trained to segment a single object. The input feature vectors are the same, but the target labels differ based on the object of interest for segmentation. The classifier for every object has access to the contextual information from the previous stage. The propagation of object information is achieved by feeding neighborhoods from the output of each classifier. The flow of contextual information among the classes enables the model to learn the geometrical relationships and

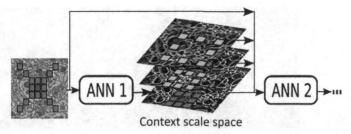

Context scale space

Fig. 3.11 Illustration of the multiscale contextual model. Each context image is sampled at different scales *(shown by the green squares)*. The *blue squares* represent the center pixel, and the *red squares* show the selected locations at original scale. (For color interpretation refer online.) *(M. Seyedhosseini, T. Tasdizen, Multi-class multi-scale series contextual model for image segmentation, IEEE Trans. Image Process. 22 (11) (2013) 4486–4496, Figure 2. Reprinted with permission.)*

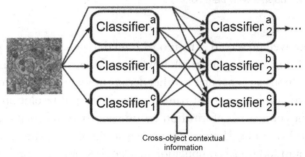

Cross-object contextual
information

Fig. 3.12 Illustration of the multiclass contextual model. Each classifier is a binary classifier that is trained for a specific object *(a, b, and c are objects)*. Each classifier takes advantage of the context images of all objects from the previous stage. The *superscripts* show object type, and the *subscripts* show the classifier number in the series. *(M. Seyedhosseini, T. Tasdizen, Multi-class multi-scale series contextual model for image segmentation, IEEE Trans. Image Process. 22 (11) (2013) 4486–4496, Figure 4. Reprinted with permission.)*

object dependencies implicitly. Their method was evaluated for membrane detection on mouse neuropil data set (National Center for Microscopy Imaging Research) and the mouse neuropil and drosophila VNC data set (Cardona Lab at HHMI Janelia Farm) [69]. Fig. 3.13 shows examples of test images and corresponding membrane detection results for single-scale and multiscale models with ground truth. The results indicate that using multiscale and cross-object contextual information can improve the segmentation results for membrane detection. Training the model is tractable because classifiers are trained separately. For unbalanced data sets, the contextual information from the large classes is beneficial for the small classes, improving the overall segmentation.

3.2 Residual deconvolutional networks for brain electron microscopy image segmentation

RDNs [24] were introduced for EM segmentation in order to learn deeper networks. RDN builds on the deconvolution scheme [59], which addresses the limitations of full-resolution

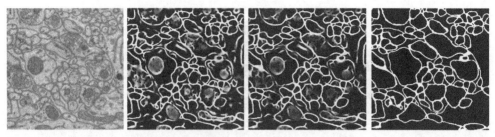

Fig. 3.13 Test results for the membrane detection experiment (mouse neuropil data set). Left: Input images, single-scale contextual model [37] and multiscale contextual model. Right: Ground-truth images. The multiscale contextual model is more successful at removing undesired areas from inside cells than the algorithms proposed in Ref. [37]. *(M. Seyedhosseini, T. Tasdizen, Multi-class multi-scale series contextual model for image segmentation, IEEE Trans. Image Process. 22 (11) (2013) 4486–4496, Figure 11. Adapted with permission.)*

features that are not well preserved. The model is used to generate dense predictions. The training framework does not rely on prior knowledge of data and uses minimum postprocessing; hence, this method can generalize to other dense output prediction problems. The network addresses two conflicting goals: namely, preserving full-resolution predictions and including sufficient contextual information by utilizing two information pathways. The residual shortcut paths are added between every few stacks of convolution or deconvolution layers, with minimum additional computation needed. It is easier to optimize a residual network [33], and the residual connections allow for training a deeper network. Using the residual paths in both the convolutional and deconvolutional stages makes it possible to acquire more multiscale contextual information while reducing the effect of the degradation problem. The resolution-preserving path is added to facilitate the reconstruction of full-resolution output. The final predictions are made by combining the features computed through both pathways. The context-growing and the resolution-preserving paths have significantly boosted the performance of nonresidual deconvolutional networks.

Evaluations were done for neurite segmentation from 3D EM images [39]. An illustration of the RDN architecture is shown in Fig. 3.14. A 3D watershed algorithm was applied to the generated probability maps to get the final segmentations. The quality of the probability maps generated by RDN plays a significant role for the 3D watershed to be able to generate the final segmentations directly without relying on any additional computations. The performance of RDN was compared with deconvolutional networks (i.e., RDNs without residual paths), and DIVE-CNN [23], where the probability maps were obtained from one of the leading teams in the ISBI 2012 2D segmentation challenge [9], and their model was used to generate probability maps for the 3D challenge data. RDN achieves a superior performance with the 3D watershed for postprocessing.

A qualitative evaluation of the performance of the models for the same slice is provided in Fig. 3.15. The regions that show improvement have been highlighted in

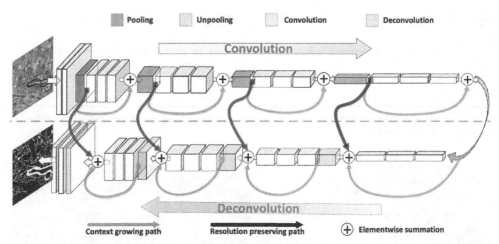

Fig. 3.14 Architecture of the residual deconvolutional network (RDN). The network consists of two pathways—namely, the context-growing path and the resolution preserving path. All convolution and deconvolution layers in the encoding and decoding stages have the size 3×3. A kernel of size 1×1 is used to implement the projection mappings. Max-pooling is used to reduce the feature map sizes in the convolution stage, while unpooling is used to restore the original size in the decoding stage. *(A. Fakhry, T. Zeng, S. Ji, Residual deconvolutional networks for brain electron microscopy image segmentation, IEEE Trans. Med. Imaging 36 (2) (2017) 447–456, Figure 1. Reprinted with permission.)*

Fig. 3.15 A qualitative comparison between the results of several models with respect to training slice number 50. Sample areas with clear differences are marked with *highlighted boxes*. Left: Raw input image and ground-truth 2D label image, with a probability map generated by team DIVE with a CNN and a probability map generated by a deconvolution network (DN), Right: a probability map generated by RDN. *(A. Fakhry, T. Zeng, S. Ji, Residual deconvolutional networks for brain electron microscopy image segmentation, IEEE Trans. Med. Imaging 36 (2) (2017) 447–456, Figure 4. Adapted with permission.)*

highlighted boxes. The RDN recovers missed borders, is less sensitive to noise, and produces better probability maps. An added advantage is that RDN does not rely on any handcrafted features throughout the entire processing pipeline and is fast, with minimum additional computations. From Table 3.4, it is evident that the RDN outperforms the other CNN-based models by a significant margin for the validation data. The testing data [39] contain segments with much larger sizes than the ones present in the training stack, and with a higher frequency. Hence, deconvolutional networks do not recognize these

Table 3.4 Comparison between various techniques applied to the validation data [39].

Method	Rand error
RDN	0.0814
DN	0.1514
DIVE-CNN	0.1541

Note: The percentage reported is after applying a 3D watershed with the best oversegmentation threshold for each set of probability maps independently.

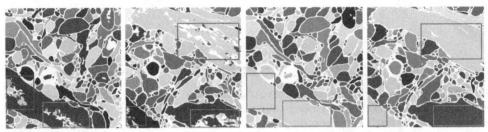

Without resolution-preserving paths   With resolution-preserving paths

Fig. 3.16 An illustration of the effect of resolution-preserving paths on the final segmentation. The results are generated for testing slices number 45 and 82 by RDN both with and without resolution-preserving paths on the left and right, respectively. *Highlighted boxes* have been placed on the compared segments. *(A. Fakhry, T. Zeng, S. Ji, Residual deconvolutional networks for brain electron microscopy image segmentation, IEEE Trans. Med. Imaging 36 (2) (2017) 447–456, Figure 6. Reprinted with permission.)*

large segments. RDNs are able to address this issue because of the presence of resolution-preserving paths. To highlight the importance of the resolution-preserving paths, the results for the RDN with and without the resolution-preserving paths are shown in Fig. 3.16. It can be seen that the resolution-preserving paths are able to reconstruct the full-resolution output effectively.

4. Conclusion

Automated methods to analyze microscopy data have been a focus of biomedical research for a long time. Hierarchical methods have been used for detection and segmentation in microscopy images, and machine learning-based classifiers were used to facilitate the desired goal. We analyzed two hierarchical methods in this chapter—one for cell detection and the other for membrane detection in microscopy images. The classifiers used for learning require a good feature set, the selection of features relies on prior knowledge about the data.

Recently, CNNs have been used extensively to address the detection and segmentation problems in microscopy images. It is challenging to capture full-resolution features with sufficient contextual information in networks. Deconvolutional networks were used to address this limitation in CNNs for biomedical applications. The limitation of training data is a critical problem for learning-based approaches. It has always been expensive to generate training data, especially for segmentation problems where pixel-level annotations are needed. Variability in the appearance of the microscopy data makes it hard to learn a model with less training data. Invariance in a predetermined set of transformations can be included during training to decrease the undesirable impact of sources of variability on the performance of the trained model. An additional layer was introduced to improve the performance of the CNNs and address the variability in the appearance of the data.

It may be beneficial to incorporate similar additional differentiable layers in the CNNs to introduce invariance to geometrical changes in microscopy data. If the layer is differentiable, then the network can be trained in an end-to-end manner. Domain adaptation methods have been used to address variability between the training and testing data, and they can be incorporated into analyzing microscopy data. Using unsupervised learning along with CNNs can help to address the problem of working with limited training data; the unsupervised features can capture structural information underlying the input data. Also, relevant loss functions can be integrated with the unsupervised data to boost the learning performance. Alternatively, multitask learning can be used to deal with the problem of limited, noisy, high-dimensional data, as seen in biomedical applications. Multitask learning aims to reduce generalization errors by training a model to fit multiple related tasks.

References

[1] R. Achanta, SLIC superpixels compared to state-of-the-art superpixel methods, IEEE Trans. Pattern Anal. Mach. Intell. 34 (11) (2012) 2274–2282.
[2] R. Adams, L. Bischof, Seeded region growing, IEEE Trans. Pattern Anal. Mach. Intell. 16 (6) (1994) 641–647.
[3] S.U. Akram, J. Kannala, L. Eklund, J. Heikkilä, Cell tracking via proposal generation and selection, CoRR (2017). abs/1705.03386.
[4] Y. Al-Kofahi, W. Lassoued, W. Lee, B. Roysam, Improved automatic detection and segmentation of cell nuclei in histopathology images, IEEE Trans. Biomed. Eng. 57 (4) (2010) 841–852.
[5] F. Amat, et al., Fast accurate reconstruction of cell lineages from large-scale fluorescence microscopy data, Nat. Methods 11 (9) (2014) 951–958.
[6] B. Andres, 3D segmentation of SBFSEM images of neuropil by a graphical model over supervoxel boundaries, Med. Image Anal. 16 (4) (2012) 796–805.
[7] D. Anoraganingrum, Cell segmentation with median filter and mathematical morphology operation, in: Proceedings 10th International Conference on Image Analysis and Processing, 1999, pp. 1043–1046.
[8] P. Arbelaez, Boundary extraction in natural images using ultrametric contour maps, in: Conference on Computer Vision and Pattern Recognition Workshop (CVPRW'06), 2006p. 182.
[9] I. Arganda-Carreras, et al., Crowdsourcing the creation of image segmentation algorithms for connectomics, Front. Neuroanat. 9 (2015) 142.

[10] C. Arteta, V. Lempitsky, J.A. Noble, A. Zisserman, Learning to detect cells using non-overlapping extremal regions, in: Medical Image Computing and Computer-Assisted Intervention—MICCAI: 15th International Conference, Nice, France, October 1–5, 2012, Proceedings, Part I, Springer Berlin Heidelberg, 2012, pp. 348–356.

[11] S. Belongie, C. Carson, H. Greenspan, J. Malik, Color and texture-based image segmentation using EM and its application to content-based image retrieval, in: Sixth International Conference on Computer Vision, 1998, pp. 675–682.

[12] E. Bernardis, S.X. Yu, Pop out many small structures from a very large microscopic image, Med. Image Anal. 15 (2011) 690–707.

[13] M. Berning, K.M. Boergens, M. Helmstaedter, SegEM: efficient image analysis for high-resolution connectomics, Neuron 87 (6) (2015) 1193–1206.

[14] S. Beucher, C. Lantuejoul, Use of watersheds in contour detection, in: International Workshop on Image Processing: Real-Time Edge and Motion Detection/Estimation, Rennes, France, 1979.

[15] T. Brox, J. Weickert, Level set based image segmentation with multiple regions, Lect. Notes Comput. Sci 3175 (2004) 415–423.

[16] J.Y. Byun, et al., Automated tool for the detection of cell nuclei in digital microscopic images: application to retinal images, Mol. Vis. 12 (105–07) (2006) 949–960.

[17] J. Canny, A computational approach to edge detection, IEEE Trans. Pattern Anal. Mach. Intell. 8 (6) (1986) 679–698.

[18] D. Chklovskii, S. Vitaladevuni, L. Scheffer, Semi-automated reconstruction of neural circuits using electron microscopy, Curr. Opin. Neurobiol. 20 (5) (2010) 667–675.

[19] D. Ciresan, A. Giusti, L.M. Gambardella, J. Schmidhuber, Deep neural networks segment neuronal membranes in electron microscopy images, in: Conference on Neural Information Processing Systems, 2012, pp. 2843–2851.

[20] D. Ciresan, A. Giusti, L.M. Gambardella, J. Schmidhuber, Mitosis detection in breast cancer histology images with deep neural networks, in: Medical Image Computing and Computer-Assisted Intervention, Nagoya, Japan, September 22–26, 2013, Proceedings, Part II, 2013, pp. 411–418.

[21] D. Cremers, Shape priors in variational image segmentation: convexity, Lipschitz continuity and globally optimal solutions, in: CVPR, 2008, pp. 1–6.

[22] C. Di Ruberto, A. Dempster, S. Khan, B. Jarra, Segmentation of blood images using morphological operators, in: International Conference on Pattern Recognition, vol. 3, 2000, pp. 397–400.

[23] A. Fakhry, H. Peng, S. Ji, Deep models for brain EM image segmentation: novel insights and improved performance, Bioinformatics 32 (15) (2016) 2352–2358.

[24] A. Fakhry, T. Zeng, S. Ji, Residual deconvolutional networks for brain electron microscopy image segmentation, IEEE Trans. Med. Imaging 36 (2) (2017) 447–456.

[25] P.F. Felzenszwalb, D.P. Huttenlocher, Efficient graph-based image segmentation, Int. J. Comput. Vis. 59 (2) (2004) 167–181.

[26] L. Fujun, X. Fuyong, Y. Lin, Robust muscle cell segmentation using region selection with dynamic programming, in: International Symposium on Biomedical Imaging, 2014, pp. 521–524.

[27] L. Fujun, et al., Robust muscle cell quantification using structured edge detection and hierarchical segmentation, in: Medical Image Computing and Computer-Assisted Intervention: 18th International Conference, Munich, Germany, October 5–9, 2015, Proceedings, Part III, Springer International Publishing, 2015, pp. 324–331.

[28] J. Funke, B. Andres, F.A. Hamprecht, A. Cardona, M. Cook, Efficient automatic 3D-reconstruction of branching neurons from EM data, in: IEEE Conference on Computer Vision and Pattern Recognition, 2012, pp. 1004–1011.

[29] Deleted in review.

[30] J. Funke, F.A. Hamprecht, C. Zhang, Learning to segment: training hierarchical segmentation under a topological loss, in: Medical Image Computing and Computer-Assisted Intervention: 18th International Conference, Munich, Germany, October 5–9, 2015, Proceedings, Part III, Springer International Publishing, 2015, pp. 268–275.

[31] R. Girshick, J. Donahue, T. Darrell, J. Malik, Rich feature hierarchies for accurate object detection and semantic segmentation, in: IEEE Conference on Computer Vision and Pattern Recognition, 2014, pp. 580–587.

[32] M.N. Gurcan, A. Madabhushi, N. Rajpoot, Pattern recognition in histopathological images: an ICPR 2010 contest, in: Recognizing Patterns in Signals, Speech, Images and Videos, 2010, pp. 226–234.

[33] K. He, X. Zhang, S. Ren, J. Sun, Deep residual learning for image recognition, in: IEEE Conference on Computer Vision and Pattern Recognition, 2016, pp. 770–778.

[34] T. Hu, et al., Electron microscopy reconstruction of brain structure using sparse representations over learned dictionaries, IEEE Trans. Med. Imaging 32 (12) (2013) 2179–2188.

[35] V. Jain, et al., Supervised learning of image restoration with convolutional networks, in: 2007 IEEE 11th International Conference on Computer Vision, 2007, pp. 1–8.

[36] V. Jain, et al., Learning to agglomerate superpixel hierarchies, Adv. Neural Inform. Proc. Syst. 24 (2011) 648–656.

[37] E. Jurrus, Detection of neuron membranes in electron microscopy images using a serial neural network architecture, Med. Image Anal. 14 (6) (2010) 770–783.

[38] E. Jurrus, et al., An optimal-path approach for neural circuit reconstruction, in: 2008 5th IEEE International Symposium on Biomedical Imaging: From Nano to Macro, 2008, pp. 1609–1612.

[39] N. Kasturi, et al., Saturated reconstruction of a volume of neocortex, Cell 162 (3) (2015) 648–661.

[40] V. Kaynig, Geometrical consistent 3D tracing of neuronal processes in ssTEM data, in: Medical Image Computing and Computer-Assisted Intervention—MICCAI 2010, Springer Berlin Heidelberg, 2010, pp. 209–216.

[41] N. Krasowski, et al., Improving 3D EM data segmentation by joint optimization over boundary evidence and biological priors, in: 2015 IEEE 12th International Symposium on Biomedical Imaging (ISBI), 2015, pp. 536–539.

[42] A. Krizhevsky, I. Sutskever, G.E. Hinton, Imagenet classification with deep convolutional neural networks, in: Conference on Neural Information Processing Systems, 2012, pp. 1097–1105.

[43] H.W. Kuhn, The Hungarian method for the assignment problem, Nav. Res. Logist. Q. 2 (1955) 83–97.

[44] R. Kumar, A. Vzquez-Reina, H. Pfister, Radon-like features and their application to connectomics, in: 2010 IEEE Computer Society Conference on Computer Vision and Pattern Recognition—Workshops, 2010, pp. 186–193.

[45] D. Laptev, Anisotropic ssTEM image segmentation using dense correspondence across sections, in: Medical Image Computing and Computer-Assisted Intervention—MICCAI 2012, Springer Berlin Heidelberg, 2012, pp. 323–330.

[46] K. Lee, A. Zlateski, A. Vishwanathan, H.S. Seung, Recursive training of 2D-3D convolutional networks for neuronal boundary detection, in: Proceedings of the 28th International Conference on Neural Information Processing Systems, vol. 2, 2015, pp. 3573–3581.

[47] K. Lee, et al., Superhuman accuracy on the SNEMI3D connectomics challenge, CoRR (2017). abs/1706.00120.

[48] F. Liu, L. Yang, A novel cell detection method using deep convolutional neural network and maximum-weight independent set, in: Medical Image Computing and Computer-Assisted Intervention—MICCAI 2015, Munich, Germany, October 5–9, 2015, Proceedings, Part III, 2015, pp. 349–357.

[49] C. Liu, J. Yuen, A. Torralba, SIFT flow: dense correspondence across scenes and its applications, IEEE Trans. Pattern Anal. Mach. Intell. 33 (5) (2011) 978–994.

[50] T. Liu, C. Jones, M. Seyedhosseini, T. Tasdizen, A modular hierarchical approach to 3D electron microscopy image segmentation, J. Neurosci. Methods 226 (2014) 88–102.

[51] T. Liu, M. Seyedhosseini, T. Tasdizen, Image segmentation using hierarchical merge tree, IEEE Trans. Image Process. 25 (10) (2016) 4596–4607.

[52] T. Liu, M. Zhang, M. Javanmardi, N. Ramesh, T. Tasdizen, SSHMT: semi-supervised hierarchical merge tree for electron microscopy image segmentation, in: 14th European Conference on Computer Vision, Amsterdam, Netherlands, October 11–14, 2016, Proceedings, Part I, Springer International Publishing, 2016, pp. 144–159.

[53] J. Long, E. Shelhamer, T. Darrell, Fully convolutional networks for semantic segmentation, in: IEEE Conference on Computer Vision and Pattern Recognition, 2015, pp. 3431–3440.

[54] D. Marr, E. Hildreth, Theory of edge detection, Proc. R. Soc. Lond. B Biol. Sci. 207 (1980) 187–217.

[55] J. Matas, O. Chum, M. Urban, T. Pajdla, Robust wide baseline stereo from maximally stable extremal regions, in: British Machine Vision Conference, 2002, pp. 36.1–36.10.

[56] E. Meijering, Cell segmentation: 50 years down the road [life sciences], IEEE Signal Process. Mag. 29 (5) (2012) 140–145.

[57] Y. Mishchenko, Automation of 3D reconstruction of neural tissue from large volume of conventional serial section transmission electron micrographs, J. Neurosci. Methods 176 (2) (2009) 276–289.

[58] S.K. Nath, K. Palaniappan, F. Bunyak, Cell segmentation using coupled level sets and graph-vertex coloring, in: Medical Image Computing and Computer-Assisted Intervention: 9th International Conference, Copenhagen, Denmark, October 1–6, 2006. Proceedings, Part I, Springer Berlin Heidelberg, 2006, pp. 101–108.

[59] H. Noh, S. Hong, B. Han, Learning deconvolution network for semantic segmentation, in: Proceedings of the 2015 IEEE International Conference on Computer Vision (ICCV), ICCV, 2015, pp. 1520–1528.

[60] J. Nunez-Iglesias, et al., Machine learning of hierarchical clustering to segment 2D and 3D images, PLoS One 8 (2013) 1–11.

[61] S. Osher, R.P. Fedkiw, Level Set Methods and Dynamic Implicit Surfaces, Springer-Verlag, 2002.

[62] N. Ramesh, M.E. Salama, T. Tasdizen, Segmentation of haematopoeitic cells in bone marrow using circle detection and splitting techniques, in: 9th IEEE International Symposium on Biomedical Imaging, 2012, pp. 206–209.

[63] N. Ramesh, F. Mesadi, M. Cetin, T. Tasdizen, Disjunctive normal shape models, in: IEEE International Symposium on Biomedical Imaging, 2015, pp. 1535–1539.

[64] N. Ramesh, T. Liu, T. Tasdizen, Cell detection using extremal regions in a semi-supervised learning framework, J. Healthcare Eng. 2017 (2017) 4080874.

[65] S. Ren, K. He, R. Girshick, J. Sun, Faster R-CNN: towards real-time object detection with region proposal networks, in: Advances in Neural Information Processing Systems, 2015, pp. 91–99.

[66] O. Ronneberger, P. Fischer, T. Brox, U-net: convolutional networks for biomedical image segmentation, in: Medical Image Computing and Computer-Assisted Intervention—MICCAI 2015: 18th International Conference, Munich, Germany, October 5–9, 2015, Proceedings, Part III, 2015, pp. 234–241.

[67] S.K. Sadanandan, P. Ranefall, C. Wählby, Feature augmented deep neural networks for segmentation of cells, in: Computer Vision—ECCV 2016 Workshops: Amsterdam, The Netherlands, October 8–10 and 15–16, 2016, Proceedings, Part I, 2016, pp. 231–243.

[68] M. Seyedhosseini, Detection of neuron membranes in electron microscopy images using multi-scale context and radon-like features, in: Medical Image Computing and Computer-Assisted Intervention—MICCAI 2011, Springer Berlin Heidelberg, 2011, pp. 670–677.

[69] M. Seyedhosseini, T. Tasdizen, Multi-class multi-scale series contextual model for image segmentation, IEEE Trans. Image Process. 22 (11) (2013) 4486–4496.

[70] J. Shi, J. Malik, Normalized cuts and image segmentation, IEEE Trans. Pattern Anal. Mach. Intell. 22 (8) (2000) 888–905.

[71] K. Sirinukunwattana, et al., Locality sensitive deep learning for detection and classification of nuclei in routine colon cancer histology images, IEEE Trans. Med. Imaging 35 (5) (2016) 1196–1206.

[72] C.O. Solorzano, et al., Cell Tracking Challenge, http://www.celltrackingchallenge.net.

[73] M.F. Stollenga, W. Byeon, M. Liwicki, J. Schmidhuber, Parallel multi-dimensional LSTM, with application to fast biomedical volumetric image segmentation, in: Proceedings of the 28th International Conference on Neural Information Processing Systems, vol. 2, 2015, pp. 2998–3006.

[74] T. Tasdizen, R. Whitaker, R. Marc, B. Jones, Enhancement of cell boundaries in transmission electron microscopy images, in: IEEE International Conference on Image Processing 2005, vol. 2, 2005, pp. II-129–32.

[75] T. Tasdizen, M. Sajjadi, M. Javanmardi, N. Ramesh, Improving the robustness of convolutional networks to appearance variability in biomedical images, in: 2018 IEEE 15th International Symposium on Biomedical Imaging (ISBI 2018), 2018, pp. 549–553.

[76] L. Ting, E. Jurrus, M. Seyedhosseini, M. Ellisman, T. Tasdizen, Watershed merge tree classification for electron microscopy image segmentation, in: International Conference on Pattern Recognition, 2012, pp. 133–137.

[77] S.C. Turaga, Convolutional networks can learn to generate affinity graphs for image segmentation, Neural Comput. 22 (2) (2010) 511–538.

[78] E. Türetken, et al., Network flow integer programming to track elliptical cells in time-lapse sequences, IEEE Trans. Med. Imaging 36 (4) (2017) 942–951.

[79] M.G. Uzunbaş, et al., Optree: a learning-based adaptive watershed algorithm for neuron segmentation, in: Medical Image Computing and Computer-Assisted Intervention: 17th International Conference, Boston, MA, USA, September 14–18, 2014, Proceedings, Part I, Springer International Publishing, 2014, pp. 97–105.

[80] A. Vazquez-Reina, et al., Segmentation fusion for connectomics, in: 2011 International Conference on Computer Vision, 2011, pp. 177–184.

[81] O. Veksler, Y. Boykov, P. Mehrani, Superpixels and supervoxels in an energy optimization framework, in: 11th European Conference on Computer Vision, Heraklion, Crete, Greece, September 5–11, 2010, Proceedings, Part V, Springer Berlin Heidelberg, 2010, pp. 211–224.

[82] S.N. Vitaladevuni, R. Basri, Co-clustering of image segments using convex optimization applied to EM neuronal reconstruction, in: 2010 IEEE Computer Society Conference on Computer Vision and Pattern Recognition, 2010, pp. 2203–2210.

[83] Q. Wu, F.A. Merchant, K.R. Castleman, Microscope Image Processing, Academic Press, Burlington, MA, 2008.

[84] W. Xie, A. Noble, A. Zisserman, Microscopy cell counting with fully convolutional regression networks, in: MICCAI Workshop on Deep Learning, 2015.

[85] Y. Xie, et al., Beyond classification: structured regression for robust cell detection using convolutional neural network, in: Medical Image Computing and Computer-Assisted Intervention—MICCAI 2015, Munich, Germany, October 5–9, 2015, Proceedings, Part III, 2015, pp. 358–365.

[86] Y. Xie, F. Xing, X. Shi, X. Kong, H. Su, L. Yang, Efficient and robust cell detection: a structured regression approach, Med. Image Anal. 1361-8415, 44 (2018) 245–254.

[87] Y. Xue, N. Ray, Cell detection with deep convolutional neural network and compressed sensing, CoRR (2017). abs/1708.03307.

[88] Y. Xue, N. Ray, J. Hugh, G. Bigras, Cell counting by regression using convolutional neural network, in: Computer Vision—ECCV 2016 Workshops: Amsterdam, The Netherlands, October 8–10 and 15–16, 2016, Proceedings, Part I, 2016, pp. 274–290.

[89] H.F. Yang, Y. Choe, Cell tracking and segmentation in electron microscopy images using graph cuts, in: 2009 IEEE International Symposium on Biomedical Imaging: From Nano to Macro, 2009, pp. 306–309.

[90] J. Yarkony, C. Zhang, C.C. Fowlkes, Hierarchical planar correlation clustering for cell segmentation, in: Energy Minimization Methods in Computer Vision and Pattern Recognition: 10th International Conference, Hong Kong, China, January 13–16, 2015, Springer International Publishing, 2015, pp. 492–504.

[91] T. Zeng, B. Wu, S. Ji, DeepEM3D: approaching human-level performance on 3D anisotropic EM image segmentation, Bioinformatics 33 (16) (2017) 2555–2562.

[92] C. Zhang, J. Yarkony, F.A. Hamprecht, Cell detection and segmentation using correlation clustering, medical image computing and computer-assisted intervention, in: Proc. MICCAI, 2014, pp. 9–16.

CHAPTER 4

Visual feature representation in microscopy image classification

Yang Song* and Weidong Cai†
*University of New South Wales, School of Computer Science and Engineering, Kensington, NSW, Australia
†The University of Sydney, School of Computer Science, Darlington, NSW, Australia

Contents

1. Introduction

Visual analysis of microscopy images is important in many biomedical applications. For example, the final diagnosis of cancers for staging and grading is regularly performed by the histopathology examination of biopsy tissue samples. The objective can be the classification of tissue samples as benign/malignant (Fig. 4.1A), or the classification of various cancer subtypes (Fig. 4.1B and C). As another example, the localization of protein expressions within a cell helps to facilitate high content screening of cellular phenotypes in biological and drug development studies. The localization problem can be approached by classifying the subcellular patterns in images generated from the knockdown of certain genes (Fig. 4.1D).

Such visual analysis has traditionally been conducted manually; however, manual analysis is time consuming and prone to individual bias. Especially with the rapid

Computer Vision for Microscopy Image Analysis
https://doi.org/10.1016/B978-0-12-814972-0.00004-7

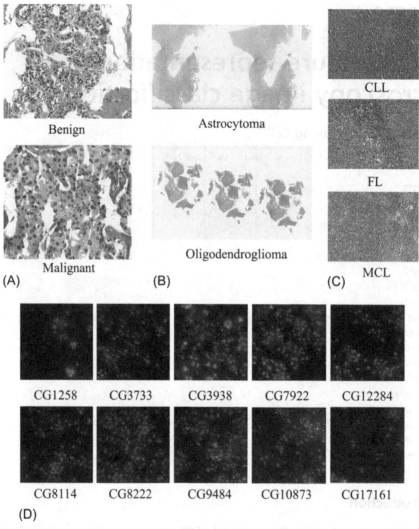

Fig. 4.1 Example images from (A) UCSB breast cancer data set, (B) MICCAI 2015 CBTC challenge data set, (C) IICBU malignant lymphoma data set, and (D) IICBU RNAi data set. Each image represents one image class.

development of microscope technology, digital images of large sizes have been increasingly acquired. There are vast amounts of digital microscopy images that are available for clinical research, and high-throughput screening is also an urgent need in digital pathology. However, manual analysis is not efficient enough to facilitate large-scale, data-driven research or high-throughput screening. Computerized approaches have the advantage of being objective and consistent, enabling standardized and reproducible analysis across cases. They can also be highly efficient, with advanced algorithm design. While many computer-aided diagnosis frameworks have been developed for radiology images over the years, automated microscopy image analysis is relatively new and less studied.

To facilitate rapid advancement in microscopy imaging research, a number of public image data sets recently have been developed and released to the research community. With public data sets, advanced computer vision algorithms can be applied and evaluated in a timely manner, and a fair comparison can be made between approaches. For example, the IICBU 2008 database [1] contains 11 separate data sets for various microscopy image classification problems, such as tissue age estimation, cancer subtyping, and protein localization. The UCSB breast cancer data set [2] is used to perform classification between benign and malignant tumors. These data sets are small, with a limited number of images; hence, the computerized method needs to be capable of performing feature discovery from limited data, which is the typical case in medical imaging research.

In addition, relatively large-scale data sets have been made available recently with high-resolution whole-slide images (WSIs), each with gigapixels. These data sets are designed for a variety of computational challenges, such as mitosis detection, structure localization and segmentation, and image classification. For example, the CAME-LYON16[1] challenge includes the task of classifying images containing normal lymph nodes and metastases. The TUPAC16[2] challenge is to classify or grade the pathology stage with tumor proliferation assessment in breast cancer images. These challenges provide large data sets, with 400 whole slide images (WSIs) in CAMELYON16 and 821 WSIs in TUPAC16. The effectiveness of image feature representation is essential with these classification tasks, and the large amount of data provided is particularly valuable for designing deep-learning methods. On the other hand, the large amount of data also introduces many challenges due to the computational cost and complexity, and this could render the standard application of deep learning models infeasible.

In the following sections, we will give a brief survey of current feature representation methods, particularly for microscopy image classification. Then we will present two supervised learning models that are designed based on Fisher vector encoding.

1.1 Feature representation

Computerized microscopy image classification approaches have been developed over the years with the aim to provide efficient and consistent image interpretation automatically. In the domain of digital pathology, approaches have been designed for grading or sub-typing of various cancers, including squamous cell carcinoma [3], prostate cancer [4], brain tumors [5], and breast cancer [6]. In these approaches, histological biomarkers are detected and quantified to encode the morphological characteristics that are critical for the histopathological analysis. For example, to determine the aggressiveness of breast

---

[1] https://camelyon16.grand-challenge.org
[2] http://tupac.tue-image.nl

cancer, the ratio of tubule nuclei to the overall number of nuclei is an important bio-marker, and a deep learning technique is designed to detect the tubule nuclei [6]. More reviews are provided in Ref. [7] as well. The advantages of these approaches are that the defined biomarker is biologically inspired and the quantification could directly correlate with the histopathological criteria used by the pathologists. However, domain-specific knowledge is required to design such methods, and in some cases, extensive ground-truth labeling is necessary to facilitate a learning-based algorithm.

On the other hand, there are also methods that are developed to perform image-level classification without detecting or quantifying a particular biomarker, and such methods are typically evaluated on a variety of different applications [2, 8–15]. For example, in one study [13], a customized feature set is designed and evaluated on nine different classifi-cation tasks, including tissue age differentiation, subcellular protein localization, lym-phoma subtyping, and pollen grain distinction. In another study [15], an image classification platform is developed for a standardized support of different problems, such as the quantification of subcellular objects, cell phenotype recognition, and histopatho-logical classification. Although such general methods are usually less effective than approaches incorporating domain-specific designs, the generalization property can be particularly useful to biomedical researchers working on new studies, when there are no customized imaging analysis tools available. The focus of this chapter is to design an image-level classification method for varying microscopy imaging applications with-out detecting biomarkers.

The key component in automated microscopy image classification, regardless of the clinical application, is the feature representation of the images. Features that are represen-tative and discriminative are fundamental to the classification performance in applications such as histopathological classification [2, 4, 5, 14, 16–21], cell detection/segmentation [22–26], event detection [27–29], and subcellular localization [13, 15, 30]. In particular, microscopy images of various classes often exhibit a high level of visual similarity, while images of the same class often show varying patterns that are difficult to summarize. Imag-ing artifacts also introduce noise. These factors make it challenging to design an effective feature representation for microscopy images. Existing studies often use a combination of standard feature descriptors, such as Haralick textures, filter banks, scale-invariant feature transforms (SIFTs), local binary patterns (LBPs), and histograms of oriented gradients (HOGs) [10, 13–15, 30–32]. Customized feature design has also been conducted to achieve better performance [2, 4, 5, 17, 27, 33, 34]. In addition, recent studies have dem-onstrated promising performance using automated feature learning based on unsupervised models such as autoencoder and its variations [16, 18, 19, 21, 24, 26, 35, 36]; and super-vised models such as the convolutional neural network (CNN) [22, 23, 25, 28, 29].

Among these features, a relatively less studied feature descriptor for microscopy image analysis is the Fisher vector (FV) [37]. FV encodes patch-level local features into a global description of the whole image by first constructing a Gaussian mixture model (GMM) from the local features with unsupervised learning, and then concatenating the differences between local features and the GMM centers as the FV descriptor. This model has demonstrated successful uses in a variety of general imaging applications, such as image classification [38], face recognition [39], object detection [40], and texture characterization [41, 42]. While dense SIFTs are typically used as the local features [43], other patch-level local features have been used to better represent microscopy images. In particular, local features learned using deconvolution networks are encoded into FV descriptors, which are used to identify subtypes of ovarian carcinomas [16]; and FV descriptors with LBP-like local features are used to classify HEp-2 cells [34]. Large performance improvement over standard handcrafted features has been demonstrated in both studies.

FV encoding can also be integrated with CNN by using a CNN model to extract the local features. Such an approach demonstrates significant improvement for texture classification over using deep learning alone or the standard FV encoding of dense SIFT local features [44]. In addition, while the CNN model can be trained from scratch on the target data set in order to reduce the method complexity, a transfer learning approach with a CNN model pretrained on the ImageNet database can also be used. Various biomedical imaging studies have found success in using pretrained CNN models (without FV encoding), and suggested that biomedical images indeed share similar low-level features with natural images, even though the high-level semantics make them appear very different [45–47].

There are, however, two issues that could affect the discriminative power of FV descriptors. First, FV descriptors are high-dimensional. An FV descriptor is constructed by pooling the difference vectors between the patch features and a number of Gaussian centers, and the resultant FV descriptor can be 64K-dimensional or even higher. The linear-kernel support vector machine (SVM) is thus regularly used with FV descriptors for the classification task. SVM is intrinsically capable of handling high-dimensional data, and the linear kernel is computationally efficient. However, in microscopy image studies, the image data set is typically much smaller than the general imaging data sets. With the limited number of images, the unsupervised learning of FV descriptors and supervised learning of SVM classifier could overfit to the training data, and the resultant model might not generalize well to unseen cases. Second, FV descriptors can have bursty visual elements. This means that there can be some artificially large elements in the FV descriptor due to large repetitive patterns in the image, and such large elements would lower the contribution from the other important elements and thus affect the representativeness of the descriptor. To solve the first issue, dimensionality reduction with principal component analysis (PCA) and large-margin, distance-metric learning have been used experimentally [39, 48]. To overcome the second issue, the intranormalization technique [49] is often applied to perform L2 normalization within each block (corresponding to one Gaussian component) of the FV descriptor, and a transfer learning-based approach [50] has been proposed.

1.2 Proposed approaches

In this chapter, we present two methods that we designed based on FV descriptors for microscopy image classification. We explore the use of FV descriptors and enhance the discriminative power of FV descriptors with learning-based dimensionality reduction. Specifically, we first construct FV descriptors with three types of local features: a dense SIFT, a deep belief network (DBN) [51] that is trained in an unsupervised manner, and a CNN model [52] that is pretrained on ImageNet. We choose these three local features as exemplars of handcrafted, unsupervised learning and supervised learning descriptors. We then apply two-dimensional reduction algorithms—namely, the separation-guided dimension reduction (SDR) [53], and supervised intraembedding (SIE) [54]—which help to reduce the high-dimensionality of FV descriptors. The SDR method is based on distance-metric learning that aims to increase the feature space separation between classes and reduce the separation within the same class. The SIE method is based on a customized convolutional neural network (CNN) model with locally connected layers to transform the FV descriptor locally into a lower dimension and reduce the bursty element effect.

The effectiveness of our methods is demonstrated on five public data sets of various clinical applications: the UCSB breast cancer data set for differentiation between benign and malignant tumors [2], the MICCAI 2015 CBTC challenge data set for classification of two brain tumor types, the IICBU malignant lymphoma data set for distinguishing three malignant lymphoma types, the IICBU RNAi data set for classifying 10 gene phenotypes [1], and the BreaKHis data set for classifying benign and malignant breast tumors [55]. We achieve improved performance over the state-of-the-art approaches reported on these data sets.

2. Fisher vector representation

FV [37] is a feature-encoding technique that aggregates a dense set of local features into a high-dimensional descriptor that represents the image-level characteristics. The underlying algorithm is based on the Fisher kernel [56]. Briefly, the generation process of the local features can be modeled by a probability density function u. Based on u, the gradient of the log-likelihood of the local features can be computed to represent the set of local features. This gradient vector is the main component in computing the FV descriptor, and u is assumed to follow a GMM model to facilitate an analytical approximation of the Fisher information.

To compute the FV descriptor, a GMM with K components is first generated based on a set of local features extracted from the training images. Each Gaussian component is represented by its mean vector μ_k, standard deviation vector σ_k, and mixture weight v_k. For a test image with N dense local features, each local feature f_n is soft-assigned to each of the Gaussian components, with the assignment weight computed as

$$\rho_n(k) = \frac{\mathcal{N}\left(f_n \mid \mu_k, \sigma_k^2\right) v_k}{\sum_{j=1}^{K} \mathcal{N}\left(f_n \mid \mu_j, \sigma_j^2\right) v_j} \tag{4.1}$$

where $\mathcal{N}(\cdot)$ is the Gaussian density function. The average first- and second-order differences between the local features and each GMM center are then computed as

$$\tau_k^{(1)} = \frac{1}{N\sqrt{v_k}} \sum_{n=1}^{N} \rho_n(k) \frac{f_n - \mu_k}{\sigma_k}, \tag{4.2}$$

$$\tau_k^{(2)} = \frac{1}{N\sqrt{2v_k}} \sum_{n=1}^{N} \rho_n(k) \left[\frac{(f_n - \mu_k)^2}{v_k^2} - 1 \right]. \tag{4.3}$$

The FV descriptor of the test image is the concatenation of all first- and second-order differences respective to the K components, expressed as follows: $x = [\tau_1^{(1)}, \tau_1^{(2)}, \ldots, \tau_K^{(1)}, \tau_K^{(2)}]$, which is also power- and L2-normalized.

The FV descriptor x has a dimension of $2KD$, where D is the dimension of the local features. The parameter K, which is the number of Gaussian components, is set to 64. While typically larger K values would increase the discriminative power of FV descriptors [37], $K=64$ is the usual setting used in texture classification [41, 42, 44], and we find that the value also provides good classification performance for our problems. A larger K value (e.g., 80 or 128) would improve the classification performance slightly, but impose higher computational cost.

Various types of local features can be integrated with FV encoding. In our design, we employ three local features, as described in the next sections.

2.1 SIFT

SIFT is the standard local feature used with FV encoding. A multiscale, dense feature extraction is performed, with spatial bins of 4, 6, 8, 10, and 12 pixels and sampling of every 2 pixels. Following the standard setup, the 128-dimensional SIFT feature is reduced to $D=64$ dimensions using principal component analysis (PCA) before FV encoding. The resultant SIFT-based FV descriptor, thus, is $2KD = 2 \times 64 \times 64 = 8192$-dimensional.

2.2 DBN

While SIFT is a highly effective yet handcrafted feature, unsupervised feature learning has become increasingly popular. In particular, DBN, which consists of multiple layers of restricted Boltzmann machines (RBMs), has been successfully applied in recent biomedical imaging studies [57, 58]. To apply DBN to our data, we construct a two-layer DBN, with each layer having 64 output neurons. A deeper DBN is not used due to the limited amount of training data. The model is trained on half-overlapping image patches of 8×8 pixels. For a test image, the learned model is applied to each patch and the 64 features from each layer are concatenated to form the local DBN feature. Similar to SIFT, PCA is also applied to reduce the feature dimension to 64. The resultant DBN-based FV descriptor is also the same: $2 \times 64 \times 64 = 8192$-dimensional. Note that we use a small patch size so that a relatively small number of neurons can be used, and subsequently, a small feature dimension is produced. Our experiments show that a higher feature dimension would result in a small degree of reduction in the classification performance.

2.3 CNN

CNN is a supervised feature-learning technique that has a multilayer neural network including convolutional and fully connected layers. It has been widely incorporated into biomedical imaging and has often demonstrated good performance [22, 23, 25]. Models that are pretrained on ImageNet have also been applied in biomedical imaging, with good results, implying that biomedical and natural images indeed exhibit similar visual characteristics at low levels [45–47]. In this study, the VGG-VD model (very deep, with 19 layers), pretrained on ImageNet [52], is applied to the image. The image is rescaled to multiple sizes, with scales of 2^s- (with $s = -3, -2.5, \ldots, 1.5$) and 512-dimensional local features are densely extracted from the last convolutional layer. These local features are then encoded using FV. The resultant CNN-based FV descriptor has $2 \times 64 \times 512 = 65{,}536$ dimensions. Note that unlike SIFT and DBN, PCA is not applied to reduce the dimension of the CNN local features because that would largely reduce the classification performance, as observed in our empirical study.

Note that when applying CNN in biomedical imaging, it is more common to train a new CNN model from the biomedical images than using the pretrained models. However, due to the small number of biomedical images available, patch-based processing and customized CNN architectures are typically required. Because our focus of this study is not about customizing the CNN design, we only experiment with simple training approaches by varying the AlexNet [59] architecture. We find that the pretrained VGG-VD model actually provides better classification performance, and the basic fine-tuning process (replacing the last layer in VGG-VD with the actual number of classes and performing backpropagation to a certain layer) decreases the classification performance as well. Therefore, we have adopted the pretrained VGG-VD model, and this approach also means that our method can be easily applied to different applications. On the other hand, we also suggest that it would be possible to design a more effective, patch-based CNN approach and use this customized CNN model as the local feature extractor.

We also note that besides these three local features, other types of features can be used, so long as they provide dense, patch-level feature descriptions. FV encoding will work with such local features in the same way.

3. Separation-guided dimension reduction

3.1 Method design

In this section, we describe our SDR method, which reduces the feature dimension of FV descriptors for SVM classification. Fig. 4.2 illustrates the overall flow of our proposed method. Formally, given a test image with a d-dimensional FV descriptor $x \in \mathbb{R}^d$, $d \in \{8192, 65536\}$, we perform a binary classification using the linear-kernel SVM:

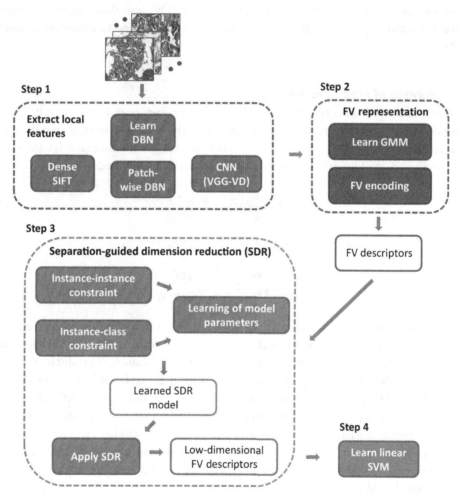

Fig. 4.2 The overall flow of our proposed SDR method. During the training phase, FV descriptors are generated based on various local features and an SDR model is trained to transform the FV descriptors to low-dimensionality, all of which are used to train a linear-kernel SVM classifier. During the testing phase, FV representation of the test image is computed and then dimension reduced using the learned SDR model, and then finally classified using the trained SVM classifier.

$$y = \text{sign}(\omega \cdot \phi(x) + b) \tag{4.4}$$

where $y \in \{-1, 1\}$ indicates the class label and $\phi(x) \in \mathbb{R}^h$ is the dimension-reduced descriptor of h dimensions ($h \ll d$). Following the standard SVM definition, $\omega \in \mathbb{R}^h$ is the weight vector and b is the bias value. The dimension-reduced descriptor $\phi(x)$ is computed as

$$\phi(x) = Mx \tag{4.5}$$

where $M \in \mathbb{R}^{h \times d}$ is the projection matrix that is learned along with the classification objective (see the next subsection for more details). The low-dimensional descriptor $\phi(x)$ is expected to provide higher discriminative power and lead to better classification results.

3.1.1 Learning of model parameters

We formulate a discriminative model to derive the parameters ω, b, and M. The model integrates dimension reduction and classification, with the objective of maximizing the separation between classes. Specifically, assume that a set of I training samples are given: $\{x_i, y_i : i = 1, \dots, I\}$. The following optimization objective is defined:

$$\arg \min_{\omega} \frac{1}{2} \|\omega\|^2 + C \sum_{i=1}^{I} \xi_i, \tag{4.6}$$

$$s.t. \quad y_i(\omega \cdot \phi(x_i) + b) \geq 1 - \xi_i, \quad \xi_i \geq 0, \quad \forall i, \tag{4.7}$$

$$\begin{aligned} \|Mx_i - Mx_j\|_2^2 > g, \quad \forall y_i \neq y_j, \\ \|Mx_i - Mx_j\|_2^2 < g, \quad \forall y_i = y_j. \end{aligned} \tag{4.8}$$

Eqs. (4.6) and (4.7) are the standard SVM formulations for optimizing the parameters ω and b, with ξ_i as the slack variable and C as the constant scalar. Eq. (4.8) is an additional constraint for the projection matrix M based on pairwise distances. This distance-metric constraint specifies that we expect a large separation (i.e., an Euclidean distance larger than a threshold g) between descriptors (x_i and x_j, $j = 1, \dots, I$) of different classes ($y_i \neq y_j$), and small separation between descriptors of the same class. In other words, this constraint encourages larger interclass distinction and lower intraclass variation in the feature space. Subsequently, by transforming the descriptors x_i into lower dimensions $\phi(x_i)$, it would be easier to establish a separation hyperplane by SVM, and hence more accurate classification would be expected.

To solve this optimization problem, we note that with $\phi(x_i)$ in Eq. (4.7), M can be considered as a latent variable in the SVM model. The distance metric in Eq. (4.8) is thus integrated with the discriminative classification of SVM. We design an alternative optimization approach to derive ω, b, M, and g.

First, assume that M is given. The low–dimensional descriptors $\phi(x_i)$ are then computed, and ω and b are derived using the standard linear SVM model defined in Eqs. (4.6) and (4.7).

Second, with known ω and b, M and g are derived based on the constraints in Eqs. (4.7) and (4.8), which are rewritten as

$$\theta_{ij}\left(g - \left\|Mx_i - Mx_j\right\|_2^2\right) + \\ \alpha\left\{y_i(\omega \cdot (Mx_i) + b) + y_j(\omega \cdot (Mx_j) + b)\right\} > 1 \tag{4.9}$$

where $\theta_{i,j}$ is 1 if $y_i = y_j$ and -1 otherwise, and α is a constant. With hinge loss, the optimization function is formulated as

$$\underset{M,g}{\operatorname{argmin}} \sum_{i,j} \max\left(1 - s_{ij}, 0\right) \tag{4.10}$$

where

$$s_{ij} = \theta_{ij}\left\{g - (x_i - x_j)^T M^T M(x_i - x_j)\right\} + \\ \alpha\left\{y_i(\omega^T Mx_i + b) + y_j(\omega^T Mx_j + b)\right\}. \tag{4.11}$$

This s_{ij} helps to encourage two objectives: (i) x_i and x_j should be classified correctly as y_i and y_j; and (ii) when x_i and x_j are from the same class (i.e., $\theta_{ij} = 1$), the distance between x_i and x_j should be less than g, and when x_i and x_j are from different classes (i.e., $\theta_{ij} = -1$), the distance between x_i and x_j should be greater than g.

A stochastic subgradient method is then used to compute M and g. In particular, at each iteration t, a pair of training data x_i and x_j is sampled and used to update M as follows:

$$M_{t+1} = \begin{cases} M_t & \text{if } s_{ij} > 1 \\ M_t - \gamma\Delta_{ij} & \text{otherwise} \end{cases} \tag{4.12}$$

where γ is a constant learning rate, and

$$\Delta_{ij} = \theta_{ij}M_t(x_i - x_j)(x_i - x_j)^T - \alpha\left(y_i\omega x_i^T + y_j\omega x_j^T\right). \tag{4.13}$$

The threshold g is also updated by

$$g_{t+1} = \begin{cases} g_t & \text{if } s_{ij} > 1 \\ g_t + \lambda\theta_{ij} & \text{otherwise} \end{cases} \tag{4.14}$$

where λ is the learning rate. The iteration continues until convergence or the maximum number of iterations is reached. Note that the objective function Eq. (4.10) is not convex in M; hence, initialization is important to obtain a good solution (described in Step 1, given next). Also, our experiments show that the classification performance is not sensitive to the learning rates γ (with values from 0.01 to 0.4) and λ (with values from 0.1 to 1), so we set $\gamma = 0.25$ and $\lambda = 1$ for fast convergence.

The overall optimization process is summarized as follows:

Step 1: Initialize $\omega = \mathbf{0}$ and $b = 0$. Initialize M by extracting the eigenvectors using PCA on the training data. Initialize g as the threshold that makes $s_{ij} > 1$ for most training pairs.

Step 2: Optimize M and g using the stochastic subgradient method with Eqs. (4.12) and (4.14).

Step 3: Optimize ω and b using linear SVM with Eqs. (4.7) and (4.8).

Steps 2 and 3 are repeated several times to obtain the final values of the model parameters.

3.1.2 Creation of training data

One important issue in the learning process is the definition of the training pairs x_i and x_j used to learn the model. We design two techniques (namely, the instance-instance and instance-class constraints) to create the training set. They are described in the next sections.

Instance-instance constraint

With the instance-instance constraint, both x_i and x_j represent the FV descriptors of training images (i.e., instances). Consider that I training samples $\{x_i : i = 1,\ldots, I\}$ are given. The straightforward training approach would be to use all combinations of data pairs as x_i and x_j. However, this approach would result in a large number of $I^2/2$ training pairs. We suggest that a large training set is not suitable for our optimization problem because with its feature space complexity, it would lead to many contradicting constraints and make it hard for the optimization process to minimize the cost while maintaining its generalizability. Existing distance-metric learning methods normally use a small set of training pairs selected randomly or predefined by the problem domain [39, 60]. In our approach, we design a classification score-based pruning technique to select a subset of the training pairs.

To do this, first, a linear SVM classifier is trained on the I training data using the original high-dimensional FV descriptors. The classification score $p_{i,l}$ of x_i for each class l is then computed as the probability estimate from the SVM classifier. Next, for each class l, three classification thresholds are computed. The first, $th_{1,l}$, is computed by sorting the classification scores $p_{i,l}$ of all x_i of class l and choosing the classification score at the c_1 percentile:

$$th_{1,l} = \text{percentile}_{c_1}\{p_{i,l} : i = 1, \ldots, I; y_i = l\}. \tag{4.15}$$

The second threshold, $th_{2,l}$, is computed similarly at the c_2 percentile. The third threshold, $th_{3,l}$, is computed at the c_3 percentile, but for all x_i not belonging to class l:

$$th_{3,l} = \text{percentile}_{c_3}\{p_{i,l} : i = 1, \ldots, I; y_i \neq l\}. \tag{4.16}$$

These thresholds help to identify x_i with high classification or misclassification scores. The c_1-, c_2-, and c_3-percentile values are constant parameters, and the settings are described in Section 3.2.

Then, three pruning rules are defined based on the classification scores and thresholds to select the training pairs.

Rule 1: If a certain x_i has a classification score p_{i, y_i} that is higher than the threshold th_{1, y_i}, it is not included in the training set. This means that we include only samples with low classification scores into the training set, so the training will focus on such data.

Rule 2: For a selected x_i, if x_j belongs to the same class as x_i and $p_{j, y_i} > th_{2, y_i}$, x_j is selected to form a training pair with x_i. Here $p_{j, y_i} > th_{2, y_i}$ means that x_j is a good positive sample with large classification margin, and we expect x_i to move closer to x_j after dimension reduction.

Rule 3: For a selected x_i, if $y_j \neq y_i$ and $p_{j, y_i} > th_{3, y_i}$, x_j is selected to form a training pair with x_i. Here, $p_{j, y_i} > th_{3, y_i}$ means that x_j is a negative sample that could be easily misclassified as class y_i, and x_i is better separated from x_j after dimension reduction.

Instance-class constraint

The instance-class constraint captures the relationship between instances and classes using a different definition of x_j. Our design is inspired by the sparse representation technique. Briefly, with sparse representation classification, a sparse reconstruction of x_i is obtained using the reference dictionary of each class l, and then x_i is classified to the class corresponding to the smallest reconstruction difference. The difference between x_i and its sparse reconstruction gives an indication of the similarity between x_i and the overall class at the global level, and by optimizing this reconstruction difference with distance metric learning, better classification results can be obtained. We thus consider that the sparse reconstruction can be used as x_j, and with the constraint in Eq. (4.8), we expect to improve the feature space separation between difference classes.

Specifically, for an x_i that is selected using Rule 1 as described previously, x_j is computed as the sparse reconstruction of x_i from the training data of class y_i (excluding x_i):

$$x_j = Rv_i \qquad (4.17)$$

where $R \in \mathbb{R}^{d \times nx}$ is the reference dictionary created by concatenating the FV descriptors of all nx number of training data of class y_i (excluding x_i). The vector $v_i \in \mathbb{R}^{nx}$ is the sparse coefficient for reconstructing x_i as x_j, and it is derived using the locality-constrained linear coding (LLC) algorithm [61]:

$$\operatorname*{argmin}_{v_i} \|x_i - Rv_i\|^2 + \beta \|e_i \odot v_i\|^2$$
$$s.t. \quad \mathbf{1}^T v_i = 1, \quad \|v_i\|_0 = q \qquad (4.18)$$

where $e_i \in \mathbb{R}^{nx}$ contains the Euclidean distance between x_i and each descriptor in R, $\beta = 0.01$ is a constant scalar, and q specifies the number of reference descriptors used in the sparse reconstruction. LLC is chosen for its computational efficiency with analytical solution and its general effectiveness in providing a good sparse reconstruction. The resultant x_j gives a class-level representation of x_i. With a small intraclass variation, x_j would be close to x_i, with small reconstruction differences. Therefore, we can label x_j as class y_i, and the training pair of x_i and x_j encourages the reduction of intraclass variation in the low-dimensional space.

In addition, another x_j is computed as the sparse reconstruction of x_i using the training data of the class $l \neq y_i$. This x_j represents the resemblance of x_i with class l, and with $l \neq y_i$, x_j is expected to be very different from x_i. Subsequently, we label this x_j as class l and include the training pair of x_i and x_j to achieve the optimization goal that x_i should be well separated from x_j after dimension reduction.

3.2 Experimental setup

For performance evaluation, we use four public data sets:

- The UCSB breast cancer data set contains 58 sections from tissue microarray images of 32 benign and 26 malignant breast cancer patients. The images are hematoxylin and eosin (H&E) stained, and each image has 896×768 pixels. This data set presents a binary classification problem of benign and malignant cases.
- The MICCAI 2015 CBTC challenge data set is for classifying two subtypes of lower-grade glioma from histopathology images. The data set with released labels contains 32 whole-slide images of varying sizes with $40 \times$ apparent magnification. Half of these images are astrocytoma, and the other half are oligodendroglioma.
- The IICBU lymphoma data set contains 374 H&E-stained image sections captured using brightfield microscopy, with 113 CLL, 139 FL, and 133 MCL cases. Each image is of 1388×1040 pixels. The images are collected from different sites, with a large degree of staining variation representing the typical clinical settings.
- The IICBU RNAi data set contains 200 fluorescence microscopy images of fly cells, acquired using a light microscope with $60 \times$ magnification. The cells are stained with DAPI for visualizing the nuclei. A total of 10 genes, with 20 images each, are selected to form the data set, and each image has 1024×1024 pixels. Classification of the gene classes helps to quantify the phenotype differences among the genes.

Example images of each data set are shown in Fig. 4.1. For all data sets, fourfold cross validation was performed. Most of the parameters were set in the same way for all data sets. Specifically, the dimension h of the dimension-reduced descriptor was set to half the number of images in the specific data set. The parameter α in Eq. (4.9) is set to 0.1, so a higher weight is allocated to the distance factor. There were three iterations for optimizing the model parameters. The sparsity factor q in Eq. (4.18) is set to 3 and 5, so that two reconstructions were obtained and the number of instance-class-based training samples doubles. The c_3 parameter used to compute the score threshold is set to 0.95 in order to reduce the number of negative samples. The only data set-specific parameters are c_1 and c_2, which are set differently for different local features (SIFT, DBN, and CNN), with values of 0.4, 0.6, or 0.8. In addition, to apply SDR for multiclass classification, the SDR algorithm is extended in a one-versus-all manner, as detailed in Ref. [53].

3.3 Results and discussion

The classification results using our SDR method are shown in Table 4.1. These results are obtained using FV descriptors of various local features: dense SIFT, patchwise DBN, and CNN features from the last convolutional layer, which are named FV-SIFT, FV-DBN, and FV-CNN. The three FV descriptors are then combined into longer descriptors: S+D (combining FV-SIFT and FV-DBN), S+C (combining FV-SIFT and FV-CNN), D+C (combining FV-DBN and FV-CNN), and S+D+C (combining all three FV descriptors). Classification using linear kernel SVM without dimensionality reduction, as well as by first applying our SDR method, are evaluated. The classification performance is measured using the overall accuracy and area under the curve (AUC). The three best results from existing studies are included for comparison as well.

The results demonstrate the benefit of our SDR method. The consistent improvement with SDR on all data sets indicates the advantage of reducing the feature dimensionality, especially for data sets of relatively small sizes. The largest performance improvement with SDR is achieved on the CBTC data set. For example, with SVM classification of the original high-dimensional FV-CNN descriptors, only 34.4% accuracy is obtained; however, after dimension reduction with SDR, the accuracy improves to 71.9%. This suggests that there is high redundancy in the FV-CNN descriptors for the CBTC data set. With the small number of images available, dimension reduction helps to enhance the discriminative power of descriptors while avoiding overfitting of the trained classifier. A similarly large improvement is obtained with the other FV descriptors and combinations of descriptors as well.

Our method outperformed the state-of-the-art approaches on these data sets. The existing studies on the UCSB data set use AUC as the performance metric, while those on the lymphoma and RNAi data sets use the accuracy measure. To the best of our knowledge, there are no published results for the CBTC data set. Our method obtains near-perfect (0.999) AUC on the UCSB data set when the FV-CNN descriptor was used, while the state-of-the-art [63] (based on joint clustering and classification in a multiple instance learning framework) is 0.95. For the lymphoma data set, the current state-of-the-art [65] proposes using a combination of LBP and CNN features based on segmented regions with an ensemble of SVM classifiers, and it provides 95.5% accuracy, while we achieve 97.9% accuracy with the S+C descriptor. For the RNAi data set,

Table 4.1 The classification accuracy (%) and AUC, comparing our method (SDR, then SVM classification) and SVM classification without dimension reduction, with FV descriptors of local features and combinations of FV descriptors

Data Set	Method	Metric	Single FV descriptor			Combinations of FV descriptors			
			FV-SIFT	FV-DBN	FV-CNN	S+D	S+C	D+C	S+D+C
UCSB	SVM	Acc	87.9	82.8	96.6	86.2	93.1	91.4	93.1
	SDR	Acc	89.7	89.7	**98.3**	91.4	94.8	96.6	94.8
	SVM	AUC	0.906	0.915	0.986	0.916	0.962	0.959	0.962
	SDR	AUC	0.925	0.928	**0.999**	0.931	**0.972**	**0.975**	**0.970**
	Others	AUC	0.92 [2]	0.93 [62]	0.95 [63]				
CBTC	SVM	Acc	53.1	62.5	34.4	50.0	37.5	56.3	46.9
	SDR	Acc	59.4	**75.0**	71.9	68.8	65.6	68.8	**75.0**
	SVM	AUC	0.500	0.551	0.262	0.434	0.324	0.461	0.398
	SDR	AUC	0.535	0.723	0.711	0.684	0.598	**0.766**	0.719
Lymphoma	SVM	Acc	90.4	88.8	93.9	91.5	95.5	94.7	95.1
	SDR	Acc	93.3	90.1	**95.7**	93.0	**97.9**	**96.5**	**96.8**
	SVM	AUC	0.961	0.951	0.984	0.976	0.991	0.990	0.990
	SDR	AUC	0.970	0.960	0.991	0.981	**0.993**	**0.993**	0.992
	Others	Acc	85 [13]	92.7 [64]	95.5 [65]				
RNAi	SVM	Acc	86.5	80.5	88.5	93.0	94.5	91.0	94.5
	SDR	Acc	88.0	81.5	90.5	**95.5**	**95.5**	91.5	**96.0**
	SVM	AUC	0.975	0.957	0.983	0.991	0.993	0.985	0.994
	SDR	AUC	0.982	0.961	0.989	0.995	0.993	0.992	**0.996**
	Others	Acc	82 [13]	90.1 [66]	92.0 [67]				

Note: For data sets with existing studies, the top three results are included for comparison. Bold values highlight the methods providing the best results.

we obtain 96% accuracy with the S + D + C descriptor, while the state-of-the-art [67] is 92% based on customized feature representations and ensemble classification.

The effects of FV descriptors in comparison with other more standard feature representations are shown in Fig. 4.3. The results are obtained using SVM classification without dimensionality reduction. For comparison, the various local features (i.e., SIFT, DBN, and CNN) are integrated with bag-of-words (BOW) encoding to evaluate the benefit of FV encoding. We choose to compare with BOW because it represents a

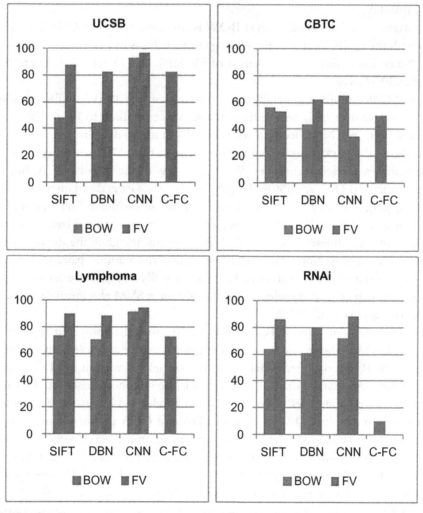

Fig. 4.3 Classification accuracy comparing FV with BOW encoding when different local features are used and SVM classification without dimensionality reduction is performed. The feature vector from the penultimate fully connected layer of the CNN model is also included for comparison (C-FC).

conventional feature-encoding technique. To compute the BOW descriptors, we experiment with 64, 128,…, 2048 feature words and find that 1024 provided the best overall results. The 4096-dimensional CNN descriptor derived from the penultimate, fully connected layer (namely, C-FC) is included as well. This C-FC shows the typical usage of CNN in classification when pretrained models are used [44].

The findings can be summarized in three points:

- FV encoding is more effective than BOW encoding for the UCSB, lymphoma, and RNAi data sets, but not for the CBTC data set. This indicates that for this small data set, the high dimension of FV descriptor gives limited discriminative and representative capability.
- The advantage of FV encoding over BOW is larger with SIFT or DBN local features than with the CNN local feature. We suggest that this is due to the lower dimension (and hence lower feature redundancy) of FV-SIFT and FV-DBN descriptors compared to FV-CNN.
- The C-FC descriptor is generally less effective than the BOW or FV encoding of CNN local features. This demonstrates the advantage of using BOW or FV encoding over the built-in CNN encoding with the fully connected layers.

Fig. 4.4 shows the performance comparison between our SDR method and the other dimensionality reduction techniques. We compare with the popular PCA, linear discriminant analysis (LDA), and ISOMAP [68] techniques. Generalized discriminant analysis (GDA) [69], as an improved version of LDA, is also included. Full matrix learning (FML) [39] is similar to SDR that the projection matrix is obtained based on distance learning. However, different from SDR, FML does not integrate the distance learning with the SVM optimization. Also, while we define the training pairs with instance-instance and instance-class constraints, FML is originally designed for face recognition and uses training pairs that are selected manually. Linear SVM classification is used with all compared approaches.

The results show that our SDR method outperformed the compared approaches on all data sets. LDA was the second best, providing performance improvement on three data sets except the RNAi data set. While GDA is a kernelized version of LDA, it actually leads to lower performance than LDA except for the lymphoma data set. This implies that when the size of data set is small, the linear model in LDA is more suitable than the kernelized model in GDA. In general, LDA and GDA perform better than PCA and ISOMAP, which indicates the advantage of having supervised dimensionality reduction for our classification problems. However, although FML is also a supervised algorithm, it results in the largest performance degradation on the UCSB, lymphoma, and RNAi data sets, and the smallest improvement on the CBTC data set as well. We suggest that this was mainly due to the large number of training pairs imposing many contradicting constraints and affecting the optimization outcome.

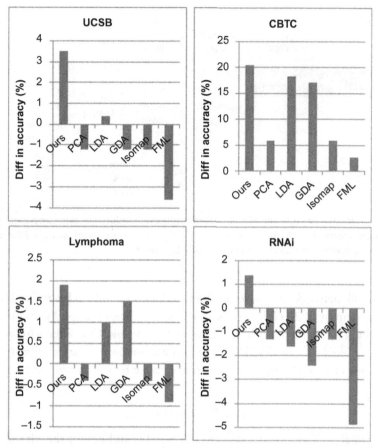

Fig. 4.4 The average change in classification accuracy after applying dimensionality reduction with different FV descriptors, compared to SVM classification without dimensionality reduction.

4. Supervised intraembedding

4.1 Method design

In this section, we present our second method for reducing the dimensionality and bursty effect of FV descriptors—namely, the supervised intraembedding (SIE) method. This SIE method is designed based on the FV encoding of CNN local features. Formally, we denote the FV-CNN descriptor as f. The objective of the supervised intraembedding method is to transform f to a lower dimension, and the transformed descriptor g is expected to provide good classification performance. For this, we design a multilayer neural network model, with locally connected layers for local transformation of descriptor blocks and a hinge loss layer for global optimization of the entire descriptor.

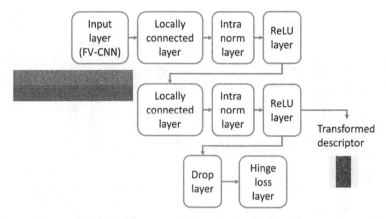

Fig. 4.5 An overview of the multilayer neural network design of our proposed supervised intraembedding method. With this network, the FV-CNN descriptor (shown as a $2K \times H$ matrix) is transformed to a lower dimension (shown as a $2K \times D_2$ matrix).

The overall network structure is illustrated in Fig. 4.5. The input layer is the FV-CNN descriptor of $2KH$ dimensions. The second layer is a locally connected layer, which is formed by $2K$ filters with each filter of D_1 neurons. One filter is fully connected to a descriptor block of $H = 512$ elements in the input layer (one descriptor block corresponds to one first- or second-order difference vector of 512 dimensions) and generates D_1 outputs:

$$f_2(i) = W_2(i)f_1(i) + b_2(i) \tag{4.19}$$

where $W_2(i) \in \mathbb{R}^{D_1 \times H}$ and $b_2(i) \in \mathbb{R}^{D_1}$ are the weights and bias of the ith filter, respectively; $f_1(i) \in \mathbb{R}^{H}$ denotes the ith block in the input layer; and $f_2(i) \in \mathbb{R}^{D_1}$ is the ith output at this locally connected layer. The output of this layer is a concatenation of outputs from all filters, and thus it has $2KD_1$ dimensions. Note that because $D_1 < H$, this layer reduces the dimensionality of the input descriptor.

The rational of designing a locally connected layer is that a FV-CNN descriptor can be considered as having $2K$ blocks, each with H dimensions and corresponding to a first- or second-order difference vector. The localized filters can help to achieve ways of transformation in different blocks. This provides more locally adaptive processing compared to the convolutional and fully connected layers in ConvNet, in which a filter is applied to the entire input. On the other hand, such local filters also significantly increase the number of learning parameters and could cause overfitting.

To reduce the number of filter parameters, we make every four consecutive filters share the same weights and bias, so there are *2K/4* unique filters altogether.

The third layer is an intranormalization layer, in which each output $f_2(i)$ from the previous layer is L2 normalized. In this way, the blocks would contribute with equal

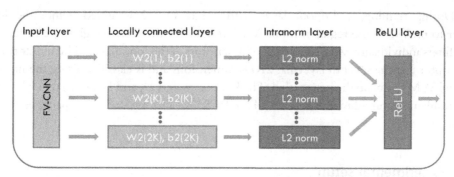

Fig. 4.6 Illustration of the locally connected and intranormalization layers.

weights in the transformed descriptor. Together with the locally connected layer, such local transformation provides a supervised learning-based approach to overcome the bursty visual elements. The fourth layer is a ReLU layer, and the ReLU activation is applied to the entire $2KD_1$-dimensional output of the third layer. Fig. 4.6 illustrates the internal structure of these layers.

Next, layers two to four are repeated as layers five to seven in the network structure in order to provide another level of transformation. Assume that the individual local filters at the fourth layer have D_2 neurons. The output f_7 at the seventh layer then has $2KD_2$ dimensions, and this is the final transformed descriptor g to be used in classification.

For the last layer, we design a hinge loss layer to impose the optimization objective of the supervised intraembedding. Typically, FV descriptors (original or dimension reduced) are classified using a linear-kernel support vector machine (SVM) to produce good classification results [44, 48]. Therefore, to align the optimization objective in our multilayer neural network with the SVM classification objective, we choose to use an SVM formulation in the loss layer. Specifically, assume that the data set contains L image classes. We construct a one-versus-all multiclass linear-kernel classification model to compute the hinge loss. Denote the weight vector as $w_l \in \mathbb{R}^{2KD_2}$ for each class $l \in \{1, \ldots, L\}$. The overall loss value based on TV input FV-CNN descriptors (for training) is computed as

$$\varepsilon = \frac{1}{2}\sum_{l=1}^{L} w_l^T w_l + C \sum_{l=1}^{L} \sum_{n=1}^{N} \max\left(1 - w_l^T f_7^n \lambda_l^n, 0\right) \tag{4.20}$$

where n is the index of the input descriptor, f_7^n is the corresponding output at the seventh layer, $\lambda_l^n = 1$ if the nth input belongs to class l and $\lambda_l^n = -1$ otherwise, and C is the regularization parameter. Minimizing this loss value ε at the last layer mimics the margin maximization in an SVM classifier. The hinge loss layer thus effectively integrates the local transformations, and local filters influence each other during the optimization.

During training, a dropout layer with a rate of 0.2 is added before the loss layer to provide some regularization. Also, to initialize the filter weights, we first train the filters individually, with one block of descriptors as the input layer. The transformed descriptor g at the seventh layer has $2KD_2$ dimensions and is classified using the linear-kernel SVM to obtain the image label. The key parameters D_1 and D_2 are set to 64; hence, the resultant feature dimension is $2 \times 64 \times 64 = 8192$. The regularization parameter C is set to 0.1.

4.2 Experimental setup

We use two public data sets in our experimental study:

- The BreaKHis data set contains 7909 hematoxylin and eosin (H&E)-stained microscopy images. The images are collected at four magnification factors ($40\times$, $100\times$, $200\times$, and $400\times$) from 82 patients with breast tumors. Each image has 700×460 pixels, and among the images, 2480 are benign and 5429 are malignant. The task is to classify the images into benign or malignant cases at both the image and patient levels, and for the individual magnification factors.
- The IICBU 2008 malignant lymphoma data set, which is the same as the one used for evaluating the SDR method.

Fig. 4.7 shows example images from the BreaKHis data set.

For training and testing, the BreaKHis data set releases five splits for cross-validation, and in each split, 70% of the images are training data and 30% are testing data. Images of the same patient are partitioned into either the training or testing set. We use the same five splits in our study. For the IICBU data set, we perform fourfold cross-validation, with 3/4 of data for training and 1/4 for testing in each split. For the supervised intraembedding, 50 epochs are trained on the BreaKHis data set and 100 epochs are trained on the IICBU data set.

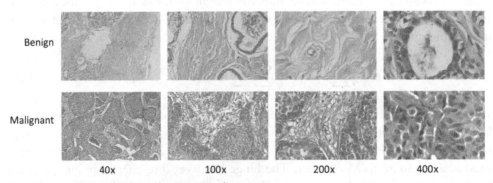

Fig. 4.7 Example images from the BreaKHis data set.

4.3 Results and discussion

We compare our results with the state-of-the-art approaches reported for these data sets, including for the BreaKHis data set, with a set of customized features [55] and with a domain-specific ConvNet model [70]; and for the IICBU data set: with a SIFT-based FV descriptor and distance metric-based dimensionality reduction [48] and with a combination of handcrafted and ConvNet features [65]. In addition, we experiment with the more standard way of using VGG-VD, which is to use the 4096-dimensional output from the last fully connected layer as the feature descriptor. Classifying the FV-CNN descriptor without supervised intraembedding is also evaluated. We also compare these with the more standard techniques to address the issues with FV descriptors: PCA for dimensionality reduction, and intranormalization for bursty visual elements.

On the BreaKHis data set, the current state-of-the-art approach [70] shows that random sampling of 1000 patches of 64×64 pixels provided the best overall result and max-pooling of four ConvNet models produced further enhancement. We thus include the results from these two techniques (rand and max [70]) in the comparison, as shown in Table 4.2. The patient-level classification is derived by majority voting of the image-level results. The original approach [55] reports the patient-level results only. Our method achieves consistently better performance than that of Spanhol et al. [55, 70], except for the image-level classification of images with $40\times$ magnification. It can be seen that while the random sampling approach [70] produces the best image-level classification for

Table 4.2 The classification accuracies (%) on the BreaKHis breast tumor data set.

		Magnification factors			
	Method	40×	100×	200×	400×
Patient-level	[55]	81.6±3.0	79.9±5.4	85.1±3.1	82.3±3.8
	[70] rand	88.6±5.6	84.5±2.4	83.3±3.4	81.7±4.9
	[70] max	90.0±6.7	88.4±4.8	84.6±4.2	86.1±6.2
	VGG-VD	86.9±5.2	85.4±5.7	85.2±4.4	85.7±8.8
	FV-CNN	90.0±5.8	88.5±6.1	85.4±5.0	86.0±8.0
	PCA	90.0±5.8	88.5±6.1	85.4±5.0	86.2±8.0
	Intranorm	90.0±5.8	87.7±5.7	86.6±5.8	86.2±6.9
	SIE	**90.2±3.2**	**91.2±4.4**	**87.8±5.3**	**87.4±7.2**
Image-level	[70] rand	**89.6±6.5**	85.0±4.8	82.8±2.1	80.2±3.4
	[70] max	85.6±4.8	83.5±3.9	82.7±1.7	80.7±2.9
	VGG-VD	80.9±1.6	81.1±3.0	82.2±1.9	80.2±3.8
	FV-CNN	86.8±2.5	85.6±3.8	83.8±2.5	81.6±4.4
	PCA	87.3±2.5	86.1±3.8	83.8±2.5	82.0±4.4
	Intranorm	87.3±2.7	86.4±4.1	83.9±2.6	82.3±4.3
	SIE	87.7±2.4	**87.6±3.9**	**86.5±2.4**	**83.9±3.6**

Bold values highlight the methods providing the best results.

Table 4.3 The classification accuracies (%) on the IICBU 2008 lymphoma data set

[48]	[65]	VGG-VD	FV-CNN	PCA	Intranorm	SIE
93.3	95.5	73.0±3.1	93.9±3.0	94.2±3.1	94.5±3.2	**96.5±2.7**

Bold values highlight the methods providing the best results.

40× magnification, its patient-level results of all magnification factors are all lower than the those of the max-pooling approach [70] and our method. Overall, the results illustrate that using FV-CNN feature representation with supervised intraembedding can outperform the handcrafted features [55] and ConvNet models [70] that are specifically designed for the particular histopathology data set.

Table 4.3 shows the result comparison with the IICBU data set. It can be seen that our SIE method achieves the best result. FV-CNN outperforms [48], indicating the advantage of using ConvNet-based patch features rather than SIFT in FV encoding, even when discriminative dimension reduction is also included. In addition, similar to our method, [65] involves an ImageNet-pretrained ConvNet model, but with additional steps for segmentation, handcrafted feature extraction, and ensemble classification. The advantage of our method illustrates the benefit of FV encoding and multilayer neural network-based dimensionality reduction. Also, compared to [65], our method is less complicated, without the need to segment the cellular objects.

With both data sets, it can be seen that our SIE method outperforms the approach with the FV-CNN descriptor only, demonstrating the benefit of supervised intraembedding. When comparing FV-CNN with VGG-VD (the 4096-dimensional descriptor), the advantage of using FV encoding of ConvNet-based patch features is evident. In addition, it can be seen that PCA and intranormalization generally improved the results compared to using the original FV-CNN descriptor. This indicates that it is beneficial to reduce the feature dimension and bursty effect of the FV-CNN descriptor, and in general, intranormalization has a greater effect on the classification performance than PCA. Our method provides more improvement over FV-CNN than PCA and intranormalization. This shows that our learning-based transformation could provide a more effective approach to address the two issues with FV-CNN.

5. Conclusions

Feature representation is the critical component in automated microscopy image classification. In this chapter, we reviewed the existing feature representation methods in microscopy image classification and presented two approaches that are based on FV descriptors. Microscopy images can be represented by FV descriptors, which are the aggregated image-level descriptor from local patch-level features using dense SIFT; patch-based DBN descriptors, which are learned in an unsupervised manner; and CNN local features that are extracted from the last convolutional layer using the pretrained VGG-VD model. To further enhance the discriminative power of the FV descriptors and decrease the impact of small data size on the classification performance, a separation-guided dimension reduction (SDR) method and a supervised intraembedding (SIE) method are applied to reduce the feature dimensionality of FV descriptors. The resultant low-dimensional descriptors are finally classified using a linear-kernel SVM to label the images. We experimented on five publicly available microscopy image data set and obtained performance improvement over the state-of-the-art techniques. We demonstrate the advantage of our methods over the commonly used dimensionality reduction techniques, as well as the benefit of FV encoding for representing microscopy images.

References

[1] L. Shamir, N. Orlov, D.M. Eckley, T.J. Macura, I.G. Goldberg, IICBU 2008: a proposed benchmark suite for biological image analysis, *Med. Biol. Eng. Comput.* 46 (9) (2008) 943–947.

[2] M. Kandemir, C. Zhang, F.A. Hamprecht, in: Empowering Multiple Instance Histopathology Cancer Diagnosis by Cell Graphs, MICCAI, 2014, pp. 228–235.

[3] J.S.J. Lewis, S. Ali, J. Luo, W.L. Thorstad, A. Madabhushi, A quantitative histomorphometric classifier (quhbic) identifies aggressive versus indolent p16-positive oropharyngeal squamous cell carcinoma, *Am. J. Surg. Pathol.* 38 (2014) 128–137.

[4] R. Sparks, A. Madabhushi, Explicit shape descriptors: novel morphologic features for histopathol-ogy classification, *Med. Image Anal.* 17 (1) (2013) 997–1009.

[5] J. Barker, A. Hoogi, A. Depeursinge, D.L. Rubin, Automated classification of brain tumor type in whole-slide digital pathology images using local representative tiles, *Med. Image Anal.* 30 (1) (2016) 60–71.

[6] D. Romo-Bucheli, A. Janowczyk, H. Gilmore, E. Romero, A. Madabhushi, Automated tubule nuclei quantification and correlation with oncotype DX risk categories in ER + breast cancer whole slide images, *Sci. Rep.* 6 (2016) 32706.

[7] A. Madabhushi, G. Lee, Image analysis and machine learning in digital pathology: challenges and opportunities, *Med. Image Anal.* 33 (1) (2016) 170–175.

[8] A.E. Carpenter, T.R. Jones, M.R. Lamprecht, C. Clarke, I.H. Kang, O. Friman, D.A. Guertin, J.H. Chang, R.A. Lindquist, J. Moffat, P. Golland, D.M. Sabatini, CellProfiler: image analysis software for identifying and quantifying cell phenotypes, *Genome Biol.* 7 (10) (2006) R100.

[9] M. Held, M.H. Schmitz, B. Fischer, T. Walter, B. Neumann, M.H. Olma, M. Peter, J. Ellenberg, D.W. Gerlich, CellCognition: time-resolved phenotype annotation in high-throughput live cell imaging, Nat. Methods 7 (9) (2010) 747–754.

[10] M. Jiang, S. Zhang, J. Huang, L. Yang, D.N. Metaxas, in: Joint Kernel-Based Supervised Hashing for Scalable Histopathological Image Analysis, MICCAI, 2015, pp. 366–373.

[11] B. Misselwitz, G. Strittmatter, B. Periaswamy, M.C. Schlumberger, S. Rout, P. Horvath, K. Kozak, W.D. Hardt, Enhanced CellClassifier: a multi-class classification tool for microscopy images, BMC Bioinform. 11 (30) (2010).

[12] G. Pau, F. Fuchs, O. Sklyar, M. Boutros, W. Huber, EBImage—an R package for image processing with applications to cellular phenotypes, Bioinformatics 26 (7) (2010) 979–981.

[13] L. Shamir, N. Orlov, D.M. Eckley, T.J. Macura, J. Johnston, I.G. Goldberg, Wndchrm—an open source utility for biological image analysis, Source Code Biol. Med. 3 (1) (2008) 13.

[14] Y. Xu, J. Zhu, E.I. Chang, M. Lai, Z. Tu, Weakly supervised histopathology cancer image segmentation and classification, *Med. Image Anal.* 18 (3) (2014) 591–604.

[15] J. Zhou, S. Lamichhane, G. Sterne, B. Ye, H. Peng, BIOCAT: a pattern recognition platform for customizable biological image classification and annotation, BMC Bioinform. 14 (291) (2013).

[16] A. Ben Taieb, H. Li-Chang, D. Huntsman, G. Hamarneh, in: Automatic Diagnosis of Ovarian Car-cinomas via Sparse Multiresolution Tissue Representation, MICCAI, 2015, pp. 629–636.

[17] S. Otalora, A. Cruz-Roa, J. Arevalo, M. Atzori, A. Madabhushi, A.R. Judkins, F. Gonzalez, H. Muller, A. Depeursinge, Combining Unsupervised Feature Learning and Riesz Wavelets for His-topathology Image Representation: Application to Identifying Anaplastic Medulloblastoma, in: in: MICCAI, 2015, pp. 581–588.

[18] U. Srinivas, H.S. Mousavi, V. Monga, A. Hattel, B. Jayarao, Simultaneous sparsity model for histopath-ological image representation and classification, IEEE Trans. Med. Imag. 33 (5) (2014) 1163–1179.

[19] T.H. Vu, H.S. Mousavi, V. Monga, G. Rao, A. Rao, Histopathological image classification using dis-criminative feature-oriented dictionary learning, IEEE Trans. Med. Imag. 36 (3) (2016) 738–751.

[20] X. Zhang, F. Xing, H. Su, L. Yang, S. Zhang, High-throughtput histopathological image analysis via robust cell segmentation and hashing, Med. Image Anal. 26 (1) (2015) 306–315.

[21] Y. Zhou, H. Chang, K. Barner, P. Spellman, B. Parvin, in: Classification of Histology Sections via Multispectral Convolutional Sparse Coding, CVPR, 2014, pp. 3081–3088.

[22] O. Ronneberger, P. Fischer, T. Brox, in: U-Net: Convolutional Networks for Biomedical Image Seg-mentation, MICCAI, 2015, pp. 234–241.

[23] K. Sirnukunwattana, S.E.A. Raza, Y. Tsang, D.R.J. Snead, I.A. Cree, N.M. Rajpoot, Locality sensitive deep learning for detection and classification of nuclei in routine colon cancer histology images, IEEE Trans. Med. Imag. 35 (5) (2016) 1196–1206.

[24] H. Su, F. Xing, X. Kong, Y. Xie, S. Zhang, L. Yang, in: Robust Cell Detection and Segmentation in Histopathological Images Using Sparse Reconstruction and Stacked Denoising Autoencoders, MIC-CAI, 2015, pp. 383–390.

[25] F. Xing, Y. Xie, L. Yang, An automatic learning-based framework for robust nucleus segmentation, IEEE Trans. Med. Imag. 35 (2) (2016) 550–566.

[26] J. Xu, L. Xiang, Q. Liu, H. Gilmore, J. Wu, J. Tang, A. Madabhushi, Stacked sparse autoen-coder (SSAE) for nuclei detection on breast cancer histopathology images, IEEE Trans. Med. Imag. 35 (1) (2016) 119–130.

[27] H. Su, Z. Yin, T. Kanade, S. Huh, in: Phase Contrast Image Restoration via Dictionary Representation of Diffraction Patterns, MICCAI, 2012, pp. 615–622.

[28] H. Wang, A. Cruz-Roa, A. Basavanhally, H. Gilmore, N. Shih, M. Feldman, J. Tomaszewski, F. Gonzalez, A. Madabhushi, Mitosis detection in breast cancer pathology images by combining hand-crafted and convolutional neural network features, J. Med. Imag. 1 (3) (2014) 034003.

[29] J. Wang, J.D. MacKenzie, R. Ramachandran, D.Z. Chen, in: Neutrophils Identification by Deep Learning and Voronoi Diagram of Clusters, MICCAI, 2015, pp. 226–233.

[30] L.P. Coelho, J.D. Kangas, A.W. Naik, E. Osuna-Highley, E. Glory-Afshar, M. Fuhrman, R. Simha, P.B. Berget, J.W. Jarvik, R.F. Murphy, Determining the subcellular location of new proteins from microscope images using local features, Bioinformatics 29 (18) (2013) 2343–2349.

[31] S.S. Abbas, T.M.H. Dijkstra, T. Heskes, A comparative study of cell classifiers for image-based high-throughput screening, BMC Bioinform. 14 (342) (2014).

[32] M. Peikari, M.J. Gangeh, J. Zubovits, G. Clarke, A.L. Martel, Pathology whole slides of breast cancer: a texture based approach, IEEE Trans. Med. Imag. 35 (1) (2016) 307–315.

[33] L. Peter, O. Pauly, P. Chatelain, D. Mateus, N. Navab, in: Scale-Adaptive Forest Training via an Effi-cient Feature Sampling Scheme, MICCAI, 2015, pp. 637–644.

[34] X. Xu, F. Lin, C. Ng, K.P. Leong, in: Adaptive Co-occurrence Differential Texton Space for HEp-2 Cell Classification, MICCAI, 2015, pp. 260–267.

[35] J. Han, Y. Wang, W. Cai, A. Borowsky, B. Parvin, H. Chang, in: Integrative Analysis of Cellular Mor-phometric Context Reveals Clinically Relevant Signatures in Lower Grade Glioma, MICCAI, 2016, pp. 72–80.

[36] A. Taalimi, S. Ensafi, H. Qi, S. Lu, A.A. Kassim, C.L. Tan, Multimodal Dictionary Learning and Joint Sparse Representation for HEp-2 Cell Classification, MICCAI, 2015, pp. 308–315.

[37] F. Perronnin, J. Sanchez, T. Mensink, in: Improving the Fisher Kernel for Large-Scale Image Classi-fication, ECCV, 2010, pp. 143–156.

[38] M. Jain, J.C. van Gemert, C.G.M. Snoek, in: What do 15000 Object Categories Tell us About Clas-sifying and Localizing Actions?, CVPR, 2015, pp. 46–55.

[39] K. Simonyan, O.M. Parkhi, A. Vedaldi, A. Zisserman, in: Fisher Vector Faces in the Wild, *BMVC*, 2013, pp. 1–12.

[40] K. Chatfield, K. Simonyan, A. Vedaldi, A. Zisserman, in: Return of the Devil in the Details: Delving Deep Into Convolutional Nets, *BMVC*, 2014, pp. 1–12.

[41] M. Cimpoi, S. Maji, I. Kokkinos, S. Mohamed, A. Vedaldi, in: Describing Textures in the Wild, *CVPR*, 2014, pp. 3606–3613.

[42] Y. Song, W. Cai, Q. Li, F. Zhang, D. Feng, H. Huang, in: Fusing Subcategory Probabilities for Texture Classification, *CVPR*, 2015, pp. 4409–4417.

[43] Y. Song, W. Cai, H. Huang, D. Feng, Y. Wang, M. Chen, Bioimage classification with subcategory discriminant transform of high dimensional visual descriptors, BMC Bioinform. 17 (465) (2016).

[44] M. Cimpoi, S. Maji, A. Vedaldi, in: Deep Filter Banks for Texture Recognition and Segmentation, *CVPR*, 2015, pp. 3828–3836.

[45] Y. Bar, I. Diamant, L. Wolf, S. Lieberman, E. Konen, H. Greenspan, in: Chest Pathology Detection Using Deep Learning With Non-Medical Training, ISBI, 2015, pp. 294–297.

[46] H. Shin, H.R. Roth, M. Gao, L. Lu, Z. Xu, I. Nogues, J. Yao, D. Mollura, R.M. Summers, Deep convolutional neural networks for computer-aided detection: CNN architecture, dataset characteristics and transfer learning, *IEEE Trans. Med. Imag.* 35 (5) (2016) 1285–1298.

[47] J. Wang, J.D. MacKenzie, R. Ramachandran, D.Z. Chen, in: A Deep Learning Approach for Semantic Segmentation in Histology Tissue Images, *MICCAI*, 2016, pp. 176–184.

[48] Y. Song, Q. Li, H. Huang, D. Feng, M. Chen, W. Cai, in: Histopathology Image Categorization With Discriminative Dimension Reduction of Fisher Vectors, *ECCV Workshops*, 2016, pp. 1–12.

[49] R. Arandjelovic, A. Zisserman, in: All About VLAD, CVPR, 2013, pp. 1578–1585.

[50] Y. Song, J. Zou, H. Chang, W. Cai, in: Adapting Fisher Vectors for Histopathology Image Classification, *ISBI*, 2017, pp. 600–603.

[51] M.A. Keyvanrad, M.M. Homayounpour, A brief survey on deep belief networks and introducing a new object oriented toolbox (DeeBNet), arXiv:1408.3264, 2014.

[52] K. Simonyan, A. Zisserman, in: Very Deep Convolutional Networks for Large-Scale Image Recognition, *ICLR*, 2015. *arXiv*:1409.1556.

[53] Y. Song, Q. Li, H. Huang, D. Feng, M. Chen, W. Cai, Low dimensional representation of fisher vectors for microscopy image classification, *IEEE Trans. Med. Imag.* 36 (8) (2017) 1636–1649.

[54] Y. Song, H. Chang, H. Huang, W. Cai, in: Supervised Intra-Embedding of Fisher Vectors for Histopathology Image Classification, MICCAI, 2017, pp. 99–106.

[55] F. Spanhol, L.S. Oliveira, C. Petitjean, L. Heutte, A dataset for breast cancer histopathological image classification, IEEE Trans. Biomed. Eng. 63 (7) (2016) 1455–1462.

[56] T. Jaakkola, D. Haussler, in: Exploiting Generative Models in Discriminative Classifiers, *NIPS*, 1999, pp. 487–493.

[57] S. Azizi, F. Imani, B. Zhuang, A. Tahmasebi, J.T. Kwak, S. Xu, N. Uniyal, B. Turkbey, P. Choyke, P. Pinto, B. Wood, M. Moradi, P. Mousavi, P. Abolmaesumi, in: Ultrasound-Based Detection of Prostate Cancer Using Automatic Feature Selection With Deep Belief Networks, MIC-CAI, 2015, pp. 70–77.

[58] T. Brosch, Y. Yoo, D.K.B. Li, A. Traboulsee, R. Tam, in: Modeling the Variability in Brain Morphology and Lesion Distribution in Multiple Sclerosis by Deep Learning, MICCAI, 2014, pp. 462–469.

[59] A. Krizhevsky, I. Sutskever, G.E. Hinton, ImageNet Classification With Deep Convolutional Neural Networks, *NIPS*, 2012, pp. 1–9.

[60] K.Q. Weinberger, L.K. Saul, Distance metric learning for large margin nearest neighbor classification, J. Mach. Learn. Res. 10 (2009) 207–244.

[61] J. Wang, J. Yang, K. Yu, F. Lv, T. Huang, Y. Gong, in: Locality-Constrained Linear Coding for Image Classification, CVPR, 2010, pp. 3360–3367.

[62] W. Li, J. Zhang, S.J. McKenna, in: Multiple Instance Cancer Detection by Boosting Regularised Trees, MICCAI, 2015, pp. 645–652.

[63] K. Sikka, R. Giri, M. Bartlett, in: Joint Clustering and Classification for Multiple Instance Learning, *BMVC*, 2015, pp. 1–12.

[64] T. Meng, L. Lin, M. Shyu, S. Chen, Histology Image Classification Using Supervised Classification and Multimodal Fusion, in: in: *ISM*, 2010, pp. 145–152.

[65] N. Codella, M. Moradi, M. Matasar, T. Sveda-Mahmood, J.R. Smith, in: Lymphoma Diagnosis in Histopathology Using a Multi-Stage Visual Learning Approach, *SPIE*, 2016, p. 97910H.

[66] B. Zhang, T.D. Pham, Phenotype recognition with combined features and random subspace classifier ensemble, BMC Bioinform. 12 (128) (2011).

[67] L. Nanni, S. Brahnam, S. Ghidoni, E. Menegatti, T. Barrier, A comparison of methods for extracting information from the co-occurrence matrix for subcellular classification, Expert Syst. Appl. 40 (18) (2013) 7457–7467.

[68] J.B. Tenenbaum, V. de Silva, J.C. Langford, A global geometric framework for nonlinear dimensionality reduction, Science 290 (2000) 2319–2323.

[69] G. Baudat, F. Anouar, Generalized discriminant analysis using a kernel approach, Neural Comput. 12 (10) (2000) 2385–2404.

[70] F. Spanhol, L.S. Oliveira, C. Petitjean, L. Heutte, in: Breast Cancer Histopathological Image Classification Using Convolutional Neural Networks, *IJCNN*, 2016, pp. 1–8.

CHAPTER 5

Cell tracking in time-lapse microscopy image sequences

Mei Chen
Microsoft, Redmond, WA, United States

Contents

As Dr. Hoeppner articulated in Chapter 1 on *A Biologist's Perspective on Computer Vision*, computer vision can compensate for the limits of human visual perception from digital images. This is especially true for time-lapse microscopy image sequences. Time-lapse images are typically recorded at a lower frame rate than that in videos, for example, every minute or every few minutes, depending on the process or phenomenon being captured. Time-lapse microscopy is an important tool for biomedical research and discovery [1] that enables the study of processes that evolve too slow or over a time duration too long for a human to observe continuously. Examples include mitosis [2–4], apoptosis [5–7], and differentiation [8] at an individual cell level. Fig. 5.1 is an example of a segment of a time-lapse microscopy image sequence that contains a cell mitosis event.

A time-lapse microscopy image sequence contains rich information about how the parameters of individual cells evolve over time. Such information is necessary to understand cell-to-cell interactions, cell behaviors such as proliferation, and how cells react to different biochemical conditions. Tracking individual cells throughout the time-lapse sequence is necessary to extract such information because otherwise, the analyses are

Computer Vision for Microscopy Image Analysis
https://doi.org/10.1016/B978-0-12-814972-0.00005-9
101

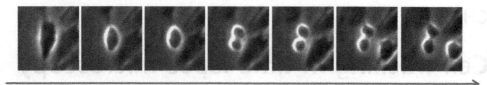

Fig. 5.1 An example of a time-lapse microscopy image sequence containing a cell mitosis event with the horizontal axis as time.

limited to population averages or snapshot measurements. Population averages do not provide any information about the variability within the populations while snapshot measurements do not capture temporal evolution. Moreover, snapshot measurements risk overestimating the variability in cell populations where temporal variations may manifest as variations between cells [9]. In fact, tracking cells in time-lapse microscopy image sequences is the only technique that captures full information about the lineage of dividing cells, which is critical for studying how and why cell populations change over time [9, 10]. The lineage tree contains the developmental history of the cells and could further the understanding of important phenomena such as cell diversity, cellular cooperation, and the stability of the phenotype. Fig. 5.2 is an example of a lineage tree of a cell population.

As set forth in Chapter 3 on *Detection and Segmentation in Microscopy Images*, there are unique challenges in analyzing microscopy images due to low signal-to-noise ratio, low contrast, overlapping objects, and variation in appearances, both spatially among different objects and temporally for the same object. Such artifacts make the task of cell tracking extra difficult because, in addition to detecting individual cells in each image frame, the correspondence between the cells in successive image frames also needs to be established to obtain the trajectory of individual cells over time. The fact that cells in vitro are living organisms that proliferate, die, and even fuse makes the tracking task more challenging than tracking most other objects such as people or cars, where one tracking error can render the rest of the lineage from that time point on unusable. Therefore, accurate and long-term cell tracking is necessary to enable the next stages of biomedical study.

Currently, in most laboratories cell tracking in time-lapse microscopy image sequences is performed manually, where human operators observe cell movements or changes in cell appearances for hours if not days to discover when, where, and how fast a given cell migrates, goes through mitosis or apoptosis, etc. This is not only tedious but also error-prone, unreproducible, and subject to both inter- and intraoperator biases. In practice, manual inspection has been limited to tracking a small number of cells over short periods of time.

With time-lapse microscopy image data ever more simply and rapidly acquired, manual tracking of hundreds to thousands of individual cells over an image sequence of

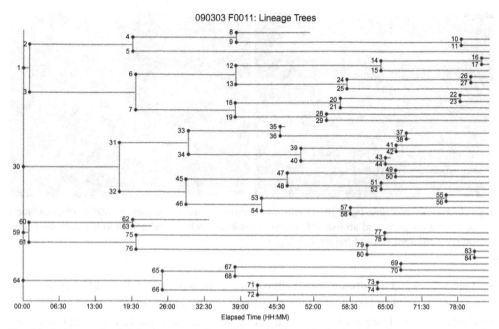

Fig. 5.2 An example of a lineage tree of a cell population with the horizontal axis as time and the vertical axis as cell identities.

hundreds to thousands of frames is practically prohibitive, if not impossible, let alone over numerous such sequences in order to evaluate the same task for different cell types or cell culture conditions. Therefore, there is a clear and urgent demand for an automated or semiautomated computer vision approach to track large cell populations over long periods of time to advance biomedical study. In addition to alleviating human labor and subjective bias as well as being reproducible, computer vision-based tracking also has the advantage of being able to capture subtle changes that are hard for a human to observe or quantify, for example, predicting the fates of neural progenitor cells by looking at their appearances and motions [11].

Research on computer vision-based cell tracking has been active for decades and there has been encouraging progress. However, more investigation is still needed as existing methods are not robust for long-term imaging experiments with significant cell populations [1]. Fig. 5.3 shows a snapshot of a time-lapse phase contrast microscopy image sequence with a cell population in the thousands and an example tracking result of each individual cell in the sequence. Such tracking problems are more challenging than tracking a few cells or over a brief time duration and will be the primary focus for discussion in this chapter.

In addition to the typical artifacts present in microscopy images, the following issues need to be addressed to achieve reliable cell tracking in time-lapse image sequences:
• Reidentification—connecting a cell in one frame to the same cell in successive frames.

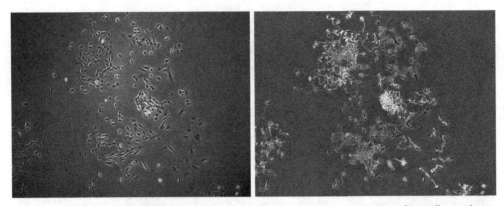

Fig. 5.3 An area of a time-lapse phase contrast microscopy image sequence with a cell population in the thousands (left), and an example tracking result of each individual cell in the area over time denoted by different colored trajectories (right).

- Appearance and disappearance—cells can move into or out of the field of view of the frame and need to be connected to cells previously seen if applicable.
- Occlusion—cells are partially or completely occluded in some frames. and need to be connected to the same cells when they come out of occlusion.
- Identity switches—when two objects cross each other, the algorithm needs to be able to discern which one is which.
- Cellular events such as division, merging, death—different from most other objects, a cell can divide into two or more cells, merge with other cells, or go through apoptosis and gradually disappear in a time-lapse image sequence. In the field of computer vision for microscopy image analysis, these are treated as distinct cellular events and tackled separately via event detection techniques, such as those discussed in depth in Chapter 6 on *Mitosis Detection in Microscopy Images and Image Sequences*, and are therefore out of the scope for this chapter. Note that in real-world applications, the cell tracking module should be integrated with the cellular event detection module so as to be able to correctly track the lineage of the cell population. Fig. 5.4 Illustrates the inherent connection between cell division detection and cell tracking in a time-lapse image sequence. Fig. 5.5 shows what a complete system with cell tracking and cellular event detection should include.

Many publications have reviewed past research on computer vision-based cell tracking [12–15]. In recent years, machine learning-based techniques, especially deep neural networks (DNN), have disrupted the field of computer vision and brought significant performance improvement to solving many problems such as detection, recognition, segmentation, and classification. In this chapter, we categorize cell tracking algorithms as *traditional*, that is, prior to the popularity of deep neural networks, and *deep*

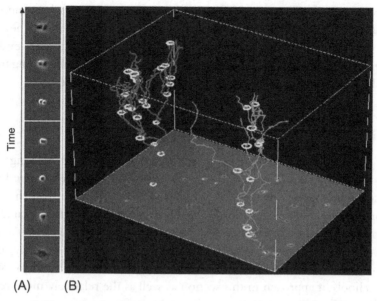

Fig. 5.4 An example illustrating the connection between cell division and cell tracking. (A) A time-lapse phase contrast microscopy image sequence that contains a mitosis event with the vertical axis as time. (B) A three-dimensional view of the trajectories of cells as they migrate and divide over time, the vertical axis. Note that the time of cell birth from each mitosis is the time stamp when the cell trajectory forks.

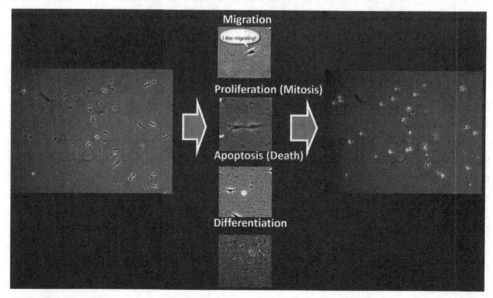

Fig. 5.5 A complete cell tracking system that is comprised of tracking cell migration and handling cellular events, including division (mitosis), death (apoptosis), and differentiation.

learning-based methods. We cover representative traditional approaches, and delve into the current developments in deep learning-based techniques because they represent the state of the art. We will also discuss challenges in the quantitative evaluation of large-scale, long-term tracking performance; the current efforts in addressing these problems; and how cell tracking enables the study of real-world problems.

1. Traditional cell tracking approaches

Similar to general object tracking in computer vision, traditional cell tracking approaches can largely be grouped as either *model-based* [16–19] or *tracking by detection* [20–24]. In model-based approaches, a mathematical representation of each cell, such as an active contour or level set, is propagated through the image sequence and updated to fit the image data at each frame. In tracking by detection, the task of tracking is done in two steps, *detection* and *track linking*. The cells are first detected independently in different image frames, then the detected cells are associated and linked into tracks. We discuss these two schools of approach in this section as well as the relatively more recent joint segmentation and tracking techniques.

1.1 Model-based tracking

Model-based tracking can work well for image sequences with high spatial magnification and high temporal resolution. For applications where cell contour is necessary, model evolution has the advantage that temporal context can be used to obtain more accurate segmentation boundaries. The mathematical representation of cells can be either parametric [25, 26] or implicit [17].

Parametric models represent cell boundaries using active meshes [26], active contours [16, 19], or Gaussian mixture models (GMM) [25]. These methods are computationally fast. However, their performance depends heavily on the empirically selected parameters, and they require separate treatment to handle cases when cells touch and when cells enter or leave the field of view. Fig. 5.6 shows examples of cells touching, overlapping, and leaving the field of view, which make cell tracking challenging. Implicit methods employ the level set of a function to represent the cell boundaries, which has the advantage of allowing not only shape but also topological changes [27]. However, implicit methods are computationally expensive. In general, because the entire cell boundary needs to be tracked, model-based algorithms are slower than tracking-by-detection algorithms where only the cell location needs to be tracked. There have been efforts to make model-based algorithms faster [14, 26].

Once a model describing the spatial pattern of pixels with the appearance of a cell is constructed, the next step is to associate the cells over successive image frames in the time

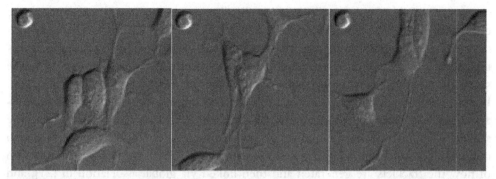

Fig. 5.6 Examples of challenging cases for cell tracking. From left to right: cells touching, overlapping/occluding, and leaving the field of view.

lapse sequence. This can be done via probabilistic approaches such as maximum a posteriori estimation [22] or stochastic expectation-maximization [28].

1.2 Tracking by detection

Methods along the line of tracking by detection are more popular for cell tracking, intuitively because they decouple the detection and tracking tasks, thereby making the approach more generalizable and flexible. First, cells are detected and/or segmented and some features are extracted to represent each detected cell. During the tracking step, detected cells in successive frames are associated with one another. Cell trajectories can then be formed by global association with all frames linked [21, 29–32], by local association linking only neighboring frames [23], or by employing a combination of the two [13].

By disassociating tracking from detection, tracking-by-detection methods have the advantage that the track-linking technique can be used with different detection or segmentation approaches and vice versa. This makes it possible for a cell tracking system to accommodate different types of data by customizing either the cell detection or segmentation module or the track linking module. Because of the variations in cell shapes and the effect of different experimental settings and culture conditions on the appearances of cells, the cell detection or segmentation step typically needs to be more application-dependent than the track-linking step. Therefore, it usually makes more sense to use the same track-linking module together with various application-specific detection or segmentation methods.

Compared to model-based tracking, tracking by detection has the advantage that it can leverage more extended temporal context to produce more accurate trajectories. Track linking faces the same challenges as any object tracking problem, namely the ambiguity of cell correspondence when cells occlude each other, switch positions, or move in or out of the field of view, as illustrated in Fig. 5.6, not to mention that there could be errors from the cell detection or segmentation step. Therefore, it is more reliable to consider extended temporal context to have both spatial and temporal information to disambiguate the aforementioned scenarios. Ideally, the entire time-lapse image sequence should be considered via global optimization when constructing the cell trajectories. In practice, global optimization can be prohibitively compute-intensive or computationally expensive. Often, *tracklets* from neighboring frames are first created throughout the sequence, then the tracklets are linked via global association over the entire sequence to optimally construct the complete cell trajectories [33, 21]. Fig. 5.7 is an illustration of how the tracklets are generated and then linked via global association in [21], and Fig. 5.8 is a three-dimensional (3D) view of the real tracklets and the trajectories formed from them.

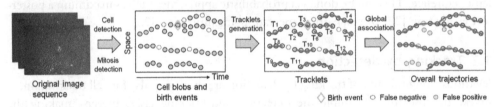

Fig. 5.7 An illustration of tracklet generation and trajectory construction in [21].

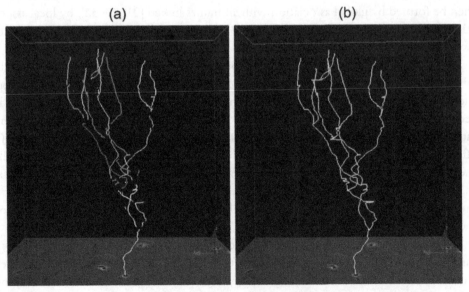

Fig. 5.8 A 3D view of the real tracklets (A) and the trajectories (B) formed from them with the vertical axes as time.

In addition to the challenge of corresponding the same cells across image frames in the time-lapse sequence, there could be errors from the cell detection or segmentation step. Leveraging temporal context helps, but it is difficult to recover from such errors during tracking. Earlier methods were not able to correct cell detection or segmentation errors in the tracking stage. More recent approaches have reported success resolving some false positives, false negatives, and undersegmentation errors in the tracking stage [21, 24, 34, 35]. However, they all achieve such at the expense of additional complexities in the algorithm, and despite this, they still fail to resolve some detection or segmentation errors.

1.3 Joint segmentation and tracking

Because it is difficult if not impossible for cell tracking to recover from errors in cell detection or segmentation, it is natural to investigate approaches integrating tracking with detection to optimize the overall performance. Proposal-based joint detection and tracking methods [36–38] first generate a large set of cell detection proposals covering multiple hypotheses for ambiguous regions; then, the detection proposals are connected via a spatiotemporal graph, also called a tracking graph, to prevent the selection of conflicting proposals. Finally, optimization schemes such as integer linear programming are employed for inference. Fig. 5.9 shows an example of a tracking graph where multiple detection proposals are associated temporally and ambiguities are resolved based on compatibility.

An object proposal is a candidate for detecting and/or segmenting an object. Object proposals enable the subsequent analysis to focus on a small set of image regions. They need to have high recall, with a corresponding candidate for as many objects as possible, without the total number of proposals being too large to be computationally intractable. Object proposals are used extensively in object tracking as a preprocessing step to focus

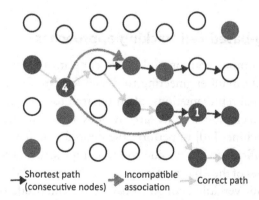

Fig. 5.9 Example of a tracking graph where multiple detection proposals are associated temporally.

the attention on regions in an image that are more likely to contain the objects. This enables an efficient representation of multiple hypotheses and significantly reduces the number of detection and association alternatives for optimization.

Compared to tracking-by-detection approaches, proposal-based joint detection and tracking methods utilize temporal information during tracking to resolve ambiguities in detection and are thereby less prone to errors in detection. They use cell proposals to represent all potential cell hypotheses and defer the detection decision until tracking. In addition to being less prone to detection errors, this has the advantage of being able to draw on the shape and appearance features of each cell candidate for more effective evaluation of multiple detection and temporal association hypotheses in ambiguous regions.

Another advantage of joint detection and tracking is that sequence-specific constraints can be incorporated in the tracking graphs to improve performance. For example, Jug et al. [36] employed exit constraints specific to the particular application and Schiegg et al. [37] used high-level cues about the number of cells in each proposal tree to improve the performance. In practical applications, these methods can also enable user-friendly interactive error correction during the track verification step as alternative detections can be viewed.

For challenging sequences with a high cell count or high level of ambiguity due to cell population density or image quality, the proposal-based tracking methods can be computationally more expensive than the detection-based methods, as the number of proposals and edges in the tracking graph linking the proposals can be large. If the proposal quality is generally good, then the additional computing expense may not be consequential. Therefore, it is important to develop effective proposal generation techniques to mitigate the computational demand. Another way to manage the computational workload is to limit the possible transitions between frames. Schiegg et al. [39] used this approach to speed up the inference for long sequences. However, this scheme may not work well for sequences with a low frame rate and high cell density.

2. Deep learning-based cell tracking approaches

Until recent years, computer vision and microscopy image analysis relied heavily on domain expertise and careful engineering to design features for transforming raw pixel values to useful internal representations, often referred to as image features. These representations were then employed either directly or by a machine-learning technique such as support vector machines [40] to perform the desired task. These internal representations are typically difficult to design due to the complexity and large variations in the appearances and shapes of the objects of interest. By the same token, the human-designed representations are not versatile enough to handle the multitude of variations found in real-world visual data.

In order to track hundreds to thousands of individual cells, multiple levels of representations are necessary to capture the characteristics of the appearances and shapes of cells for tracking to be robust to challenges such as occlusion, although shallow representations were more common because they were more intuitive for humans to design. The lower level representations were typically gradient-based feature descriptors, such as scale-invariant feature transform (SIFT) [41] and the histogram of oriented gradients (HOG) [42]. The commonly used higher-level representations included deformable part models (DPM) [43] that represented objects using a collection of parts. These shallow representations had some success but were not sufficiently robust for most real-world applications.

2.1 Power of deep learning

In the last decade, the phenomenal development in deep neural networks (DNN), that is, deep learning, largely disrupted the field of computer vision, first in tasks such as classification then in object detection and more. In fact, deep learning has improved the accuracy and analysis power of object detection by an order of magnitude where it was traditionally difficult to design the higher-level discriminative representations. DNNs learn a hierarchy of representations by concatenating nonlinear modules that each transform their input into a more abstract level of representation. By concatenating a sufficiently large number of such modules, typically referred to as the *depth* of the DNNs, complex and comprehensive representations can be obtained. It has been shown that the first modules extract low-level image representations generally equivalent to edges, corners, etc. The middle modules extract mid-level representations such as wheels, eyes, etc., based on the input from the first modules. The last modules extract higher-level representations based on input from the middle modules, sufficient to locate and recognize complex objects or structures such as cats or cars while being robust to variations in illumination, pose, scale, occlusion, etc., as illustrated in Fig. 5.10 [44, 45].

Deep learning has had some success in microscopy image analysis as well. It has demonstrated improvement for mitosis detection compared to conventional approaches [46–52]. Moreover, U-Net [53], a semantic segmentation network, is considered to produce a state-of-the-art performance for cell segmentation in microcopy images [54, 55].

2.2 Deep learning for object tracking

For current deep learning techniques to be successful, in addition to a well-designed neural network architecture and an efficient computing platform such as graphic processing units (GPUs), two factors are important:

1. Large labeled training dataset(s) that are well distributed to capture the potential variability in the data.

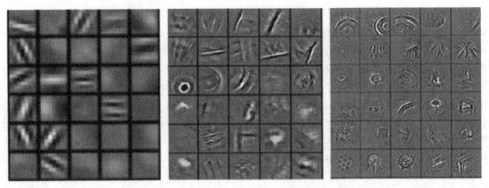

Fig. 5.10 A visualization of the representations learned at increasing depths of a convolutional neural network (CNN) from left to right, low-level, mid-level, and higher-level [44, 45].

2. The distribution of the training data needs to be representative of the test data that the model will be applied on.

Despite the sweeping success of deep learning in applications such as image classification and object detection, its performance in object tracking had been less dominant until around 2019. Results from tracking approaches employing handcrafted features were competitive, even outperforming deep learning-based trackers on standard benchmarks [56, 57].

There are two key challenges to leveraging the power of deep features in object tracking. First, as mentioned above, compared to traditional handcrafted features, DNN models need well-distributed labeled data to learn strong deep features. This is a nontrivial obstacle because a large number of human-labeled images are scarce and expensive in general. By adding the spatiotemporal nature of the object tracking task where a complete labeling entails tracing each individual object throughout its appearances in the sequence, this challenge is more pronounced. This likely explains why it is was not until recently that deep learning-based approaches demonstrated superior performance for multiple object tracking [58] because where training data is inadequate, the model is learned from sparse data. Even though pretrained deep networks are typically employed to initialize the weights in the target neural network to give a head start, the target model still needs to learn the discriminative representations that are invariant to changes in appearances, shape, occlusion, etc., from adequate labeled data. The second challenge in utilizing deep learning-based features for object tracking is accurate target prediction. Not only is precise target localization crucial for tracking performance because in most tracking systems new frames are annotated by the tracker itself, but it also affects the learning of the deep features. Inaccurate target predictions may lead to DNN model drift and eventual tracking failure.

Most deep learning-based object tracking algorithms adopt the *tracking by detection* paradigm explained in Section 1.2, and deep neural networks are typically employed in the *detection* step, that is, to detect and/or segment the object and extract features to represent each detected object. Although the specific techniques for object detection and track association may vary, the most common overall framework and deep neural network architectures for object tracking are, Simple Online and Real-time Tracking (SORT) [59], Generic Object Tracking Using a Regression Network (GOTURN) [60], and the Multidomain Network (MDNet) [61].

SORT relies mainly on the object detection engine, and it can plug into any object detection algorithm such as YOLO [62], Mask R–CNN [63], and Faster R–CNN [64]. It associates the objects in each frame with those detected in previous frames using simple heuristics such as maximizing the IOU (intersection-over-union) metric between object bounding boxes in neighboring frames. An extension based on SORT, DeepSORT [65], integrates appearance information based on a deep appearance descriptor. The intuition behind it is that humans track objects over time based on not only how far and how fast the movement is, but also what the object looks like. DeepSORT incorporates the appearance information by computing deep features for every bounding box from the object detection engine and factor the similarity between deep features into the tracking logic.

GOTURN is trained by comparing pairs of cropped frames from thousands of sequences, as illustrated in Fig. 5.11. In the "previous frame," the location of the object is known together with its bounding box, and the frame is cropped to twice the size of the bounding box around the object, with the object centered. The algorithm then tries to predict the location of the same object in the subsequent "current frame." The same double-sized bounding box is used to crop the second frame. A convolutional neural network (CNN) is trained to predict the location of the bounding box in the "current frame." Note that different from the SORT approaches, GOTURN is an offline learning tracker based on a convolutional neural network that does not learn online. Once the

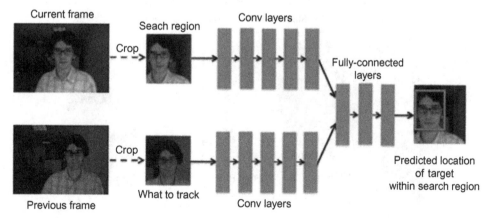

Fig. 5.11 An illustration of the GOTURN algorithm [60].

tracker is trained using thousands of videos for general object tracking, it can be used to track most objects without retraining/finetuning, even if those objects were not part of the training set. Another advantage of GOTURN is that it runs fast, for example, 100 fps on a GPU.

As alluded to above, CNNs are computationally expensive to train. To use a CNN in online training, smaller networks need to be adopted to train at fast speed during deployment. However, smaller networks are known to not have adequate discriminative power compared to larger networks. One solution is to train the entire larger network offline, and during inference to use the first few layers as the feature extractor while only changing the weights of the last few layers online. This has the benefit of the representation power of larger CNNs as the feature extractor, and the fast training of the last few layers online.

The goal of training the CNN is to distinguish between the target and the background. However, the target in one video could be the background in another. MDNet [61] tackles this by splitting the network into two parts, where the first part is trained over multiple training sets and learns to distinguish objects from their background, that is, the *shared layers* in Fig. 5.12, The second part is trained on a specific training set and learns to identify objects within frames in the sequence, that is, the *domain-specific layers* in Fig. 5.12. This makes it possible to only modify the weights of the last few CNN layers during online training, thereby reducing computation time. MDNet was originally designed as a single object tracker, and Gan et al. [66] extended it for multiobject tracking.

It would be remiss to leave out object trackers that employ long short-term memory (LSTM) networks [67] along with convolutional neural networks. LSTM networks are known for being effective at learning historical patterns and not computationally expensive, making them potentially suitable for visual object tracking. Recurrent YOLO (ROLO) [68] is a single object, online, tracking-by-detection algorithm. It employs a

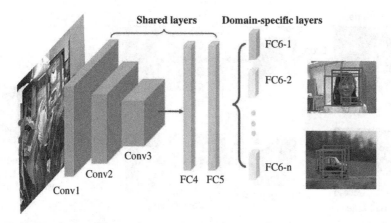

Fig. 5.12 The MDNet architecture [61].

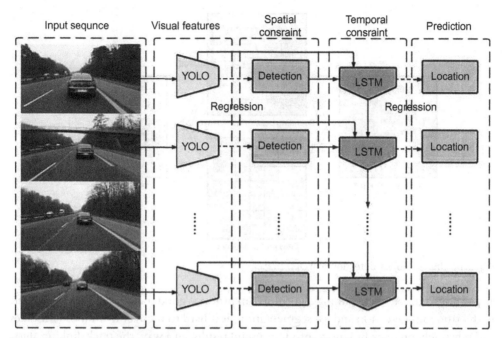

Fig. 5.13 The architecture of the recurrent YOLO network (ROLO) [68].

YOLO network for object detection and an LSTM network to determine the trajectory of the target object, as shown in Fig. 5.13.

YOLO divides the input image into a grid, and if the center of an object falls into a grid cell, that grid cell is responsible for detecting that object, as shown in Fig. 5.14. Each grid cell predicts bounding boxes and the corresponding confidence scores for those boxes (that is, the class probability map). The preliminary location inference from YOLO, that is, the image features and the coordinates of the object bounding boxes, helps the LSTM network to attend to relevant visual elements. This enables ROLO to exploit the spatiotemporal history of visual features and makes it possible for ROLO tracking to be robust even when YOLO detection is flawed or when the target object is occluded.

To be sure, there are many, many published works employing deep learning for object tracking. We discussed a few representatives of the different lines of attack. Given this chapter's focus on cell tracking, the list above is not intended to be exhaustive.

2.3 Deep learning for cell tracking in time-lapse microscopy images

As discussed in Section 1, for traditional approaches good cell detection and/or segmentation is a necessary condition for robust tracking. The same applies to deep learning-based approaches at the time of this writing. With perfect detection and/or segmentation,

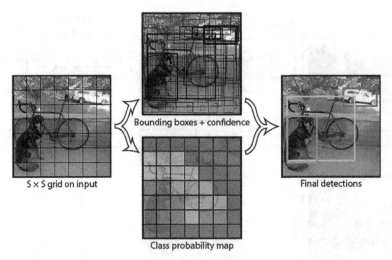

S × S grid on input   Bounding boxes + confidence   **Final detections**

Class probability map

Fig. 5.14 Unified object detection in YOLO [62].

any well-grounded track-linking algorithm can produce good tracking results. However, with erroneous detection and/or segmentation, it is hard to recover from those mistakes and rely solely on track linking to produce useful results. In a way, the track-linking algorithm determines how poor the detection and/or segmentation results can be before the tracking breaks down. The detection and/or segmentation algorithm decides if some semblance of automated tracking is attainable, or how much manual correction would be needed to achieve reasonable performance. In order to track a cell population over a meaningful time duration, the algorithm also needs to be able to handle the additional challenges brought upon by cellular events such as division (mitosis), fusion, death (apoptosis), and differentiation, as illustrated in Fig. 5.5.

2.3.1 Deep learning-based cell detection/segmentation

For cell detection and segmentation in microscopy images, CNNs such as U-Net [53] have been shown to achieve state-of-the-art performance (more details in Chapter 3 *Detection and Segmentation in Microscopy Images*). However, the training of such networks is complicated and data-hungry, so the methods have not been widely adopted. Another line of attack with good performance is to model the optics of the microscope and solve an inverse problem to find the optical thickness of the cells at each pixel [69, 70] (more details in Chapter 2 on *Microscopy Image Formation, Restoration, and Segmentation*). Such methods do require considerable knowledge about the optics employed during image capture and therefore have not been widely employed either. For fluorescence microscopy, thanks to fluorescent stains, simple algorithms based on filtering techniques, such as the difference of Gaussians filtering or Laplacian of Gaussians filtering, followed by thresholding can produce competitive cell detection and segmentation results. Recent works leveraging the easier-to-obtain segmentation results from fluorescence microscopy and applying panoptic-level domain adaptation to transfer the knowledge from fluorescence microscopy images to histopathology images have shown promise to achieve state-of-the-art segmentation results [71].

2.3.2 Deep learning-based cell mitosis detection

Both recurrent neural networks (RNN) such as LSTM and CNNs with sequential saliency have demonstrated state-of-the-art performance for in vitro cell mitosis detection in microscopy image sequences [48, 52] (more details in Chapter 6 on *Mitosis Detection in Microscopy Images and Image Sequences*, and [47]). As shown in Fig. 5.4, identifying exactly when and where each cell division event occurs is of critical importance for accurate tracking of in vitro cells and their daughter cells as well as for the construction of cell population lineage over time.

2.3.3 Deep learning-based cell tracking

There have been efforts employing deep learning for cell tracking in microscopy image sequences. Likely due to the challenges articulated in earlier sections of this chapter, most works focus on single-cell [72] or few-cell [73] tracking. The success of deep learning has yet to dominate the tracking of a large population of hundreds to thousands of cells over an extended time duration of multiple days, which is not an uncommon setting for research and development in drug discovery, stem cell engineering and regenerative medicine.

Like the application of deep learning to general object tracking, most works utilizing deep learning for cell tracking adopt the *tracking-by-detection* framework. Hernandez et al. [73] employed a fully convolutional neural network specifically designed for cell segmentation called DeepCell [74], followed by the *Viterbi algorithm* for cell tracking based on Magnusson et al. [35], as illustrated in Fig. 5.15. The tracking algorithm represents the sequence of images using a Hidden Markov Model with individual cell locations as the hidden states and the cell segmentations from the fully convolutional network as the observations. The Viterbi algorithm is used to determine the most likely state transitions between each time step. This approach leverages information from the full image sequence for each individual track and adds tracks only when they increase the overall score of a probabilistic scoring function. The authors demonstrated good results on an *Escherichia coli* dataset. However, it does not explicitly tackle cellular events such as mitosis, and the Viterbi algorithm makes a strong assumption that cells move according to the Brownian motion model, which is known to be inadequate. In many real-world settings, instead of moving small random distances between frames, cells exhibit motions with a clear direction as well as sometimes sudden changes in both direction and speed.

Akram et al. [75] adopted a *joint-detection-and-tracking* approach based on proposal selection [38] that represents multiple hypotheses for ambiguous regions using cell proposals. It employs a fully convolutional neural network to propose candidates for cell

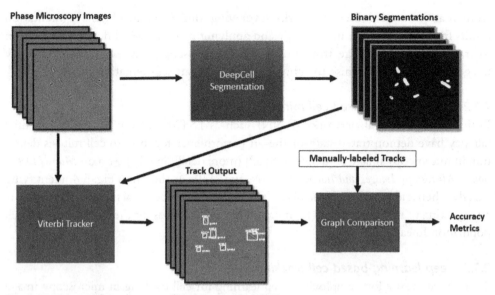

Fig. 5.15 The workflow diagram of Hernandez et al. [73].

bounding boxes and their corresponding scores, and a variant of U–Net to produce cell segmentation masks. Cell tracks are characterized as a directed acyclic graph where the nodes include all cells in the sequence, with *source* nodes marking the initiation of new tracks and *sink* nodes indicating the termination of existing tracks. The edges of the directed acyclic graph represent cellular events such as migration, mitosis, and death. It poses the problem of joint cell detection and tracking as the selection of a subset of cell and edge proposals. *Integer linear programming* is applied to select the optimal set of cell and edge proposals to generate cell tracks. Although not yet published at a peer-reviewed venue (only on *ArXiv*), this work demonstrated competitive or superior performance on several publicly available datasets. This approach has the potential of being able to handle various cellular events that happen in an in vitro setting. However, it makes a strong assumption on the appearance, position, and motion of the daughter cells after mitosis, which limits its generalization power to different cell types or different cell culture conditions.

Ramesh and Tasdizen [76] proposed a semisupervised framework for learning classifiers to predict cell division and transitions/migrations. It applies an unsupervised loss to support the learning of classifiers to predict cell divisions and transitions by imposing constraints on the incoming and outgoing track links for all detected cells, that is, only one of the incoming links can be active and at most two of the outgoing links can be active. It achieved superior performance on predicting cell division compared to Türetken et al. [38], and can be incorporated as an additional block into existing learning–based algorithms for cell tracking to better handle cell division events.

Tsai et al. [77] presented a semiautomated system, Usiigaci, for cell segmentation and tracking. It employs a mask regional CNN (Mask R–CNN) [63] for segmentation, and segmented cells are linked using the nearest neighbor search in the Trackpy library [78]. The segmentation and tracking results can be manually verified via a graphical user interface (GUI). As reported by the authors on their datasets, the valid track ratio in Usiigaci is 19.5% without manual verification, and 54% after manual verification.

3. Metrics for evaluating and comparing cell tracking performance

It has been difficult to quantitatively evaluate and compare the performance of cell tracking algorithms. There has not been consensus about which performance measures to use. Therefore, most published algorithms have been assessed using a variety of different metrics. To gauge the tracking performance on a population of cells in an image sequence, it is common to compare the computer-generated tracks against the manually generated ground truth using a number of different performance measures, a few of which are discussed below.

Bise et al. [21] proposed *track purity*, *target effectiveness*, and *mitosis branching correctness* as metrics to measure large-scale long-term cell tracking performance. *Track purity*, a concept coined by Mori et al. [79], computes the percentage of correctly associated measurements in a given track, that is, a measure of the degree to which the computer-generated tracks follow the manual ground truth labeling, and therefore evaluates the association/tracking performance and *penalizes false positive* tracks. The track purity of a single trajectory is computed by finding the cell that the track follows in most images in the sequence and dividing the number of images where the cell is followed computationally by the total length of the manually labeled track, as illustrated in Fig. 5.16. Although track purity can be evaluated for each single track, it is more meaningful to compute the statistics of track purity over all cell tracks in the image sequence. Smith et al. [80] assessed the track

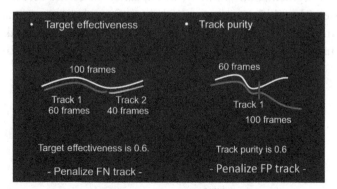

Fig. 5.16 Illustration of the target effectiveness and track purity metrics as defined in Bise et al. [21]. Here, FN stands for false negatives, and FP stands for false positives.

purity of a set of tracks by averaging the values of track purity for each individual track in the set. Another way to compute the statistics could be a weighted average where the individual cell tracks are weighed by their corresponding lengths to prevent short tracks from skewing the statistics, thus providing a normalized measurement.

Target effectiveness is defined in Bise et al. [21] as the number of the assigned track observations over the total number of image frames containing the target cell. It indicates how many frames of the target cell are followed by the computer-generated tracks, and therefore *penalizes false negative* tracks, as illustrated in Fig. 5.16.

The *mitotic branching correctness* measure is defined in Bise et al. [21] to assess the accuracy of mother-daughter relationships between mitotic branches in cell trajectories. Fig. 5.17 shows an example of a mitosis branching where the black lines are ground truth cell tracks and the red dashed lines denote computer generated tracks. In the ground truth, there is a cell division event at time t in which cell i divides into daughter cells j and k. If the computer-generated cell tracking results indicate a cell division event of the cell i' that corresponds to cell i, and children j' and k' of the cell i' correspond to daughter cells j and k, and the time distance between the two cell division events $\varepsilon = |t - t'|$ is smaller than a preset threshold, then this mitosis branching is considered to be correctly detected. The mitotic branching correctness metric is computed as the number of correctly detected mitosis branchings over the total number of the ground truth mitotic events.

Although the adoption of the aforementioned metrics has been seen in the cell tracking research literature, more effort is necessary to seek further consensus on how to quantitatively, effectively, and comprehensively evaluate and compare the performances of computer vision-based tracking of in vitro cell populations in microcopy image sequences. The Cell Tracking Challenge [14] is one such effort that combined different types of tracking errors into a single performance measure, the *tracking measure (TRA)*.

The goal of the TRA is to evaluate how well the computer vision tracking algorithms detect the cells and follow them in time. Although the TRA does not directly evaluate the detection or segmentation accuracy, as explained in earlier sections, reliable cell detection is essential to this measurement. Different from the pure accuracy-based metrics proposed in Bise et al. [21], Maška et al. [14] defined the TRA to take into consideration how much time it would take for a human to correct all tracking errors.

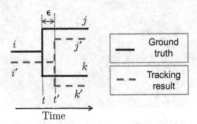

Fig. 5.17 The mitotic branching correctness metric ε as defined in Bise et al. [21].

Moreover, TRA gives more weight to tracking errors where the cells are missing, and less weight to sole track-linking errors.

Like Akram et al. [75] and Matula et al. [81], Maška et al. [14] represents cell tracking results using acyclic-oriented graphs. The nodes of the graphs correspond to the detected cells while the edges of the graphs denote the temporal relations between the nodes. They consider two types of edge semantics: *track links* where the cell continues with the same label in the consecutive frames, and *parent links* where the cell continues with a different label, not necessarily in the consecutive frames. Nondividing cells have one or no successor (e.g., in the event that the cell leaves the field of view), whereas cells that undergo mitosis have two or more successors (e.g., in the case of a division with more than two daughter cells). The TRA quantifies the difference between the acyclic-oriented graph generated by a computer vision algorithm and the graph manually produced as ground truth.

To measure how much time it would take for a human to correct all tracking errors, TRA computes the least number of operations it would take to make the computer-generated and human-produced graphs identical. The permissive operations are weighed differently based on the human effort that would be required. The permissive operations and their respective weights (w) are defined as: delete a node ($w = 1$, requires one mouse click); split a node ($w = 5$, requires drawing a divider); add a node ($w = 10$, requires adding a segmentation mask); delete an edge ($w = 1$, requires one mouse click); change edge semantics ($w = 1$, requires one mouse click); and add an edge ($w = 1.5$, requires determining both nodes of the edge). The TRA is the weighted sum of the least number of operations needed to make the computer-generated graph equal to the human-generated ground truth. To enable meaningful comparison between cell tracking performance on datasets with different numbers of cells, the weighted sum is further normalized by the number of markers, that is, by the number of nodes annotated in the ground truth graph. Given its emphasis on how much human intervention is needed to obtain perfect cell tracking, the TRA is a useful metric for evaluating and comparing complete cell tracking systems. It is not designed to evaluate the different aspects or submodules of the tracking system separately.

Drawn from the above performance evaluation metrics, Magnusson et al. [35] adopted track purity, object purity (the same as *target effectiveness* in Bise et al. [21]), and the precision and recall for both mitosis and apoptosis detection as performance measures (where *mitosis recall* is the same as *mitosis branching correctness* in Bise et al. [21]).

4. A note on particle tracking

In time-lapse microscopy image sequences, besides understanding how cells behave, biologists are also interested in the movements of subcellular objects, such as a single molecule, a macromolecular complex, an organelle, a virus, or a microsphere. These objects are generally referred to as *particles* in this context. The task of detecting and tracing individual particles in a time lapse microscopy image sequence is referred to as *particle tracking*. Analogous to large-scale cell tracking, given that the number of particles is typically in the hundreds to thousands, manual detection or tracking is time-consuming, subjective, and difficult to reproduce. It is therefore of interest to develop computer vision-based particle tracking systems.

For biologists, particle tracking is key to the quantitative study of intracellular dynamic processes. The particles are generally smaller than the diffraction limit and their appearances are determined by the point spread function of the microscope. They are typically small enough to be represented as point objects, and their identities are solely determined and traced based on their motion as they share the same appearances. The states of individual particles are often estimated using Kalman filters with motion models assuming Brownian motion, directed motion with constant velocity, or random switching between different types of motions. Note that such motion models are not sufficient for cell tracking due to the interaction between cells. The biggest challenge in accurate particle tracking is data association to trace the particle identities between image frames in the sequence.

Chenouard et al. [82], Meijering et al. [12], and Rohr et al. [15] provided literature surveys on computer vision-based particle tracking techniques prior to the popularity of deep learning. Chenouard et al. [83] generated different motion hypotheses for each particle and then searched for a set of hypotheses that maximized an objective function. Integer programming is used to find a set of nonoverlapping tracks among the hypotheses for all particles. Jaqaman et al. [84] generated short, nonoverlapping tracks that were assumed to not have linking errors and linked them into longer tracks by solving a global optimization problem. Most traditional particle-tracking techniques employ ad hoc rules for the initiation and termination of particle tracks.

The advances in deep learning have brought investigations for its application to particle tracking [85–87]. Although particle tracking and cell tracking are related but different research problems, there is a parallel in the observation that deep learning-based tracking approaches have advantages, particularly in terms of end-to-end automation, but are not yet definitively superior to traditional algorithms. Newby et al. [86] employed a three-layer CNN trained on synthetic data for particle localization, and demonstrated its robustness to certain changing conditions that do not deviate too far from the training data. Yao et al. [87] presented a deep learning-based method for data association. It combines a CNN and an LSTM to learn particle dynamics to predict the motion of particles and the cost of linking particles from frame to frame. Kowalek et al. [85] compared CNN and classical approaches that feed human-engineered features to classifiers such as random forest for the classification of diffusion modes, and concluded that although CNN performs better in general, at the cost of longer processing times, there are still borderline cases where classical methods outperform CNN.

Similar to the current status in cell tracking research, it has been difficult to effectively and comprehensively evaluate and compare different particle-tracking algorithms due to the lack of recognized benchmark datasets and standardized performance metrics. Different from the state of current cell tracking research, particle tracking algorithms have claimed to achieve higher accuracy than manual analysis [88].

5. Future directions for computer vision-based cell tracking

Automated tracking of a large population of in vitro cells over an extended time is still a relatively young research field. Compared to nature images, the disruptive impact of deep learning on microscopy image analysis has been more limited. Cells in general have large variability in their shapes and appearances across images from different experiments and under different culture conditions, and their shapes can deform depending on the cell types. As evidenced in several works discussed in this chapter, accurate cell detection and/or segmentation is crucial to cell tracking performance. When tracking errors occur, it is often caused by detection or segmentation errors. A fully automated cell tracking system that can handle biological, chemical, and imaging variabilities is an ambitious goal, and there are some concrete steps that we can take toward achieving it.

5.1 Data is oxygen

In image classification, object detection, and natural language processing, it has been shown again and again that larger neural networks trained on larger datasets can achieve superior performance. It is conceivable that the same is true for microscopy images and cell tracking. More datasets with ground truth covering a broad range of imaging, chemical, and biological variabilities are needed for the development and assessment of robust cell-tracking algorithms. There has been increasing efforts to methodologically acquire, annotate, and benchmark diverse microscopy image datasets and make them freely available to the public. Chapter 9 on Open Data and Software for Microscopy Image Analysis introduces a few of such datasets.

Besides investing more resources to acquire and annotate datasets, simulated data should be developed to model the variability and the complexity in real cell image data. With simulated datasets, variables such as the signal-to-noise ratio and cell density can be tuned systematically, and the ground truth is free. The accuracy of the ground truth will become more and more important as the algorithms improve. When the algorithms outperform human annotators, using simulated data will be the only option to further improve and evaluate the algorithms. In particle tracking and human tracking, synthetic data have been shown to be effective.

5.2 Less dependency on labeled data

No matter how many resources are invested in data acquisition and labeling, large annotated data are expensive and not always viable, so researchers have been investigating approaches that are less dependent on fully labeled data. In image classification, object detection, and video classification, algorithms employing self-supervised, unsupervised, or weakly supervised learning techniques have already shown to approximate or even outperform fully supervised machine learning approaches in certain settings. This is an encouraging development and should be investigated for cell-tracking applications.

5.3 Interactive systems toward automation

With constantly improving microscope hardware, more and more time-lapse microscopy image sequences of cells will be acquired expeditiously. The datasets are likely to become larger and larger to enable large-scale, long-term, sufficiently varied, and statistically significant investigations. The research community has so far been primarily focusing on algorithms and software for automated cell tracking, and systems do not yet exist that can handle the tremendous diversity and variability that time-lapse experiments exhibit. Specialized systems are only applicable to the specific application they are developed for, while generic approaches typically do not achieve state-of-the-art performance on challenging data from specific applications. Because current approaches do not yet produce perfect results on a wide variety of data, user-friendly and interactive systems may be useful to correct and improve the computer-generated results so that they are useful for the user [89]. Further, because ground truth microscopy data is still limited, such an interactive system can also serve as a semiautomated data annotation tool with reduced manual labor required to obtain more labeled data.

In less than two decades, thanks to the progress in both time-lapse microscopy image acquisition and image analysis algorithms, computer vision-based cell tracking has come a long way. Tremendous efforts on algorithm development, open source software, and benchmark datasets as well as more standardized performance evaluation metrics are enabling faster prototyping and assessment of cell-tracking techniques. There is more awareness of the importance of developing self-contained, biologist-friendly cell-tracking systems, and more and more biologists are open to leveraging computer software to accelerate data analysis.

The demands for user-friendly cell-tracking systems with high performance will only increase and thereby further stimulate the development of better performing systems. Once the cells are segmented and tracked, they can be analyzed to extract biologically meaningful information such as cell sizes, lineage trees, migration speeds, and mitotic rate to facilitate biological research and investigation. Fig. 5.18 shows an illustration of a computer vision cell tracking system that outputs a cell lineage measurement and stemness metric to provide feedback for adaptive subculturing that is important for stem cell

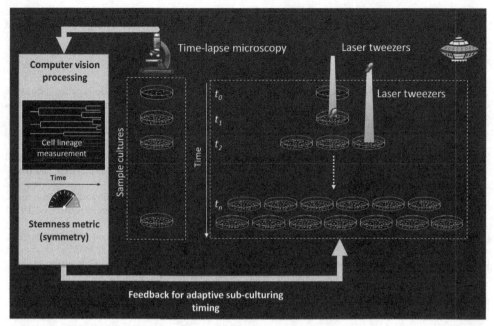

Fig. 5.18 An illustration of computer vision cell tracking providing feedback for adaptive subculturing timing that is important for stem cell engineering.

engineering, to the extent of manipulating individual cells using laser tweezers. This vision is closer to reality than it might appear. Computer vision-based cell tracking is already orders of magnitude more efficient than manual tracking, so it is only a matter of time before it outperform human experts in accuracy.

References

[1] D.L. Coutu, T. Schroeder, Probing cellular processes by long-term live imaging—historic problems and current solutions, J. Cell Sci. 126 (Pt 17) (2013) 3805–3815, https://doi.org/10.1242/jcs.118349. Epub 2013 Aug 1323943879.

[2] B. Neumann, T. Walter, J.K. Hériché, J. Bulkescher, H. Erfle, C. Conrad, P. Rogers, I. Poser, M. Held, U. Liebel, Phenotypic profiling of the human genome by time-lapse microscopy reveals cell division genes, Nature 464 (7289) (2010) 721–727, https://doi.org/10.1038/nature08869. 20360735 PMCID: PMC3108885.

[3] S. Huh, R. Bise, M. Chen, T. Kanade, Automated mitosis detection of stem cell populations in phase-contrast microscopy images, IEEE Trans. Med. Imaging 30 (3) (2010) 586–596.

[4] S. Huh, M. Chen, Detection of mitosis within a stem cell population of high cell confluence in phase-contrast microscopy images, in: IEEE Conference on Computer Vision and Pattern Recognition (CVPR), 2011.

[5] H.M. Ellis, H.R. Horvitz, Genetic control of programmed cell death in the nematode *C. elegans*, Cell 44 (6) (1986) 817–829, https://doi.org/10.1016/0092-8674(86)90004-8.3955651.

[6] S. Huh, D. Ker, H. Su, T. Kanade, Apoptosis detection for adherent cell populations in time-lapse phase-contrast microscopy images, in: International Conference on Medical Image Computing and Computer-Assisted Intervention (MICCAI), 2012.

[7] S. Huh, T. Kanade, Apoptosis detection for non-adherent cells in time-lapse phase contrast microscopy, in: International Conference on Medical Image Computing and Computer-Assisted Intervention (MICCAI), 2013.

[8] S. Huh, H. Su, M. Chen, T. Kanade, Efficient phase contrast microscopy restoration applied for muscle myotube detection, in: International Conference on Medical Image Computing and Computer-Assisted Intervention (MICCAI), 2013.

[9] M. Etzrodt, M. Endele, T. Schroeder, Quantitative single-cell approaches to stem cell research. Cell Stem Cell 15 (5) (2014) 546–558, https://doi.org/10.1016/j.stem.2014.10.015 ISSN 1934–5909.

[10] K. Li, M. Chen, T. Kanade, Cell population tracking and lineage construction with spatiotemporal context, in: International Conference on Medical Image Computing and Computer-Assisted Intervention (MICCAI), 2007.

[11] M. Cohen, M. Georgiou, N.L. Stevenson, M. Miodownik, B. Baum, dynamic filopodia transmit intermittent Delta-Notch signaling to drive pattern refinement during lateral inhibition, Dev. Cell 19 (1) (2010) 78–89.

[12] E. Meijering, O. Dzyubachyk, I. Smal, Methods for cell and particle tracking, Meth. Enzymol. 504 (2012) 183–200, https://doi.org/10.1016/B978-0-12-391857-4.00009-4.22264535.

[13] T. Kanade, Z. Yin, R. Bise, S. Huh, S. Eom, M.F. Sandbothe, M. Chen, Cell image analysis: algorithms, system and applications, in: IEEE Workshop on Applications of Computer Vision (WACV), IEEE, 2011, , pp. 374–381.

[14] M. Maška, V. Ulman, D. Svoboda, P. Matula, P. Matula, C. Ederra, A. Urbiola, T. España, S. Venkatesan, D.M.W. Balak, P. Karas, T. Bolcková, M. Štreitová, C. Carthel, S. Coraluppi, N. Harder, K. Rohr, K.E.G. Magnusson, J. Jaldén, H.M. Blau, O. Dzyubachyk, P. Křížek, G.M. Hagen, D. Pastor-Escuredo, D. Jimenez-Carretero, M.J. Ledesma-Carbayo, A. Muñoz-Barrutia, E. Meijering, M. Kozubek, C. Ortiz-de Solorzano, A benchmark for comparison of cell tracking algorithms, Bioinformatics 30 (11) (2014) 1609–1617.

[15] K. Rohr, W.J. Godinez, N. Harder, S. Wörz, J. Mattes, W. Tvarusko, R. Eils, Tracking and quantitative analysis of dynamic movements of cells and particles, Cold Spring Harb. Protoc. 2010 (6) (2010) 1–16.

[16] R. Bise, K. Li, S. Eom, T. Kanade, Reliably tracking partially overlapping neural stem cells in DIC microscopy image sequences, in: Proceedings of the International Conference on Medical Image Computing and Computer Assisted Intervention (MICCAI), 2009.

[17] O. Dzyubachyk, W.A. van Cappellen, J. Essers, W.J. Niessen, E. Meijering, Advanced level-set-based cell tracking in time-lapse fluorescence microscopy, IEEE Trans. Med. Imaging 29 (3) (2010) 852–867.

[18] K. Li, E.D. Miller, M. Chen, T. Kanade, L.E. Weiss, P.G. Campbell, Cell population tracking and lineage construction with spatiotemporal context, Med. Image Anal. 12 (5) (2008) 546–566.

[19] C. Zimmer, E. Labruyere, V. Meas-Yedid, N. Guillen, J.-C. Olivo-Marin, Segmentation and tracking of migrating cells in video microscopy with parametric active contours: a tool for cell-based drug testing, IEEE Trans. Med. Imaging 21 (10) (2002) 1212–1221.

[20] O. Al-Kofahi, R.J. Radke, S.K. Goderie, Q. Shen, S. Temple, B. Roysam, Automated cell lineage construction: a rapid method to analyze clonal development established with murine neural progenitor cells, Cell Cycle 5 (3) (2006) 327–335.

[21] R. Bise, Z. Yin, T. Kanade, Reliable cell tracking by global data association, in: Proceedings of the IEEE international symposium on biomedical imaging (ISBI), IEEE, 2011, , pp. 1004–1010.

[22] N.N. Kachouie, P. Fieguth, J. Ramunas, E. Jervis, Probabilistic model-based cell tracking, Int. J. Biomed. Imaging 2006 (2006) 1–10.

[23] D. Padfield, J. Rittscher, B. Roysam, Coupled minimum cost flow cell tracking for high-throughput quantitative analysis, Med. Image Anal. 15 (4) (2011) 650–668.

[24] M. Schiegg, P. Hanslovsky, B.X. Kausler, L. Hufnagel, F.A. Hamprech, Conservation tracking, in: IEEE International Conference on Computer Vision, 2013.

[25] F. Amat, W. Lemon, D.P. Mossing, K. McDole, Y. Wan, K. Branson, E.W. Myers, P.J. Keller, Fast, accurate reconstruction of cell lineages from large-scale fluorescence microscopy data, Nat. Methods 11 (9) (2014) 951–958, https://doi.org/10.1038/nmeth.3036. Epub 2014 Jul 2025042785.

[26] A. Dufour, R. Thibeaux, E. Labruyère, N. Guillén, J.C. Olivo-Marin, 3-D active meshes: fast discrete deformable models for cell tracking in 3-D time-lapse microscopy, IEEE Trans. Image Process. 20 (7) (2011) 1925–1937, https://doi.org/10.1109/TIP.2010.2099125. 21193379 Epub 2010 Dec 30.

[27] K. Li, E.D. Miller, L.E. Weiss, P.G. Campbell, T. Kanade, Online tracking of migrating and proliferating cells imaged with phase-contrast microscopy, in: IEEE Computer Society Workshop on Mathematical Methods in Biomedical Image Analysis (MMBIA), 2006.

[28] K. Minoura, K. Abe, Y. Maeda, et al., Model-based cell clustering and population tracking for time-series flow cytometry data. BMC Bioinf. 20 (2019) 633, https://doi.org/10.1186/s12859-019-3294-3.

[29] X. Lou, M. Schiegg, F.A. Hamprecht, Active structured learning for cell tracking: algorithm, framework, and usability. IEEE Trans. Med. Imaging 33 (4) (2014) 849–860, https://doi.org/10.1109/TMI.2013.2296937.

[30] K.E.G. Magnusson, J. Jaldén, A batch algorithm using iterative application of the Viterbi algorithm to track cells and construct cell lineages, in: Proceedings of the IEEE International Symposium on Biomedical Imaging (ISBI), IEEE, 2012, , pp. 382–385.

[31] R. Bise, T. Kanade, Z. Yin, S. Huh, Automatic cell tracking applied to analysis of cell migration in wound healing assay, in: Proceedings of the Annual International Conference of the IEEE Engineering in Medicine and Biology Society (EMBC), IEEE, 2011, , pp. 6174–6179.

[32] L. Zhang, Y. Li, R. Nevatia, Global data association for multi-object tracking using network flows, in: Proceedings of the IEEE Conference on Computer Vision and Pattern Recognition (CVPR), IEEE, 2008, , pp. 1–8.

[33] G.W. Pulford, B.F. La Scala, Multihypothesis Viterbi data association: algorithm development and assessment. IEEE Trans. Aerosp. Electron. Syst. 46 (2) (2010) 583–609, https://doi.org/10.1109/TAES.2010.5461643.

[34] C. Haubold, J. Aleš, S. Wolf, F.A. Hamprecht, A generalized successive shortest paths solver for tracking dividing targets, in: Proceedings of the European Conference on Computer Vision (ECCV), Springer, 2016, , pp. 566–582.

[35] K.E.G. Magnusson, J. Jaldén, P.M. Gilbert, H.M. Blau, Global linking of cell tracks using the Viterbi algorithm, IEEE Trans. Med. Imaging 34 (4) (2015) 911–929.

[36] Florian Jug, Tobias Pietzsch, Dagmar Kainmüller, Jan Funke, Matthias Kaiser, Erik van Nimwegen, Carsten Rother, Gene Myers. Optimal Joint Segmentation and Tracking of *Escherichia coli* in the Mother Machine. Workshop on Bayesian and Graphical Models for Biomedical Imaging, Springer, 2014.

[37] M. Schiegg, P. Hanslovsky, C. Haubold, U. Köthe, L. Hufnagel, F.A. Hamprecht, Graphical model for joint segmentation and tracking of multiple dividing cells, Bioinformatics 31 (6) (2015) 948–956.

[38] E. Türetken, X. Wang, C.J. Becker, C. Haubold, P. Fua, Network flow integer programming to track elliptical cells in time-lapse sequences, IEEE Trans. Med. Imaging 36 (4) (2017) 942–951.

[39] M. Schiegg, B. Heuer, C. Haubold, S. Wolf, U. Koethe, F.A. Hamprecht, Proof-reading guidance in cell tracking by sampling from tracking-by-assignment models, in: Proceedings of the IEEE International Symposium on Biomedical Imaging (ISBI), 2015, pp. 394–398.

[40] C. Cortes, V. Vapnik, Support-vector networks, Mach. Learn. 20 (3) (1995) 273–297.

[41] D. Lowe, Object recognition from local scale-invariant features, in: Proceedings of the International Conference on Computer Vision, 2 1999, pp. 1150–1157.

[42] N. Dalal, B. Triggs, Histograms of oriented gradients for human detection, in: IEEE Conference on Computer Vision and Pattern Recognition, 2005.

[43] P. Felzenszwalb, D. McAllester, D. Ramanan, A discriminatively trained, multiscale, deformable part model, in: IEEE Conference on Computer Vision and Pattern Recognition, 2008.

[44] J. Yosinski, J. Clune, A. Nguyen, T. Fuchs, H. Lipson, Understanding neural networks through deep visualization, in: International Conference on Machine Learning, Deep Learning Workshop, 2015.

[45] M. Zeiler, R. Fergus, Visualizing and understanding convolutional networks, in: European Conference on Computer Vision (ECCV), 2014.

[46] V. Dodballapur, Y. Song, H. Huang, M. Chen, W. Cai, Mask-driven mitosis detection in histopathology images, in: 16th IEEE International Symposium on Biomedical Imaging (ISBI), 2019.

[47] A. Liu, Y. Lu, M. Chen, Y. Su, Mitosis detection in phase contrast microscopy image sequences of stem cell populations: a critical review, IEEE Trans. Big Data 3 (4) (2017) 443–457.

[48] Y. Lu, A.A. Liu, M. Chen, W.Z. Nie, Y.T. Su, Sequential saliency guided deep neural network for joint mitosis identification and localization in time-lapse phase contrast microscopy images, IEEE J. Biomed. Health Inform. 24 (5) (2020) 1367–1378, https://doi.org/10.1109/JBHI.2019.2943228. 31545751 Epub 2019 Sep 23.

[49] Y. Mao, Z. Yin, A hierarchical convolutional neural network for mitosis detection in phase-contrast microscopy images, in: International Conference on Medical Image Computing and Computer-Assisted Intervention, 2016.

[50] Y. Mao, Z. Yin, Two-stream bidirectional long short-term memory for mitosis event detection and stage localization in phase-contrast microscopy images, in: International Conference on Medical Image Computing and Computer-Assisted Intervention, 2017.

[51] Y. Mao, L. Han, Z. Yin, Cell mitosis event analysis in phase contrast microscopy images using deep learning, Med. Image Anal. 57 (2019) 32–43.

[52] Y. Su, Y. Lu, M. Chen, A. Liu, Spatiotemporal Joint Mitosis Detection Using CNN-LSTM Network in Time-Lapse Phase Contrast Microscopy Images, vol. 5, IEEE Access, 2017, pp. 18033–18041.

[53] O. Ronneberger, P. Fischer, T. Brox, U-net: convolutional networks for biomedical image segmentation, in: Medical Image Computing and Computer-Assisted Intervention (MICCAI), LNCS, vol. 9351, Springer, 2015, , pp. 234–241.

[54] F. Long, Microscopy cell nuclei segmentation with enhanced U-Net, BMC Bioinf. 21 (2020) 8.

[55] A. Vuola, S. Akram, J. Kannala, Mask-RCNN and U-Net ensembled for nuclei segmentation, in: IEEE International Symposium on Biomedical Imaging (ISBI), 2019.

[56] Y. Wu, J. Lim, M.H. Yang, Object tracking benchmark, IEEE Trans. Pattern Anal. Mach. Intell. 37 (9) (2015) 1834–1848.

[57] M. Kristan, A. Leonardis, J. Matas, M. Felsberg, R. Pflugfelder, L. Čehovin Zajc, T. Vojir, G. Häger, A. Lukežič, G. Fernandez, Computer Vision – ECCV 2016 Workshops, Springer, 2016.

[58] M. Kristan, J. Matas, A. Leonardis, et al., The seventh visual object tracking vot2019 challenge results, in: International Conference on Computer Vision Workshop, 2019.

[59] A. Bewley, Z. Ge, L. Ott, F. Ramos, B. Upcroft, Simple online and realtime tracking, in: Proceedings of the International Conference on Image Processing, 2016.

[60] D. Held, S. Thrun, S. Savarese, Learning to track at 100 FPS with deep regression networks, in: European Conference on Computer Vision (ECCV), 2016.

[61] H. Nam, B. Han, Learning multi-domain convolutional neural networks for visual tracking, in: Proceedings of the IEEE Conference on Computer Vision and Pattern Recognition (CVPR), 2016.

[62] J. Redmon, S. Divvala, R. Girshick, A. Farhadi, You only look once: unified, real-time object detection, IEEE Conference on Computer Vision and Pattern Recognition (CVPR), 2016.

[63] K. He, G. Gkioxari, P. Dollar, R. Girshick, Mask R-CNN, in: International Conference on Computer Vision (ICCV), 2017.

[64] S. Ren, K. He, R. Girshick, J. Sun, Faster R-CNN: towards real-time object detection with region proposal networks, in: Neural Information Processing Systems (NIPS), 2015.

[65] N. Wojke, A. Bewley, D. Paulus, Simple online and realtime tracking with a deep association metric, in: 2017 IEEE International Conference on Image Processing, 2017, pp. 3645–3649.

[66] W. Gan, S. Wang, X. Lei, M. Lee, C.-C. Kuo, Online CNN-based multiple object tracking with enhanced model updates and identity association, Signal Process. Image Commun. 66 (2018) 95–102.

[67] S. Hochreiter, J. Schmidhuber, Long short-term memory, Neural Comput. 9 (8) (1997) 1735–1780, https://doi.org/10.1162/neco.1997.9.8.1735.9377276.

[68] G. Ning, Z. Zhang, C. Huang, Z. He, X. Ren, H. Wang, Spatially Supervised Recurrent Convolutional Neural Networks for Visual Object Tracking, arXiv, 2016 1607.05781v1, July.

[69] Z. Yin, T. Kanade, M. Chen, Understanding the phase contrast optics to restore artifact-free microscopy images for segmentation, Med. Image Anal. 16 (5) (2012) 1047–1062.

[70] Z. Yin, K. Li, T. Kanade, M. Chen, Understanding the optics to aid microscopy image segmentation, in: Proceedings of the International Conference on Medical Image Computing and Computer Assisted Intervention (MICCAI), Springer, 2010, , pp. 209–217.

[71] D. Liu, D. Zhang, Y. Song, F. Zhang, L. O'Donnell, H. Huang, M. Chen, W. Cai, Unsupervised instance segmentation in microscopy images via panoptic domain adaptation and task re-weighting, in: IEEE Conference on Computer Vision and Pattern Recognition (CVPR), 2020.

[72] J.B. Lugagne, H. Lin, M.J. Dunlop, DeLTA: automated cell segmentation, tracking, and lineage reconstruction using deep learning, PLoS Comput. Biol. 16 (4) (2020) e1007673https://doi.org/10.1371/journal.pcbi.1007673 32282792 PMCID: PMC7153852.

[73] D. Hernandez, S. Chen, E. Hunter, E. Steager, V. Kumar, Cell tracking with deep learning and the viterbi algorithm, in: International Conference on Manipulation, Automation and Robotics at Small Scales (MARSS), July, 2018.

[74] D.A. Van Valen, T. Kudo, K.M. Lane, D.N. Macklin, N.T. Quach, M.M. DeFelice, I. Maayan, Y. Tanouchi, E.A. Ashley, M.W. Covert, Deep learning automates the quantitative analysis of individual cells in live-cell imaging experiments, PLoS Comput. Biol. 12 (11) (2016) e1005177.

[75] S. Akram, J. Kannala, L. Eklund, J. Heikkilä, Cell Tracking Via Proposal Generation and Selection, (2017)preprint arXiv:1705.03386.

[76] N. Ramesh, T. Tasdizen, Semi-supervised learning for cell tracking in microscopy images. 2018 IEEE 15th International Symposium on Biomedical Imaging (ISBI 2018), Washington, DC, (2018) pp. 948–951, https://doi.org/10.1109/ISBI.2018.8363727.

[77] H. Tsai, J. Gajda, T. Sloan, A. Rares, A.S. Usiigaci, Instance-aware cell tracking in stain-free phase contrast microscopy enabled by machine learning. SoftwareX (2019), https://doi.org/10.1016/j.softx.2019.02.007.

[78] D. Allan, C. van der Wel, N. Keim, T.A. Caswell, D. Wieker, R. Verweij, et al., soft-matter/trackpy: Trackpy v0.4.2 (Version v0.4.2). Zenodo (2019), https://doi.org/10.5281/zenodo.3492186.

[79] S. Mori, K.C. Chang, C.Y. Chong, K.P. Dunn, Tracking performance evaluation: prediction of track purity, in: Proc. SPIE, 1096 1989.

[80] K. Smith, D. Gatica-Perez, J.-M. Odobez, S. Ba, Evaluating multi-object tracking, in: Proceedings of the IEEE Conference on Computer Vision and Pattern Recognition (CVPR), IEEE, 2005, pp. 36–43.

[81] P. Matula, M. Maška, D.V. Sorokin, P. Matula, C. Ortiz-de Solórzano, M. Kozubek, Cell tracking accuracy measurement based on comparison of acyclic oriented graphs, PLoS One 10 (12) (2015) 1–19.

[82] N. Chenouard, I. Smal, F. de Chaumont, M. Maška, I.F. Sbalzarini, Y. Gong, J. Cardinale, J. Carthel, S. Coraluppi, M. Winter, A.R. Cohen, W.J. Godinez, K. Rohr, Y. Kalaidzidis, L. Liang, J. Duncan, H. Shen, Y. Xu, K.E.G. Magnusson, J. Jaldén, H.M. Blau, P. Paul-Gilloteaux, P. Roudot, C. Kervrann, F. Waharte, J.-Y. Tinevez, S.L. Shorte, J. Willemse, K. Celler, G.P. van Wezel, H.-W. Dan, Y.-S. Tsai, C. Ortiz de Solórzano, J.-C. Olivo-Marin, E. Meijering, Objective comparison of particle tracking methods, Nat. Methods 11 (3) (2014) 281–289.

[83] N. Chenouard, I. Bloch, J.-C. Olivo-Marin, Multiple hypothesis tracking for cluttered biological image sequences, IEEE Trans. Pattern Anal. Mach. Intell. 35 (11) (2013) 2736–2750.

[84] K. Jaqaman, D. Loerke, M. Mettlen, H. Kuwata, S. Grinstein, S.L. Schmid, G. Danuser, Robust single-particle tracking in live-cell time-lapse sequences, Nat. Methods 5 (8) (2008) 695–702.

[85] P. Kowalek, H. Loch-Olszewska, J. Szwabiński, Classification of Diffusion Modes in Single-Particle Tracking Data: Feature-Based Versus Deep-Learning Approach, arXiv, September 2019 1902.07942v4.

[86] J. Newby, A. Schaefer, P. Lee, M. Forest, S. Lai, Convolutional neural networks automate detection for tracking of submicron-scale particles in 2D and 3D. Proc. Natl. Acad. Sci. 115 (36) (2018) 9026–9031, https://doi.org/10.1073/pnas.1804420115.

[87] Y. Yao, I. Smal, I. Grigoriev, A. Akhmanova, E. Meijering, Deep-learning method for data association in particle tracking, Bioinformatics (2020) btaa597.

[88] I. Smal, K. Draegestein, N. Galjart, W. Niessen, E. Meijering, Particle filtering for multiple object tracking in dynamic fluorescence microscopy images: application to microtubule growth analysis, IEEE Trans. Med. Imaging 27 (6) (2008) 789–804.

[89] M. Li, Z. Yin, Debugging object tracking results by a recommender system with correction propagation, in: Asian Conference on Computer Vision, Springer International Publishing, 2014, pp. 214–228.

CHAPTER 6

Mitosis detection in biomedical images

Yao Lu, An-An Liu*, and Yu-Ting Su
Tianjin University, School of Electrical and Information Engineering, Tianjin, China
*Corresponding author: e-mail: anan0422@gmail.com

Contents

1. Mitosis process and the detection problem

Detection of mitosis events plays an important role in many biomedical activities, such as biological research and medical diagnosis. Cell division is an important process in the life cycle of cells, and mitosis detection can provide important information about cell behaviors and thus lay the foundation for automatic analysis with computer vision methods. Modern biomedical applications always must deal with large amounts of microscopy image data about cells; manual analysis with such big data is time consuming and cannot guarantee consistent detection accuracy. Mitosis detection with computer vision and machine learning methods is commonly used in automated analysis systems for cellular behavior analysis.

The mitosis detection problem can be classified further into three levels:

1. *Classification of mitotic images/sequences.* The goal of mitosis image/sequence classification is to detect if a mitotic event occurs in the sequence.

2. *Spatial and/or temporal localization of mitotic events in microscopy images.* To better analyze cell behavior, we need to further locate the spatial and temporal positions of mitotic events in microscopy images.

Computer Vision for Microscopy Image Analysis
https://doi.org/10.1016/B978-0-12-814972-0.00006-0

131

3. *Temporal segmentation of mitosis into stages.* In the continuous process of mitosis, cells undergo a number of stages during division. The observation of cell state changes during mitosis also provides significant information for the analysis of cell behavior. This requires the mitosis detection system to be able to segment mitosis sequence into temporal stages.

1.1 Evaluation metric

In this section, we introduce the commonly used metric to evaluate mitosis detection results. As shown in Fig. 6.1, detection results are categorized into four types:
1. *True positive.* Mitotic candidates that are correctly identified as positive (mitotic).
2. *False positive.* Nonmitotic candidates that are incorrectly classified as positive (mitotic).
3. *True negative.* Nonmitotic candidates that are correctly identified as negative (nonmitotic).
4. *False negative.* Mitotic candidates that are incorrectly classified as negative (nonmitotic).

Based on the above definitions, the detection results are commonly evaluated in two aspects: *precision* and *recall*. As defined in Eqs. (6.1) and (6.2), precision (*positive predictive value*) measures the fraction of true positive samples among positive detection results, and recall (*sensitivity*) measures the fraction of retrieved true positive samples among all positive samples. To consider both precision and recall in a single metric, we calculate the harmonic average of the precision and recall score, which is called the F_1 score, as shown in Eq. (6.3):

$$\text{Precision} = \frac{\text{True Positive}}{\text{True Positive} + \text{False Positive}} \tag{6.1}$$

$$\text{Recall} = \frac{\text{True Positive}}{\text{True Positive} + \text{False Negative}} \tag{6.2}$$

$$F_1 = \frac{2 \times \text{Precision} \times \text{Recall}}{\text{Precision} + \text{Recall}} \tag{6.3}$$

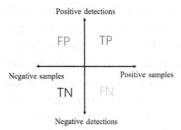

Fig. 6.1 Samples are categorized into four groups according to their ground-truth type and detection result: True positive, false positive, true negative, and false negative.

2. Medical image for mitosis detection

Considering the widespread application of mitosis detection in the biomedical field, computer vision methods for mitosis detection need to handle various models of image data. In this section, we introduce several common microscopy imaging methods for cells in practical applications, including static imaging and time-lapse imaging.

2.1 Phase contrast microscopy image

Phase contrast microscopy transforms phase variations of light caused by transparent specimens into light amplitude changes, which can be observed directly by the human eye or a camera. Because phase contrast imaging will not cause damage to cell structures, phase contrast microscopy can be used for continuous observation of cellular activity. The time-lapse microscopy images provide valuable information during the detection of cellular activities with computer vision methods. Fig. 6.2 presents an image showing a dynamic process of cell division continuously captured by phase contrast microscopy.

2.2 Differential interference contrast microscopy image

Differential interference contrast (DIC) is another technique that can enhance the contrast of transparent specimens. Based on the principle of interferometry, DIC microscope converts the length of optical paths through transparent specimens into identifiable intensity information. The image of DIC microscopy is similar to phase contrast microscopy, but without the bright diffraction halo around cells. Interested readers could refer to https://www.microscopyu.com/galleries/dic-phase-contrast for some examples and more detailed information about DIC images.

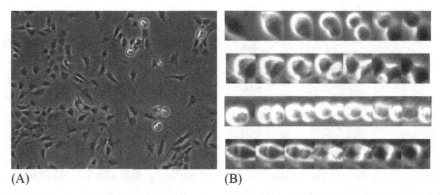

(A)   (B)

Fig. 6.2 Cells in phase contrast microscopy image. (A) Mitotic cell in a single frame of microscopy images. (B) Dynamic mitotic process in time lapse images.

2.3 Fluorescence microscopy image

Fluorescence imaging uses fluorescence and phosphorescence to study specimens under a microscope. Fluorophore in a specimen can absorb light with specific wavelengths and then emit light with longer wavelengths, which will be used for fluorescence imaging.

Indirect immune fluorescence (IIF) can be used to search for antibodies in the serum, making it a powerful method of antinuclear autoantibody (ANA) testing used for the diagnosis of autoimmune diseases. In this test, specialists need to analyze the intensity and pattern of cells in the image, as well as the presence and type of mitotic cells. Depending on the type of autoantibody, the cells can be categorized into six patterns: (1) centromere; (2) nucleolar, (3) homogeneous, (4) fine speckled, (5) coarse speckled, and (6) cytoplasmic. Readers could find more detailed description and samples of different ANA patterns at https://www.anapatterns.org.

2.4 Histological imaging

In histopathology research, a specimen is dyed with stains [e.g., hematoxylin-eosin] to highlight components of the tissue under a microscope. Histopathology is an important tool for the accurate diagnosis of cancer diseases. According to the Nottingham Grading System, assessment of breast cancer is mainly based on three morphological features in histology sections: (1) tubule formation, (2) nuclear pleomorphism, and (3) the number of mitotic cells.

In recent years, several public data sets of breast cancer histological images have been proposed for the assessment of a computer automatic diagnosis algorithm, including the MITOSIS contest at ICPR 2012 [1], the AMIDA13 contest at MICCAI 2013 [2], and the MITOS-ATYPIA challenge at ICPR 2014. Fig. 6.3 shows examples of mitotic cells in histological images.

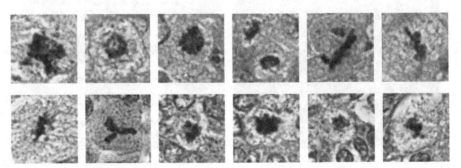

Fig. 6.3 Examples of mitotic cells in histological images. *The images are from https://mitos-atypia-14. grand-challenge.org/Description/.*

3. Mitosis detection approaches

We categorize the mitosis detection methods for time series image sequences into four types: (1) tracking-based methods, (2) tracking-free methods, (3) hybrid methods, and (4) deep-learning methods. We describe each type in detail in the rest of this section.

3.1 Tracking-based methods

Some microscopy imaging methods can observe cells without affecting their structure (such as phase contrast microscopy imaging), which allows observers to monitor behaviors of live cells continuously over time. The dynamic changes of cell appearance can be used along with their static appearance for the detection of mitosis.

Some cell behaviors can be detected by analyzing the cell trajectories of in time-lapse microscopy images. As shown in Fig. 6.4, cell trajectories will split during cell division. Therefore, the detection of mitotic events can be achieved by analyzing the bifurcation of cell trajectories.

Since cell movement and division are closely related cellular activities, they can be incorporated into the same detection system, as shown in Fig. 6.5.

3.2 Tracking-free methods

As tracking is a challenging task in microscope images (especially when cell confluence is high), inaccurate cell-tracking results can interfere with the detection of cell division

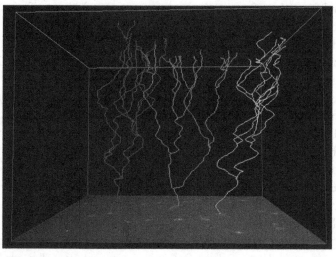

Fig. 6.4 Three cell trajectories detected in the cell tracking system. Each branch point of the trajectories corresponds to a mitotic event.

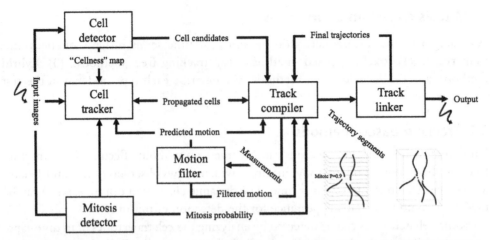

Fig. 6.5 A tracking system with mitosis detection. *(The image is from "Kang Li, Eric D Miller, Mei Chen, Takeo Kanade, Lee E Weiss, Phil G Campbell, Computer vision tracking of stemness, in: 2008 5th IEEE International Symposium on Biomedical Imaging: From Nano to Macro, IEEE, 2008, pp. 847–850.")*

behaviors. In addition, some microscopy imaging methods can generate only static images of cells, which makes it impossible to detect mitosis events with cell-tracking methods. In this section, we introduce some methods that achieve independent mitosis detection without the extra complexity of a cell-tracking system. These methods usually rely on efficient feature expression of the shapes and textures of mitotic cells, and classification methods to classify region candidates as mitotic or not.

The general procedure for mitosis detection on a single image frame without cell-tracking can be described as follows:

1. Candidate segmentation. Most mitosis detection approaches are based on the classification of image areas containing a single cell. We need to first extract region candidates that can contain mitotic cells from microscopy image.

2. Feature extraction. With the region candidates, feature extraction can find the most discriminative visual information to describe cell images in feature spaces of lower dimensions. This is an essential step before performing classification to find mitotic cells.

3. After the extraction of visual features from cell images, we can apply a set of different classifiers, such as Support Vector Machine (SVM), Random Forest, and Ada-Boost, to detect mitosis in candidates.

Detailed comparison for mitosis detection methods are described in Refs. [3] (IIF images), [2] (histological images), and [4] (phase contrast images).

Because visual feature extraction plays an important role in the process of mitosis detection, we give our description of feature extraction approaches in the rest of this section.

3.2.1 Morphological descriptors

Cells in the mitosis process usually undergo significant changes in their shapes, so shape information is important to identifying mitotic cells. Morphological features are commonly used to describe the shape of the cells in the images. Some commonly used morphological features are used in mitosis detection approaches. These features include area, major axis length, minor axis length, eccentricity, orientation, convex area, filled area, equivalent diameter, solidity, extend, and perimeter of the mitotic region candidate.

3.2.2 Texture feature

In addition to the descriptors about cell shapes, image textures of cell regions provide important information to distinguish mitotic cells in microscopy images. In applications, LBP and GLCM are commonly used for creating texture description of images.

Local binary patterns (LBPs)

The LBP feature assigns each pixel of the image a value according to its contrast of the value with neighborhood pixels.

Taking the 3×3 neighborhood, for example, for a pixel at position (x_c, y_c), the LBP pattern is defined as

$$\text{LBP}(x_c, y_c) = \sum_{p=0}^{7} 2^p s(g_p - g_c) \tag{6.4}$$

where p represents the position for one of the 8 pixels in the neighborhood and g_p and g_c represent gray values.

$$s(x) = \begin{cases} 1, & \text{if } x \geq 0 \\ 0, & \text{otherwise} \end{cases} \tag{6.5}$$

Based on the calculated values, we divide the image into cells (e.g., 16×16 pixels in each cell) and compute the histogram of LBP values over each cell. Concatenated histogram vectors are finally used to represent the texture features in the image.

Gray-level cooccurrence matrix (GLCM)

The Gray-Level Cooccurrence Matrix feature is based on the statistics of pixel intensity distributions in the image. GLCM describes the joint probability of certain sets of pixels with specific values and spatial relationship in the image.

GLCM is a square matrix $\mathbf{C}$ with a size of $N \times N$, here N indicates the number of gray levels. Each element c_{ij} in the matrix is defined as

$$c_{ij} = \sum_{x=1}^{W} \sum_{y=1}^{H} 1(\boldsymbol{I}(x, y), i) * 1(\boldsymbol{I}(x + \Delta x, y + \Delta y), j) \qquad (6.6)$$

here Δx and Δy define the relationship between two pixels; W and H represent the width and height of image $\boldsymbol{I}$, respectively; and $1(i, j)$ is defined as

$$1(i, j) = \begin{cases} 1, & \text{if } i = j \\ 0, & \text{otherwise} \end{cases} \qquad (6.7)$$

Based on the GLCM matrix, some second-order statistics features (e.g., energy, entropy, correlation) are commonly used to describe textures of image in mitosis detection approaches.

Scale-invariant feature transform (SIFT)

Scale-invariant feature transform (SIFT) is a broadly adopted feature extraction method in image classification tasks. The feature is invariant to scale and orientation of images and robust to illumination fluctuations, noise, partial occlusion, and minor viewpoint changes in the images. These characteristics are important for mitosis detection when cells in the image have different sizes and orientations. The SIFT feature is composed of several key points in the image with an orientation and the corresponding descriptor of the area around the selected key points. SIFT key points are searched through different image scales, known as the Difference of Gaussian (DoG) pyramid. Key points are selected by picking local maxima points in the 3D neighborhood of the image scale pyramid. For each key point, the dominant orientation is determined to achieve rotation invariance. SIFT descriptors are calculated as a histogram of image gradients around key points to characterize the local appearance of each selected key point. Readers can find more detailed material about the SIFT feature in Ref. [5]. Liu et al. [6] applied SIFT in mitosis detection task to describe the appearance of mitotic cells in phase contrast microscopy images.

3.2.3 GIST

The gist of a scene is an abstract representation of it, which spontaneously activates memory representation of the category of the scene. GIST is a popular feature for image classification problems. GIST features can represent different levels of description for images, from low-level features (e.g., color, spatial frequencies) to intermediate image properties (e.g., image surface, volume) and high-level information (e.g., objects, activation of semantic knowledge). GIST describes the structure of the scene (Spatial Envelope) in the image with a set of properties: naturalness, openness, roughness, ruggedness, and expansion. With these properties, GIST can provide a holistic description of the global scene without local information. Because GIST can extract coarsely localized information and generate a holistic representation of entire images without a precise boundary of the object in the image, this element is considered to be suitable for feature extraction on deformable cell images.

An example of the adoption of the GIST feature for mitosis detection can be found in Ref. [7]. Readers can refer to Ref. [8] for a detailed description of the concept of *Spatial Envelope* and GIST feature extraction.

3.2.4 Sparse representation

Considering the irregular appearance changes of cells in microscope images, traditional low-level visual features such as the intensity, texture, or shape cannot represent cells discriminatively. Some methods use sparse representation of low-level features to formulate a higher-level visual feature of cells.

Given a training set $\mathbf{X}$, we need to build a dictionary of bases ($\phi = \{\phi_i\}_{i=1}^{M}$) so any image can be represented with the linear combination of the bases in the dictionary. The proposed sparse representation method consists of two steps: (1) build a dictionary of bases (dictionary learning), and (2) find a linear combination of them to represent a new sample (sparse decomposition). These steps are discussed next.

Dictionary learning

With the given training set, the dictionary ϕ^* and the reconstruction coefficients $\mathbf{W}^*$ can be obtained by the following optimization process:

$$\min_{\phi \in \mathbb{C},\, \mathbf{W} \in \mathbb{R}^{M \times N}} \sum_{i=1}^{N} \left(\|\mathbf{X}_i - \phi \cdot w_i\|_2^2 + \gamma_1 \|w_i\|_1 + \gamma_2 \|w_i\|_2^2 \right) \tag{6.8}$$

where $\mathbf{W} = \{w_i\}_{i=1}^{M}$, and $\phi \in \mathbb{C} = \{\mathbb{R}^{d \times M}, s.t. \|\phi_i\|_2^2 \leq 1\}$. The objective function consists of three parts: the first is a reconstruction term that forces the algorithm to provide good representation of X_i, the second is the lasso regularization term that ensures the sparsity of the learned representation, the third is the ridge regularization term that ensures the consistence for the decomposed coefficient.

Sparse decomposition

After we build the dictionary of bases ϕ^*, we can use it to reconstruct any given sample y in the sparse decomposition step:

$$\min_{w_y \in \mathbb{R}^M} \|\mathbf{Y} - \phi^* \cdot w_y\|_2^2 + \gamma_1 \|W_y\|_1 + \gamma_2 \|w_y\|_2^2 \tag{6.9}$$

With the sparse representation of cell images, we can use a widely used classifier method (such as Support Vector Machine, SVM) to detect mitosis from image candidates. Liu et al. [9] gives a more detailed description of the application of sparse representation to the mitosis detection problem.

Furthermore, if we build basis dictionaries with cell images of different classes, we can compare the reconstruction loss of a test sample with different dictionaries for classification. Huang [10] proposed using the eXclusive Independent Component Analysis (XICA) method for mitosis detection in histological images.

With a given input $\mathbf{y}$ and basis dictionaries $\{\phi_1, \ldots \phi_N\}$ built with different image classes, the class of the sample $\mathbf{y}$ can be determined by

$$k^* = \arg \min_k \|\mathbf{y} - \phi_k w_k\|_1, k = 1, \cdots, N \tag{6.10}$$

where w_k is the sparse representation of $\mathbf{y}$ with corresponding dictionary ϕ_k on class k.

3.2.5 3D filtering

One commonly used tracking-free method on time-lapse microscopy images is the spatial-temporal sliding window. By expanding the 2D convolution operation into 3D convolution on spatial-temporal volumes, we can apply the convolution operations with a series of 3D filters in order to extract patterns of local spatial-temporal information from the sequence of microscopy images. For example, Li et al. [11] used a series of 3D Haar-like filters to extract features for mitosis detection, as shown in Fig. 6.6.

3.2.6 Convolutional neural networks (CNNs)

As a popular deep-learning architecture, the convolutional neural network (CNN) has been implemented in many computer vision problems. In this section, we introduce how we can use this technique for mitosis detection. Further, we will introduce the implementation of a deep-learning method on dynamic images (image sequence) for mitosis detection in Section 3.4.

Traditional classification methods tend to separate feature extraction and classification as two independent steps, but a deep-learning method such as CNN can predict the detection area candidate using raw RGB values. As shown in Fig. 6.7, CNN is a feed-forward

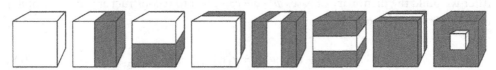

Fig. 6.6 A series of 3D Haar-like filters for spatial-temporal information extraction. *(This image is from "Kang Li, Eric D Miller, Mei Chen, Takeo Kanade, Lee E Weiss, Phil G Campbell, Computer vision tracking of stemness, in: 2008 5th IEEE International Symposium on Biomedical Imaging: From Nano to Macro, IEEE, 2008, pp. 847–850.")*

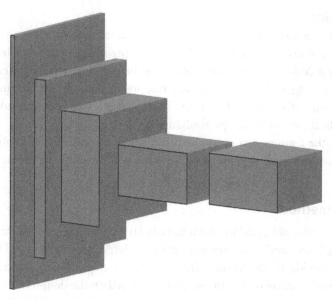

Fig. 6.7 A simple illustration of the CNN network structure for static images. Each layer represents the convolution operations with a series of kernels, as well as the subsequent pooling operations. After each convolution layer, the spatial resolution of the feature map gradually decreases, while the depth increases.

network consisting of multiple convolution layers and pooling layers, followed by fully connected layers for final classification. Each convolution layer performs 2D convolution operations with multiple filters on the input raw image or feature map to produce a new feature map, and then it will be passed through a nonlinear activation function as the input of the next convolution layer. Between convolution layers, pooling layers are generally introduced to select the most important activation in a local spatial neighborhood (e.g., the maximum activation in the max-pooling layer). The parameters of the filters in each layer are learned during training by use of the gradient descent algorithm during backward propagation. Cires et al. and Chen et al. [12, 13] used the CNN network for mitosis detection in histological images for breast cancer diagnosis.

Furthermore, considering the network structure of CNNs, the output feature maps from convolution layers can preserve spatial relationships of various areas. With the upsampled feature map of the convolution layer, we can obtain classification results in different regions of the microscopy image (e.g., pixel level segmentation). Because we use only the convolution part of the network (without fully connected layers), this network structure is called a *fully convolutional network (FCN)*. Li et al. [14] described the application of FCN for cell image segmentation and classification tasks on IIF images.

3.2.7 Conclusion

In this section, we introduce some methods that detect mitotic cells without tracking them. These methods can be applied when time-lapse image sequences are not available or there is a great deal of interference with long-term tracking of cells. Extraction of visual features on cell images plays an important role in these methods. We introduce some classic visual features for mitosis detection. These features will be jointly adopted in some detection applications for better performance.

Moreover, the features can be applied to other methods, such as probabilistic graph models for detection in time-lapse images which we introduce in the next section.

3.3 Hybrid methods

Recent years, a series of hybrid methods have been proposed to address the limitations of both tracking-based and tracking-free mitosis detection methods. These methods employ *graph models* to determine the conditional dependence structures among a sequence of visual features of the mitosis process. Based on the design of the graph model, some methods can further segment a mitosis process into different phases, as well as identifying mitotic sequences.

3.3.1 Structure overview

A classical system for mitosis detection using hybrid methods is shown in Fig. 6.8. As the image shows, the detection framework with a hybrid method can be divided into three parts: (1) candidate extraction, which generates sequence candidates that contain a sequence of image patches of single cells for further detection in subsequent steps;

(2) feature extraction, which extract more representative visual features from images in the previously generated sequence candidate; and (3). modeling the sequential dynamic process of mitosis using a temporal model (typically a graph model), and then obtain the final detection result. Earlier in this chapter, we introduced several visual feature extraction methods for mitosis detection on static images in Section 3.2. Based on this information, we focus on the first and third steps in the rest of this section.

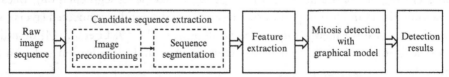

Fig. 6.8 An overview of the graph models for mitosis detection in image sequences.

Image preconditioning

Considering the image artifacts introduced by the microscope during imaging (e.g., phase contrast imaging), it is necessary to first preprocess the input image with prior knowledge of microscopy imaging in order to generate better candidates for the mitotic sequence.

Due to the optical principle and imperfections of the imaging process, microscopy imaging can introduce artifacts that will cause difficulties with further segmentation and detection. For example, cell images under phase contrast microscope contain halos and shade-offs. The imaging model can be generally formulated as

$$\mathbf{g} = \mathbf{P} \circledast \mathbf{f} + \mathbf{C} \tag{6.11}$$

where $\mathbf{f}$ represents the ideal image (the artifact-free image to be restored), $\mathbf{g}$ represents the observed images that must be dealt with during detection, $\mathbf{C}$ is a constant matrix representing the additive noise during imaging, $\circledast$ denotes the convolution operation, and $\mathbf{P}$ is the point spread function (PSF) which corresponds to the microscope:

$$\mathrm{PSF}(u, v) = \delta(u, v) - \mathrm{airy}\left(\sqrt{u^2 + v^2}\right) \tag{6.12}$$

More detailed information about an imaging model of phase contrast microscopy can be found in Ref. [15].

Based on the physical principles of the microscope, the preconditioning of microscopy images can be formulated as the minimization of nonnegative constrained convex objective function with smoothness and sparseness regularization. The objective function can be formulated as

$$\mathbf{O}(\mathbf{f}) = \|\mathbf{g}^* - \mathbf{Hf}\|_2^2 + \gamma \mathrm{Smoothness}(\mathbf{f}) + \beta \mathrm{Sparsity}(\mathbf{f}), \mathrm{s.t.} \mathbf{f} \geq 0 \tag{6.13}$$

where γ controls the smoothness term of the objective function and β controls the sparseness part of the objective function. More detailed introduction about the nonnegative convex optimization method for image preconditioning can be found in Ref. [16].

Sequence segmentation

With the image preconditioning step removing artifacts, candidate cell regions can be generated via simple segmentation methods. Candidate cell image sequences are then obtained by concatenating spatial overlapped cell regions in adjacent frames. The candidate sequence generation process is shown in Fig. 6.9.

3.3.2 Hidden Markov model (HMM)

The hidden Markov model (HMM) is widely used to model the dynamic process of sequence input. Gallardo et al. [17] applied the HMM to the detection of mitotic cells. As an extension of the first-order Markov chain, the HMM model assumes that the

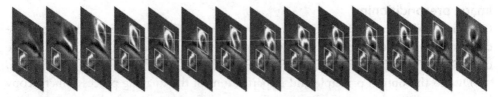

Fig. 6.9 Cell image sequence candidate extraction. *(This image is from "Seungil Huh, Ryoma Bise, Mei Chen, Takeo Kanade, et al. Automated mitosis detection of stem cell populations in phase-contrast microscopy images. IEEE Trans. Med. Imaging, 30(3):586– 596, 2011.")*

current stage in the sequence only depends on that of the preceding one. The HMM process can be described by a probability transition matrix $\mathbf{A} = \{a_{ij}\}$:

$$a_{ij} = P\big(q_t = S_j \mid q_{t-1} = S_i\big), 1 \leq i, j \leq N.$$

$$a_{ij} \geq 0, \sum_{j=1}^{N} a_{ij} = 1 \qquad (6.14)$$

where q_t is the state at time t and N is the number of states.

In the Markov process, the initial state can be expressed as

$$\pi_j = P\big(q_1 = S_j\big), 1 \leq j \leq N. \qquad (6.15)$$

Unlike the Markov chain model, the states in the HMM model cannot be directly observed. Instead, we use the conditional probability matrix $(\mathbf{B} = \{b_{jk}\})$ to model the relationship between observations and hidden states as follows:

$$b_{jk} = P\big(v_{kt} \mid q_t = S_j\big), 1 \leq j \leq N, 1 \leq k \leq M. \qquad (6.16)$$

here v_{kt} indicates the observation v_k at time t and M indicates the number of observation symbols.

To classify cell sequences using HMM in practical applications, multiple HMM models are independently trained with different type of sequence candidates to model different cellular dynamic processes. Given a cell sequence candidate, the visual features at each time step are extracted and then fed into all the trained HMM models to predict the type of the candidate sequence.

3.3.3 Conditional random field (CRF)

The HMM model assumes that the observations at each time step in the sequence are independent, and this limits the model's ability to make better use of the context information between different cell frames in the sequence. To deal with this problem, we can use the CRF model to exploit more contextual information in mitosis sequence candidates (as proposed in Ref. [18]).

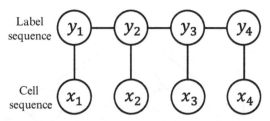

Fig. 6.10 The CRF model structure.

Given an input sequence of length T: $\mathbf{x} = (\mathbf{x}_1, \mathbf{x}_2,..., \mathbf{x}_T)$, we need to build a CRF model that maps input sequence $\mathbf{x}$ into a sequence of labels ($\mathbf{y} = (y_1, y_2,..., y_T)$), indicating the phases of mitotic cells for each frame in the sequence. The conditional probability distribution of y is defined as

$$p(\mathbf{y}|\mathbf{x}, \theta) = \frac{e^{\Psi(\mathbf{y}, \mathbf{x}; \theta)}}{\mathbf{Z}(\mathbf{x})} \tag{6.17}$$

where θ indicates the parameter vector of the CRF model, $\Psi(\mathbf{x}, \mathbf{y}, \theta)$ indicates the potential function, and $\mathbf{Z}(\mathbf{x}) = \Sigma_y\, \Psi(\mathbf{y}, \mathbf{x}; \theta)$ indicates the partition function.

The CRF model assumes that the cell state depends on the observation at the current time, as well as the adjacent cell states of the current state (Fig. 6.10). Therefore, the potential function in the CRF model can be defined as

$$\Psi(\mathbf{y}, \mathbf{x}; \theta) = \sum_{i=1}^{T} \phi(\mathbf{x}_i) \cdot \theta(y_i) + \sum_{i, j \in E} \theta(y_i, y_j) \tag{6.18}$$

where $\phi(\mathbf{x}_i) \in \mathbb{R}^d$ indicates the feature vector of the cell image $\mathbf{x}_i$, $\theta(k) \in \mathbb{R}^d$ indicates the compatibility between image x_i, and state label y_i, $\theta(i, j) \in \mathbb{R}$, $i, j \in \{0, 1\}$ indicates the compatibility between different cell states.

3.3.4 Hidden conditional random field (HCRF)

During the training of a CRF model, we find that we need to label each frame in the training data sequences, which means that we need to have a good definition of each state of mitotic cell images in the data set and accurately annotate each frame in the sequence. This can significantly increase the cost of generating a training data set.

A significant drawback of using the CRF model is that the model assumes the label of each time in the sequence must be observable. The HCRF model has been used to address the mitosis detection problem [19]. By introducing hidden states $\mathbf{h}$ to model the latent structure of the mitosis sequence, HCRF models the mitotic process with sequence-level labels in the training data. This means that we can apply this mitosis detection method in more practical applications.

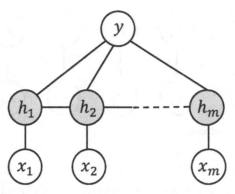

Fig. 6.11 The HCRF model structure.

As shown in Fig. 6.11, the conditional probability of the sequence label y in the HCRF model can be defined as

$$p(y|\mathbf{X}, \theta) = \sum_h p(y, \mathbf{h}|\mathbf{X}, \theta)$$

$$= \frac{\sum_h e^{\Psi(y, \mathbf{h}, \mathbf{X}; \theta)}}{\sum_{y' \in \mathbf{Y}, \mathbf{h} \in \mathbf{H}} e^{\Psi(y', \mathbf{h}, \mathbf{X}; \theta)}} \tag{6.19}$$

where $\mathbf{h} = \{h_1, h_2, \cdots, h_T\}$ indicates the hidden state vector, $\Psi(y, \mathbf{h}, \mathbf{X}; \theta) \in \mathbb{R}$ indicates the function, and θ represents parameters in the HCRF model.

The potential function is defined as

$$\Psi(y, \mathbf{h}, \mathbf{X}; \theta) = \sum_{j=1}^m \sum_{l \in L_1} f_{1,l}(j, y, h_j, \mathbf{X})\theta_{1,l}$$

$$+ \sum_{(j,k) \in E} \sum_{l \in L_2} f_{2,l}(j, k, y, h_j, h_k, \mathbf{X})\theta_{2,l} \tag{6.20}$$

where L_1 is the node feature set; L_2 is the edge feature set; $\theta_{1,l}, \theta_{2,l}$ are the components of θ that correspond to the node and edge parameters, respectively; $f_{1,l}$ is the feature function depending on a single hidden state and $f_{2,l}$ is the feature function depending on a pair of hidden states.

3.3.5 Event detection conditional random field (EDCRF)

Because the HCRF model has less constraint on the labels of each frame in the sequence, it lacks the ability to locate the exact frame where the cell split happens during the mitosis process, which is a common demand in practical applications. To solve this problem, an event detection conditional random field (EDCRF) has been proposed [20]. As a combination of HCRF and the latent-dynamic conditional random field (LDCRF) model, the EDCRF uses both the sequence-level label as a global constraint, and the frame-level labels as local constraints, which enables it to temporally locate the time of the cell division among the image frames in a sequence candidate. The graph structures of LDCRF and EDCRF are displayed in Fig. 6.12.

As shown in this figure, given the sequence $\mathbf{x}$, the global label y in EDCRF is defined as

$$y = \begin{cases} p, & \text{if the } p\text{th patch of } \mathbf{x} \text{ contains birth event} \\ 0, & \text{if } \mathbf{x} \text{ is not a mitosis sequence} \end{cases} \qquad (6.21)$$

the sublabel $\mathbf{s}$ is defined as

$$s_j = \begin{cases} N(\text{no event}), & \text{if } y = 0 \\ B(\text{before event}), & \text{if } y > 0 \text{ and } j < y \\ A(\text{after event}), & \text{if } y > 0 \text{ and } j \geq y \end{cases} \qquad (6.22)$$

Based on the label detection, the conditional probability distribution of the label y in EDCRF is defined as

$$P(y|\mathbf{x}, \theta) = P(\mathbf{s}|\mathbf{x}, \theta) = \sum_{\mathbf{h}} P(\mathbf{s}|\mathbf{h}, \mathbf{x}, \theta) P(\mathbf{h}|\mathbf{x}, \theta) \qquad (6.23)$$

To facilitate the training of the model, EDCRF requires that each sublabel s is associated with a disjointed set of hidden states, defined as $\mathcal{H}_s$ as follows:

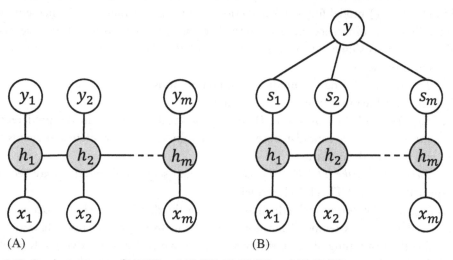

Fig. 6.12 Graph structures of LDCRF and EDCRF. (A) LDCRF and (B) EDCRF.

$$P(\mathbf{s}|\,\mathbf{h},\mathbf{x},\theta)=\begin{cases}1, & \text{if}\,\forall h_j \in \mathcal{H}_{s_j}\\0, & \text{otherwise}\end{cases} \tag{6.24}$$

Thus, the EDCRF model can be simplified as follows:

$$P(y|\,\mathbf{x},\theta)=\sum_{\mathbf{h}:\forall h_j \in \mathcal{H}_{s_j}}P(\mathbf{h}|\,\mathbf{x},\theta) \tag{6.25}$$

Finally, $P(\mathbf{h}|\mathbf{x},\theta)$ can be defined as a typical CRF formulation:

$$
\begin{aligned}
P(\mathbf{h}|\,\mathbf{x},\theta)=&\frac{1}{Z}\exp\left(\sum_{j=1}^{m}f^{(s)}\left(h_j,\mathbf{x},j\right)\cdot\theta^{(s)}\left(h_j\right)\right)\\
&+\sum_{j=2}^{m}f^{(t)}\left(h_{j-1},h_j,\mathbf{x},j\right)\cdot\theta^{(t)}\left(h_{j-1},h_j\right))
\end{aligned}
\tag{6.26}
$$

where Z is the partition function, $f^{(s)}(h_j,\mathbf{x},j)$ is the state function defined with the feature vector of cell image in Eq. (6.27), and $f^{(t)}(h_{j-1},h,\mathbf{x},j)$ is the transition function defined in Eq. (6.28). Further, $\mathcal{U}=(\mathcal{H}_N \times \mathcal{H}_N)\cup(\mathcal{H}_B \times \mathcal{H}_B)\cup(\mathcal{H}_B \times \mathcal{H}_A)\cup(\mathcal{H}_A \times \mathcal{H}_A)$ represents the set of sublabel transitions: $\{(N \to N), (B \to B), (B \to A), (A \to A)\}$.

$$f^{(s)}\left(h_j,\mathbf{x},j\right)=\phi\left(x_j\right) \tag{6.27}$$

$$f^{(t)}\left(h_{j-1},h_j,\mathbf{x},j\right)=\begin{cases}1, & \text{if}\,\left(h_{j-1},h_j\right)\in\mathcal{U}\\0, & \text{otherwise}\end{cases} \tag{6.28}$$

3.3.6 Two-labeled hidden conditional random field (TL-HCRF)

Based on the EDCRF, Huh [21] proposed a two-labeled hidden conditional random field (TL-HCRF) model for better detection of mitosis in a high-confluence environment. When cell confluence increases in the late stage of cell culturing, it becomes more difficult to identify single mitotic cells. To deal with this problem, the TL-HCRF detects mitosis in three steps:

1. *Predetection.* During the predetection phase, mitosis candidates are detected with only static visual features in each single frame.

2. *Sequence candidate construction.* Based on the locations found in the predetection phase, mitotic sequence candidates are constructed by tracking pre-detected events forward and backward along time.

3. *Detection with the TL-HCRF model.* Extracted sequence candidates are fed into the specially designed TL-HCRF model.

Unlike the EDCRF model, which assumes that the division of cells can occur at any time, TL-HCRF uses temporal location information from predetection phase to help determine the real timing of cell birth events. As shown in Fig. 6.13, two kinds of labels are defined in the TL-HCRF model: $y \in \{0, 1\}$ indicates whether the input sequence contains mitotic event, and z represents the cell division time in the sequence.

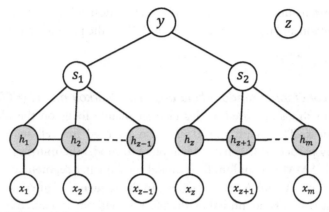

Fig. 6.13 The TL-HCRF model structure.

There are also two sublabels (s_1, $s_2 \in \{N, B, A\}$) corresponding to the two subsequences split by the cell division time z:

$$\begin{cases} s_1 = N(\text{no event}), s_2 = N(\text{no event}) & \text{if } y = 0 \\ s_1 = A(\text{before event}), s_2 = B(\text{after event}) & \text{if } y = 1 \end{cases} \quad (6.29)$$

With these label definitions, the conditional model of TL–HCRF can be defined as

$$P(y \mid \mathbf{x}, z; \theta) = P(s_1, s_2 \mid \mathbf{x}, z; \theta) = \sum_{\mathbf{h}} P(\mathbf{h}, s_1, s_2 \mid \mathbf{x}, z; \theta) \quad (6.30)$$

$$P(\mathbf{h}, s_1, s_2, \mid \mathbf{x}, z, \theta) = \frac{1}{Z} \exp\left(\Psi(\mathbf{h}, s_1, s_2, \mathbf{x}, z; \theta)\right) \quad (6.31)$$

where Z is the partition function, and $\Psi(\mathbf{h}, s_1, s_2, \mathbf{x}, z; \theta)$ is the potential function which can be defined as:

$$\begin{aligned} \Psi(\mathbf{h}, s_1, s_2, \mathbf{x}, z; \theta) =& \sum_{j=1}^{m} f^{(s)}\left(h_j, \mathbf{x}, j\right) \cdot \theta^{(s)}\left(h_j\right) \\ &+ \sum_{j=2}^{z-1} f^{(t)}\left(h_{j-1}, h_j, \mathbf{x}, j\right) \cdot \theta^{(t)}\left(h_{j-1}, h_j, s_1, s_1\right) \\ &+ f^{(t)}\left(h_{z-1}, h_z, \mathbf{x}, k\right) \cdot \theta^{(t)}\left(h_{z-1}, h_z, s_1, s_2\right) \\ &+ \sum_{j=z+1}^{m} f^{(t)}\left(h_{j-1}, h_j, \mathbf{x}, j\right) \cdot \theta^{(t)}\left(h_{j-1}, h_j, s_2, s_2\right) \\ &+ \sum_{j=1}^{z-1} \theta^{(l)}\left(h_j, s_1\right) + \sum_{j=z}^{m} \theta^{(l)}\left(h_j, s_2\right) \end{aligned} \quad (6.32)$$

where $f^{(s)}$ is the state function; $f^{(t)}$ is the transition function; $\theta^{(s)}$ and $\theta(t)$ are the parameters of the state function and transition function; and $\theta(l)$ is the parameter associated with the sublabels s_1, s_2.

3.3.7 Hidden conditional random field and semi-Markov model (HCRF and SMM)

The previous methods discussed in this chapter mainly focus on the identification of mitotic sequences. The graph model can also be used for cell state segmentation. A semi-Markov model (SMM) has been applied to model the mitosis process with different stages [6]. SMM is a random field model for sequence segmentation by modeling the state transition as a semi-Markov process. In the sequence segmentation framework, mitotic sequences are first identified by the HCRF method, as defined in Section 3.3.4. Based on the detection results from the HCRF model, SMM further segments the sequence into different stages, which are defined by the transition of cell appearance during the mitosis process. Generally, we can define four stages of the cell appearance transition: (1) interphase, (2) the start of mitosis, (3) formation of daughter cells, and (4) separation of daughter cells. The four stages of mitosis are illustrated in Fig. 6.14.

As shown in Fig. 6.15, given the input sequence $\mathbf{X} = \{\mathbf{x}_t\}_{t=1}^{T}$, SMM divides the sequence into segments $\mathbf{S} = \{s_i\}_{i=1}^{s}$. Each segment s_i is represented by a pair of integers

Stage 1   Stage 2   Stage 3   Stage 4

Fig. 6.14 The four stages of the mitosis process. (*This image is from "Anan Liu, Kang Li, Takeo Kanade, A semi-Markov model for mitosis segmentation in time-lapse phase contrast microscopy image sequences of stem cell populations, IEEE Trans. Med. Imaging 31(2) (2012) 359–369."*)

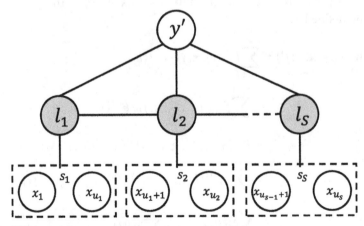

Fig. 6.15 The HMM model structure.

(u_i, l_i), where u_i indicates the position of the last frame in s_i and l_i represents the state of s_i.

The SMM also generates an overall prediction of the whole sequence as $y' \in \{0, 1\}$:

$$p(y' | \mathbf{X}, \gamma) = p(y' | \mathbf{S}, \gamma) \cdot p(\mathbf{S} | \mathbf{X}, \gamma) \tag{6.33}$$

where γ is the parameter vector for the SMM learned during training.

The sequence is considered to be a valid mitosis process only if the sequence contains the complete state transition process from stage 1 to stage 4. Thus, we define $y' = 1$ when $\mathbf{S}$ contains one (and only one) complete stage transition process, and $y' = 0$ in other cases. With this definition, Eq. (6.33) can be simplified as

$$p(y' | \mathbf{X}, \gamma) = p(\mathbf{S} | \mathbf{X}, \gamma) = \frac{\exp(\gamma^{\mathrm{T}} \cdot \psi(\mathbf{X}, \mathbf{S}))}{\sum_{\mathbf{S}'} \exp(\gamma^{\mathrm{T}} \cdot \psi(\mathbf{X}, \mathbf{S}'))} \tag{6.34}$$

The potential function $\gamma^{\mathrm{T}} \cdot \psi(\mathbf{X}, \mathbf{S})$ can be defined as

$$\gamma^{\mathrm{T}} \cdot \psi(\mathbf{X}, \mathbf{S}) = \sum \gamma^{\mathrm{T}} \cdot \psi\left(l_{i-1}, l_i, \mathbf{X}_{u_{i-1}:u_j}\right)$$
$$= \sum \sum_{a, b \in L} \gamma_{a,b}^{\mathrm{T}} \cdot \begin{bmatrix} \psi_1(\mathbf{X}_{u_{i-1}.u_i}) \\ \psi_2(\mathbf{X}_{u_{i-1}.u_i}) \end{bmatrix} \cdot 1_a(l_{i-1}) \cdot 1_b(l_i) \tag{6.35}$$

where $\psi_1(\cdot)$ indicates the averaged feature vectors, $\psi_2(\cdot)$ indicates the standard deviation of feature vectors, and $[\cdot]$ represents vector concatenation operation.

3.3.8 Conclusion

In this section, we introduced a few hybrid methods for mitosis detection in time-lapse microscopy images. The hybrid methods use handcrafted features (e.g., HoG) to extract visual information from each cell image, and then use a designed graph model to model the temporal dynamics of mitosis. By designing the probability graph model during detection, we can achieve the identification, accurate temporal localization, and stage segmentation of mitotic sequences. As we add prior knowledge of mitosis to the design of the graph model, the increased complexity of the model increases the mitosis detection accuracy accordingly.

3.4 Deep-learning methods

In recent years, deep learning-related methods have been greatly developed in the computer vision field and achieved great improvements of the results of many problems. One big advantage of deep learning-related methods is that they are generally better suited to problems with big data. Most of the methods that we have introduced in previous sections generally rely on specially designed features (such as HoG, SIFT, and GIST), but these handcrafted features are designed for general purposes and thus cannot perfectly suit specific tasks and data types. However, deep learning-related methods can solve this problem by training a deep neural network for both feature extraction and classification tasks in a data-driven manner.

3.4.1 Two-stream CNN

Compared with mitosis detection on static images, the difference of the detection problem on image sequence is that the input data contains both static visual information and temporal dynamic information. One solution is to use two separate CNNs to extract features of the input data under various modalities: one from the original images and another from their optical flow images. The visual appearance and temporal dynamic features are then fused for the detection of mitotic events. Readers can find more detailed information for the application of two-stream CNNs for action recognition in Ref. [22].

Specifically, Mao and Yin [23] proposed a mitosis detection method that takes both static image sequence and optical flow image sequence as input. The architecture of a two-stream CNN for mitosis detection is illustrated in Fig. 6.16. Given a sequence of cell images, we feed the original cell images into the appearance branch of the two-stream network, extract optical flow images from original images as motion information, and feed them into the motion branch of the two-stream network. Deep features from both branches are then concatenated together as hybrid features for the classification of the overall sequence as mitosis or not.

3.4.2 3-Dimensional convolutional network (C3D) for mitosis detection

Another important variation of a deep-learning model for image sequence event detection is 3D convolutional network (C3D). Instead of extraction motion information from image sequence with optical flow methods, C3D uses 3D kernels in convolution layers to learn the spatiotemporal information directly.

Compared with traditional 2D convolution layers in CNN, the C3D network directly takes a sequence of images (with shape $h \times w \times t \times c$) as input. Here, h and w represent the height and width of the input image, respectively; t represents the temporal

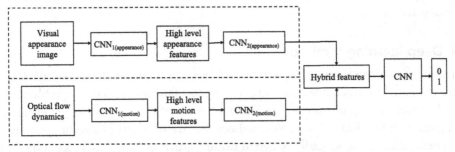

Fig. 6.16 Illustration of the two-stream CNN architecture for mitosis detection.

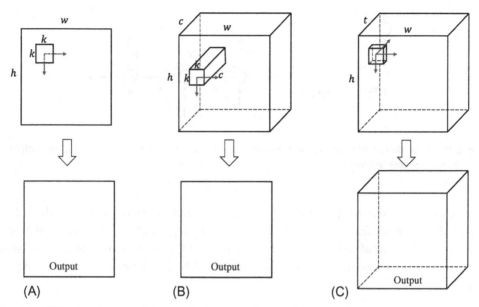

Fig. 6.17 Difference between 2D convolution operations and 3D convolution operation.

length of the input sequence; and c represents the number of channels for each pixel in the image. In each layer, convolution operations are applied along both spatial and temporal dimensions with 3D kernels on the input sequences. The difference between 2D convolution operation and 3D convolution operation is shown in Fig. 6.17.

A detailed description of the C3D network can be found in Refs. [24, 25].

The C3D network has been applied to mitosis detection problems in phase contrast microscopy images as described in Ref. [26]. The C3D network is specifically designed for detection on cell image sequences. The network contains five convolution layers (each followed by a pooling layer) and two fully connected layers. The output of the network is used as the sequence feature for mitosis detection (Fig. 6.17).

3.4.3 Long short-term memory network (LSTM) for mitosis detection

Just like CNN can be applied to single static images, a recurrent neural network (RNN) can be used to model the temporal dynamics of time-lapse sequences in a deep-learning way. Unlike CNN, which takes independent images as input, RNN takes a sequence of image features to model the temporal information in the sequence. The RNN unit maintains the memory state throughout all the time steps in the sequence (as shown in Fig. 6.18):

$$s_t = f(\mathbf{U}x_t + \mathbf{W}s_{t-1}) \tag{6.36}$$

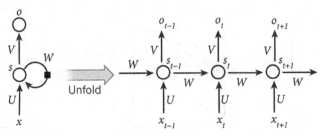

Fig. 6.18 Illustration of RNN. Left: recurrent representation of the RNN unit; right: a temporal unfolded version of the representation.

where $f(\cdot)$ is a nonlinear function such as ReLU; $\mathbf{U}$ and $\mathbf{W}$ are parameters of the RNN network, which are shared across all time steps; and s_t represents the memory of RNN at time t, which is calculated based on the current feature input (x_t) and the memory state from the previous time step s_{t-1}. The output of the RNN network at time step t is represented as

$$o_t = \text{softmax}(\mathbf{V}s_t) \tag{6.37}$$

As the temporal length of input sequence increases, the gradients propagate over time during training. A traditional RNN suffers gradient exploding and gradient vanishing problems in actual applications, several modifications of the RNN structure have been proposed. A long short-term memory (LSTM) network is a popular extension of the vanilla design of RNN units. The original design of the LSTM network is proposed at 1997 [27]. The LSTM expands the RNN unit with three gate functions controlling the information flow of cell state over time. Given a sequence input of $\mathbf{X} = (x_1, x_2, \ldots, x_T)$, the memory state of the LSTM unit at time t is controlled by three gate functions: (1) the *input gate* function $i(\mathbf{x}_t, h_{t-1}; \mathbf{W}_i, \mathbf{b}_i)$; (2) the *forget gate* function $f(\mathbf{x}_t, \mathbf{h}_{t-1}; \mathbf{W}_f, \mathbf{b}_f)$; and (3) the *output gate* function $o(\mathbf{x}_t, \mathbf{h}_{t-1}; \mathbf{W}_o, \mathbf{b}_o)$, as shown in Eq. (6.38). In this equation, $\mathbf{c}_t$ represents the memory of an LSTM unit at current time t and $\mathbf{h}_t$ represents the hidden state output of the LSTM network at time step t:

$$
\begin{aligned}
\mathbf{i}_t &= \sigma(\mathbf{W}_{xi}\mathbf{x}_t + \mathbf{W}_{hi}\mathbf{h}_{t-1} + \mathbf{b}_i) \\
\mathbf{f}_t &= \sigma(\mathbf{W}_{xf}\mathbf{x}_t + \mathbf{W}_{hf}\mathbf{h}_{t-1} + \mathbf{b}_f) \\
\mathbf{o}_t &= \sigma(\mathbf{W}_{xo}\mathbf{x}_t + \mathbf{W}_{ho}\mathbf{h}_{t-1} + \mathbf{b}_o) \\
\mathbf{c}_t &= \mathbf{f}_t \odot \mathbf{c}_{t-1} + \mathbf{i}_t \odot \tanh(\mathbf{W}_{xc}\mathbf{x}_t + \mathbf{W}_{hc}\mathbf{h}_{t-1} + \mathbf{b}_c) \\
\mathbf{h}_t &= \mathbf{o}_t \odot \tanh(\mathbf{c}_t)
\end{aligned}
\tag{6.38}
$$

The joint of the CNN and LSTM architecture can be applied for mitosis detection, as shown in Fig. 6.19. The architecture has been applied for mitosis detection [28], and

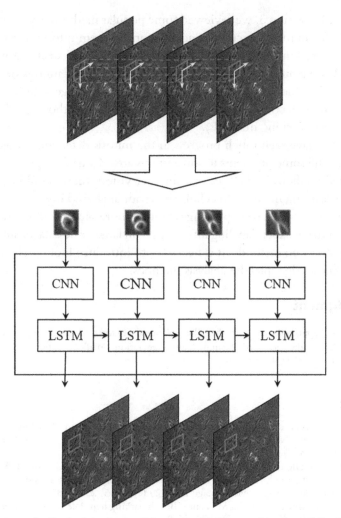

Fig. 6.19 Overview of mitosis detection architecture with the combination of the CNN and LSTM networks.

achieved significant improvement of detection accuracy compared with previous methods with handcrafted visual features.

4. Conclusion

In Section 1 of this chapter, we described the mitosis detection problem and introduced some commonly used metrics for evaluating detection algorithms. In Section 2, we gave an overview of some common microscopy imaging methods that are related to mitosis detection tasks. In Section 3, we reviewed some popular methods for cell behavior analysis (especially for mitosis detection), and categorized them into four classes: tracking-based methods, tracking-free methods, hybrid methods, and deep-learning methods. In Section 3.2, we mainly focused on the methods that detect mitosis on static images. In Sections 3.1, 3.3, and 3.4, we discussed how to take advantage of time-series dynamic images for mitosis detection (with the traditional tracking method, graph model-based method, and deep-learning methods).

Although we have seen much progress in the mitosis detection problems in recent years, there are still some problems to solve in this area. Considering the success of deep learning-related methods in the area of computer vision, there should be more studies applying deep-learning methods to cellular behavior analysis. However, compared with natural images, medical microscope images require more specialized knowledge; thus, it is more difficult to get expert labeling information on large-scale data for supervised training with deep-learning methods. It is necessary to introduce biologically and medically related prior knowledge into the analysis methods.

Acknowledgment

This work was supported in part by the National Natural Science Foundation of China (61772359,61472275), the grant of Tianjin New Generation Artificial Intelligence Major Program (19ZXZNGX00110,18ZXZNGX00150).

References

[1] L. Roux, D. Racoceanu, N. Lome´nie, M. Kulikova, H. Irshad, J. Klossa, F.´d.´r. Capron, C. Genestie, G. Le Naour, M. Gurcan, Mitosis detection in breast cancer histological images, J. Pathol. Inform. 4 (8) (2013).

[2] M. Veta, P.J. Van Diest, S.M. Willems, H. Wang, A. Madabhushi, A. Cruzroa, F.A. Gonzalez, A.B. L. Larsen, J.S. Vestergaard, A.B. Dahl, et al., Assessment of algorithms for mitosis detection in breast cancer histopathology images, Med. Image Anal. 20 (1) (2015) 237–248.

[3] P. Foggia, G. Percannella, P. Soda, M. Vento, Benchmarking hep-2 cells classification methods, IEEE Trans. Med. Imaging 32 (10) (2013) 1878–1889.

[4] A.-A. Liu, Y. Lu, M. Chen, Y.-T. Su, Mitosis detection in phase contrast microscopy image sequences of stem cell populations: a critical review, IEEE Trans. Big Data 3 (4) (2017) 443–457.

[5] D.G. Lowe, Distinctive image features from scale-invariant keypoints, Int. J. Comput. Vis. 60 (2) (2004) 91–110.

[6] A. Liu, K. Li, T. Kanade, A semi-Markov model for mitosis segmentation in time-lapse phase contrast microscopy image sequences of stem cell populations, IEEE Trans. Med. Imaging 31 (2) (2012) 359–369.

[7] A. Liu, K. Li, T. Hao, A hierarchical framework for mitosis detection in time-lapse phase contrast microscopy image sequences of stem cell populations, 2011.

[8] A. Oliva, A. Torralba, Modeling the shape of the scene: a holistic representation of the spatial envelope, Int. J. Comput. Vis. 42 (3) (2001) 145–175.

[9] A. Liu, Z. Gao, H. Tong, Y. Su, Z. Yang, Sparse coding induced transfer learning for hep-2 cell classification, Biomed. Mater. Eng. 24 (1) (2014) 237–243.

[10] C.H. Huang, H.K. Lee, Automated mitosis detection based on exclusive independent component analysis, in: *Pattern Recognition (ICPR), 2012 21st International Conference on*, IEEE, 2012, pp. 1856–1859.

[11] K. Li, E.D. Miller, M. Chen, T. Kanade, L.E. Weiss, P.G. Campbell, Computer vision tracking of stemness, in: *2008 5th IEEE International Symposium on Biomedical Imaging: From Nano to Macro*, IEEE, 2008, pp. 847–850.

[12] H. Chen, Q. Dou, X. Wang, J. Qin, P.-A. Heng, Mitosis detection in breast cancer histology images via deep cascaded networks, in: *Proceedings of the Thirtieth AAAI Conference on Artificial Intelligence*, AAAI Press, 2016, pp. 1160–1166.

[13] D.C. Cireşan, A. Giusti, L.M. Gambardella, J. Schmidhuber, Mitosis detection in breast cancer histology images with deep neural networks, in: *International Conference on Medical Image Computing and Computer-assisted Intervention*, Springer, 2013, pp. 411–418.

[14] Y. Li, L. Shen, S. Yu, Hep-2 specimen image segmentation and classification using very deep fully convolutional network, IEEE Trans. Med. Imaging 36 (7) (2017) 1561–1572.

[15] Z. Yin, K. Li, T. Kanade, M. Chen, Understanding the Optics to Aid Microscopy Image Segmentation, Springer Berlin Heidelberg, Berlin, Heidelberg, 2010, pp. 209–217.

[16] K. Li, T. Kanade, Nonnegative mixed-norm preconditioning for microscopy image segmentation, in: International Conference on Information Processing in Medical Imaging, vol. 21, 2009, pp. 362–373.

[17] G.M. Gallardo, F. Yang, F. Ianzini, M. Mackey, M. Sonka, Mitotic cell recognition with hidden markov models, in: Medical Imaging 2004, International Society for Optics and Photonics, 2004, pp. 661–668.

[18] L. Liang, X. Zhou, F. Li, S.T.C. Wong, J. Huckins, R.W. King, Mitosis cell identification with conditional random fields, in: *Life Science Systems and Applications Workshop, 2007. LISA 2007. IEEE/NIH*, IEEE, 2007, pp. 9–12.

[19] K.L. Anan Liu, T. Kanade, Mitosis sequence detection using hidden conditional random fields, in: 2010 IEEE International Symposium on Biomedical Imaging: From Nano to Macro, IEEE, 2010, pp. 580–583.

[20] S. Huh, R. Bise, M. Chen, T. Kanade, et al., Automated mitosis detection of stem cell populations in phase-contrast microscopy images, IEEE Trans. Med. Imaging 30 (3) (2011) 586–596.

[21] S. Huh, M. Chen, Detection of mitosis within a stem cell population of high cell confluence in phase-contrast microscopy images, in: *Computer Vision and Pattern Recognition (CVPR), 2011 IEEE Conference on*, IEEE, 2011, pp. 1033–1040.

[22] K. Simonyan, A. Zisserman, Two-stream convolutional networks for action recognition in videos, in: Advances in Neural Information Processing Systems, 2014, pp. 568–576.

[23] Y. Mao, Z. Yin, A hierarchical convolutional neural network for mitosis detection in phase-contrast microscopy images, in: *International Conference on Medical Image Computing and Computer-Assisted Intervention*, Springer, 2016, pp. 685–692.

[24] S. Ji, W. Xu, M. Yang, K. Yu, 3D convolutional neural networks for human action recognition, IEEE Trans. Pattern Anal. Mach. Intell. 35 (1) (2013) 221–231.

[25] D. Tran, L. Bourdev, R. Fergus, L. Torresani, M. Paluri, Learning spatiotemporal features with 3d convolutional networks, in: *Computer Vision (ICCV), 2015 IEEE International Conference on*, IEEE, 2015, pp. 4489–4497.

[26] W.Z. Nie, W.H. Li, A. Liu, T. Hao, Y.T. Su, 3d convolutional networks-based mitotic event detection in time-lapse phase contrast microscopy image sequences of stem cell populations, in: Proceedings of the IEEE Conference on Computer Vision and Pattern Recognition Work-shops, 2016, pp. 55–62.

[27] S. Hochreiter, J. Schmidhuber, Long short-term memory, Neural Comput. 9 (8) (1997) 1735–1780.

[28] Y.-T. Su, Y. Lu, M. Chen, A.-A. Liu, Spatiotemporal joint mitosis detection using cnnlstm network in time-lapse phase contrast microscopy images, IEEE Access 5 (2017) 18033–18041.

CHAPTER 7

Object measurements from 2D microscopy images

Peter Bajcsy*, Joe Chalfoun*, Mylene Simon*, Marcin Kociolek[†], and Mary Brady*
*Information Technology Laboratory, National Institute of Standards and Technology, Gaithersburg, MD, United States
[†]Lodz University of Technology, Lodz, Poland

Contents

1. Background

Two-dimensional (2D) image measurements are an integral part of quantitative microscopy imaging and image informatics. Such measurements are computed over a set of connected image pixels (region of interest, or ROI) using a wide variety of mathematical operations applied to pixel location and intensity values. Numerical results of these computations are frequently denoted as image or object features. To compute a 2D object feature, one needs the following:

(1) An input digital image

(2) A mask image defining each ROI by a unique label assigned to a set of connected pixels

Computer Vision for Microscopy Image Analysis
https://doi.org/10.1016/B978-0-12-814972-0.00007-2

(3) Mathematical operations applied to the pixels forming a ROI

(4) Parameters for the mathematical operations (model).

Every image can yield very many extracted features, as the combinatorial number of ROIs, mathematical operations, and their parameters can be extremely large. As the imaging field advances, the object feature extraction faces challenges not only in the number of measurements per image, but also in the number of images that must be processed for each experiment. To address the issue of an extremely large number of feature extractions in quantitative imaging, object measurements from 2D microscopy images have been automated by using software. As a consequence, automation has led to the creation of many software libraries for feature extraction.

For example, the microscopy community has been using several open-source libraries, including the Python scikit-image [1], CellProfiler [2], MaZda [3], ImageJ/Fiji [4], and WND-CHARM [5], and feature extractors built in house using open-source libraries (e.g., OpenCV [6], Java ImageIO [7]) and commercial libraries (e.g., MATLAB, Wolfram Mathematica). The use of some of these libraries in scholarly publications is illustrated in Table 7.1. The table was created based on Google Scholar queries and documents the usage of intensity, shape, and textural image features extracted by using one of the four libraries. The large counts in Table 7.1 motivate us to study the feature variability across feature extraction libraries, as the scientific conclusions derived here might be biased by the choice of library.

Given this motivation, the goal of this chapter is to characterize object feature variability across software libraries and to demonstrate the impact of such a numerical variability on feature-based classification. By analyzing feature variability across software libraries, one can answer the following questions for scientists:

(1) What image features do not vary with software implementations in open-source software libraries?

Table 7.1 Total counts of scholarly publications published since 2013 and since 2017 until 2018

Google scholar query key phrases	Since 2017	Since 2013
"CellProfiler image intensity features"	482	1860
"MaZda software image intensity features"	233	912
"Python scikit-image intensity features"	764	1800
"MATLAB image intensity features"	12,200	19,900
"CellProfiler shape features"	406	1590
"MaZda software shape features"	312	1600
"Python scikit-image shape features"	1760	4110
"MATLAB shape features"	17,800	29,300
"CellProfiler texture features"	104	484
"MaZda software texture features"	129	489
"Python scikit-image texture features"	385	942
"MATLAB texture features"	5900	19,400

(2) What is the ranking of features based on the magnitude of their numerical variability?

(3) What are the sources of numerical feature variability?

(4) How much does feature variability affect feature-based classification outcomes?

We are not answering these questions related to the absolute accuracy of feature values because we are not creating any evaluation ground truths. Our goal is to quantify the relative feature differences and investigate the sources of those differences in order to emphasize the importance of gathering computational provenance information and noting possible biases in scholarly publications based on the selection of a particular feature extraction library.

This chapter tackles the following goals:

- Introduce 2D image feature extraction and classification.
- Describe an overall approach to numerical evaluation of feature variability and classification.
- Outline the integration of open-source software implementations of 2D image feature extractors.
- Present representative microscopy images collected to extract features determining the heterogeneity of stem cell colonies from terabyte (TB)-sized videos [8, 9].
- Quantify and explain sources of numerical variability of image features across image feature extraction libraries.
- Illustrate the impact of the feature variability on classification outcomes in the context of a biological imaging experiment.

In addition to the insights provided in this chapter, we have prepared an open-source client-server software system called a *web image processing pipeline (WIPP)* [10], which integrates multiple feature extraction libraries. It is available for download at https://isg.nist. gov. By reading this chapter and using WIPP, scientists can evaluate feature variability across software libraries on their own. Scientists can also use WIPP for gathering provenance information about their feature extractions to make their work reproducible.

2. Introduction to 2D image measurements

Many image feature extractors have been implemented in academic environments [5, 11, 12], commercial platforms [13], and publicly available image libraries [1, 4, 6]. These extractors generate image features that are used primarily for (1) classification, (2) discovery in scientific pursuits, or both. In the context of feature-based classification, one is searching for the most discriminative or predictive features considering a certain number of classes. In the context of discovery, one is trying to understand statistical and semantic object characteristics based on image features.

In general, feature extractors can provide:

(1) Low-level image descriptors, such as scale-invariant feature transform (SIFT) [14], speeded-up robust features (SURFs) [15], histograms of oriented gradients

(HOGs) [16], local phase quantization (LPQ), binarized statistical image features (BSIFs) [17], local binary patterns (LBPs) [18], and local ternary patterns (LTPs) [19].

(2) High-level object descriptors (e.g., average intensity, location, size, perimeter, change of location).

We are interested in high-level object descriptors because they correspond to image-based measurements of semantically meaningful objects. Nonetheless, a computation of low-level features might be part of the computation to derive a high-level descriptor. Computations of high-level descriptors might also include image transformations. For example, Fourier transform (FT) changes the semantic meaning of the underlying Cartesian coordinate space of raster images to represent periodic structures for direct object measurements.

High-level object features can describe the spectral, spatial, textural, or temporal properties of an object. Spectral intensity features are typically statistical measurements of a probability distribution computed from pixel intensity (i.e., central moments). Similarly, spatial shape features are spatial moments derived from coordinates of pixels included in one ROI. Intensity and shape features have relatively well defined mapping between visual perception and their mathematical formula. On the other hand, perception of image texture is only coarsely mapped to the mathematical formulas of textural features. Computations of textural features typically include some transformation to a space where periodically repeating patterns and scale-dependent primitives can be quantified (e.g., Texton theory [20]). Temporal motion features capture dynamic changes of object appearance and location properties, such as biological cell states (e.g., mitosis, differentiation, apoptosis, migration). While computations of all feature types require 2D ROIs, motion features also require tracking information between two time-adjacent images. The tracking information defines the correspondence between object identifiers in labeled masks at time t and at time $(t+1)$.

In addition to the feature types, there are many other ways to establish ROIs that represent semantically meaningful objects. ROIs can be defined as rectangular fields of view (FOVs), arbitrarily shaped ROIs resulting from image segmentation, grid squares or grid hexagons subdividing ROIs obtained from image segmentation, and many other space filling 2D shapes subdividing an image. Fig. 7.1 illustrates the options for extracting image features from a cell colony with or without a mask, as well as other suboptions. In our work, we assume that users create ROIs according to their application needs and provide them as input masks (labeled images).

The process of designing, extracting, and selecting features is called *feature engineering*. Feature engineering is a scientific problem on its own, which faces challenges in terms of the following:

(a) Segmenting an image into semantically meaningful ROIs

(b) Devising mathematical models for operating on pixels in each ROI

(c) Selecting the most application-relevant features and computational parameters

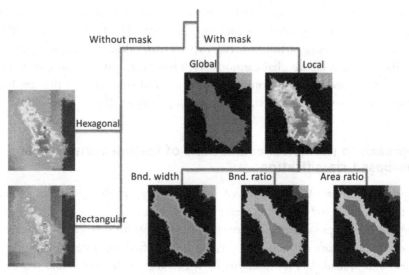

Fig. 7.1 Possible options to creating ROIs for computing 2D image features.

(d) Selecting the feature-based classification model and model parameters

(e) Optimizing all selections with respect to some reference data with known classification outcomes

If the end goal is to obtain the most accurate classification, then the feature engineering problem might be replaced by the problem of designing a convolutional neural network (CNN) architecture and the associated problem of creating a sufficiently large reference data set [21–24]. However, if the end goal is to gain insights into the characteristics of a phenomenon, then feature engineering remains a challenge [25, 26]. In our work, we consider the latter end goal and assume that a scientist has identified semantically meaningful ROIs and selected image measurements over ROIs. Our main concern is only the feature variability and its classification impact in the context of a feature engineering problem.

The feature variability across software libraries is of concern not only to the microscopy imaging community, but also to the medical imaging community. For example, Bhadriraju et al. [8] studied the reproducibility of quantitative imaging features used for classifying lung tumors in computed tomography (CT) images. The variability of features was determined independent of segmentation over repeated acquisitions of lung CT data sets. The study used commercial features implemented in C/C++ and MATLAB, which makes it hard to understand the sources of numerical variability. Thus, we limited our study to open-source feature extraction libraries.

The feature variability study can be related to a sensitivity study from a statistical perspective. Given all software implementation variables (factors), full factorial experimental designs would establish the sensitivity of the numerical features to the factors.

Such studies are frequently conducted with medical imaging devices (ultrasound, computer tomography, or magnetic resonance imaging) [10, 11]. Our feature variability study cannot be executed using a full factorial experimental design because many software libraries have hidden factors that cannot vary. However, our analysis can demonstrate the impact of feature variability on the classification of cell colonies that are heterogeneous from already-published stem cell microscopy images [5].

3. Approach to numerical evaluations of feature variability and feature-based classification

We approach numerical evaluations of image feature variability and its classification impact by executing the following steps:

(1) Identify overlapping image features in multiple feature extraction libraries.

(2) Integrate all feature extraction libraries into a unified software framework.

(3) Select and upload data sets that yield a wide range of feature values.

(4) Set all exposed algorithmic inputs to the same values.

(5) Establish metrics of feature and classification variabilities.

(6) Quantify numerical variability of intensity, shape, and textural features and classification outcomes.

(7) Analyze sources of variability.

These steps are illustrated in Fig. 7.2 (feature variability) and Fig. 7.3 (classification variability), with an emphasis on the analysis flow while the feature extraction libraries are the only element in the flow varying during the numerical evaluations. As shown

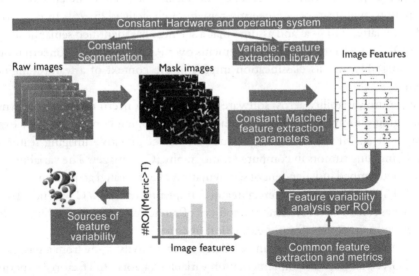

Fig. 7.2 Variability analysis of image features; arrows show analysis flow.

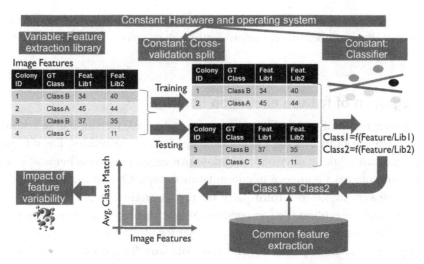

Fig. 7.3 Variability analysis of feature-based classification; arrows show analysis flow.

in Fig. 7.2, hardware, segmentation, and feature extraction parameters are kept constant. In Fig. 7.3, we indicated that hardware, cross-validation split, and classifier models are constant. Note that we evaluated the results from multiple nonstochastic classifiers.

We manually identified overlapping image features in multiple feature extraction libraries (step 1) by considering image features extracted using ImageJ/Fiji [4], Python scikit-image [1], CellProfiler [2, 12], MaZda [27–29], and feature extractors developed in-house using Java ImageIO [30]. Integration of all the feature extraction libraries to a WIPP framework [10] (step 2) allowed us to establish an identical computational environment, gather provenance information, and rerun feature extractors as many times as needed after test images were uploaded to the WIPP client-server system (step 3). These efforts are described in Section 4 (step 2) and in Section 5 (step 3). To set feature extraction algorithmic inputs, we identified exposed and hidden parameters, kept the default value of hidden parameters, and modified exposed parameters to comparable values with other feature extractors (step 4). The comparison metrics for feature and classification variabilities (step 5), together with the numerical results (step 6) and our insights about sources of numerical variability (step 7), are provided in Sections 6 and 7.

4. Integration of open-source libraries for 2D image measurements

We first integrated image feature extraction algorithms from open-source libraries into WIPP [10]. We unified the application programming interface (API) to feature extraction algorithms via a common Extensible Markup Language (XML) file with input and output specifications (see Section 4.1). Next, we summarized all the features for each type and counted the number of common features per pairs of software libraries (see Section 4.2).

4.1 Integration of feature extraction libraries

Although integration of feature libraries was the main goal, we also had to consider the computational scalability and traceability of image feature executions. For this purpose, we leveraged past work on scientific workflow management systems because image features are computed as a sequence of computational steps. One of these steps is the execution of software found in a third-party feature extraction library with the specified inputs. To enable execution (i.e., integration of heterogeneous software), we predefine a common file interface for inputs, design a parser for input parameters in the programming language of each image library, and automate launching third-party software via a command-line interface. The execution of feature extractions is then scheduled, monitored, and managed by a scientific workflow system.

In an effort to provide access to traceable image features, we designed the WIPP architecture shown in Fig. 7.4. The main capabilities of this web-based framework for traceable image feature extraction are (1) extensibility to include image feature extraction libraries written in any programming language via a file interface, (2) data management to

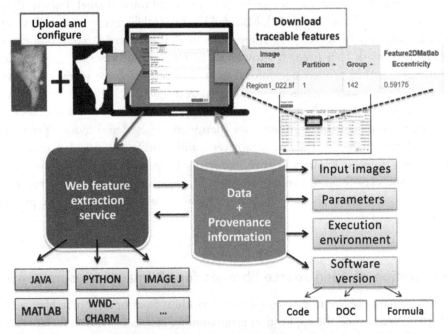

Fig. 7.4 Architecture of a client-server system for traceable image feature extraction.

upload collections and download feature values, (3) configuration and execution interface to feature extractors registered in the system, (4) collaborative access to traceable image feature values that are hyperlinked to their provenance information, and (5) access to all downloadable computational artifacts that are needed for reexecution.

In this client-server application, the server side has a representational state transfer (REST) or RESTful API, built using the Java Spring framework. It is coupled with the MongoDB database and a scientific workflow management system (WMS) called Pegasus [31] to manage the feature extraction jobs. The client side is a light web application written in JavaScript using the AngularJS framework. The client side communicates via the REST API with the server side.

4.2 Summary of features in all integrated libraries

We evaluated five open-source libraries of feature extractors that have been integrated in WIPP. Table 7.2 summarizes the number of overlapping features per software library and the total number of features per feature type. These five libraries offer extractions of 472 unique intensity, shape, and textural features. The split of 472 unique features across the five libraries is the Python scikit-image (45), CellProfiler (125), MaZda (192), Java (77), and ImageJ/Fiji (33). Of the total number of 472 features, there are 301 textural features that are split across the four libraries as follows: Python (24 out of 45), CellProfiler (53 out of 125), MaZda (172 out of 192), and in-house Java (52 out of 77). Features in Python were calculated on top of an existing image-processing library (scikit-image). The features in ImageJ/Fiji were computed as a plug-in using the ImageJ API [4], and Java features were implemented from scratch at the National Institute of Standards and Technology (NIST) [30]. MaZda and CellProfiler are stand-alone software libraries that have a defined API to access a variety of features.

Table 7.2 Integrated software libraries and their counts of the common intensity, shape, and textural features with other software libraries (#common) and of the total number of features (#total)

Feature type	Library count	Python	CellProfiler	MaZda	Java	ImageJ/Fiji
Intensity feature	#common	3	5	4	6	8
	#total	3	23	13	9	10
Shape feature	#common	18	11	3	12	14
	#total	18	49	7	16	23
Textural feature	#common	16	44	44	0	X
	#total	24	53	172	52	X

X—stands for not included in the analyses.
Note: Due to the manual work involved in integrating features, we have not included all features in all libraries. For example, the Python scikit-image and MaZda libraries contain more features than those integrated in WIPP for quantitative comparison.

5. Image features in scientific use cases

To illustrate numerical variations of intensity, shape, and textural features, as well as the classification impact, we chose data from a published imaging experiment [8]. The ultimate goal of this experiment was to measure the presence and classify the distribution of Oct4 pluripotency markers in living cell colonies over a large field of view. The image processing in this experiment is based on extracting colony features and then classifying them based on those features. The use of object features in this experiment is common to many other published microscopy experiments (e.g., cancer diagnosis from immunohistochemistry images [32]).

As documented in Bhadriraju et al. [8], the images of cell colonies were taken every 45 min for 5 days (161 time points) in both phase-contrast and fluorescent-imaging modalities. At every time point, one grid of 16×22 individual fields of view (FOVs) was taken with a 10% overlap between FOVs in both the x- and y-directions. A subset of all cell colonies was manually classified into three categories (homogeneous, heterogeneous, and dark), based on the distribution of the Oct4 marker in each colony. The class labels correspond to the visual assessment of Oct4 intensities within each cell colony. The *homogeneous* label refers to the case when the majority of pixel intensities have a high value (white). The *dark* label refers to the majority of low pixel intensities (black) and the *heterogeneous* label refers to a mixture of pixel intensities.

To automate the processing of terabyte-sized images, the colony features were extracted from the fluorescent channel and the colony masks were obtained from the coregistered phase contrast channel. A gigapixel image at each time point was created by using published background correction [33], stitching [34], segmentation [35], tracking [36], and feature-extraction methods [37]. To predict classification labels, a supervised logistic regression model was developed using colony features extracted from 140 stem cell colonies that were manually categorized as homogeneous, heterogeneous, or dark. Fig. 7.5 illustrates colony examples for each classification category in both acquired imaging modalities [i.e., phase contrast and green fluorescent protein (GFP) channels].

The inputs into our study were as follows:
(1) 140 manually annotated cell colonies from 161 stitched and background corrected fluorescent Oct4 images
(2) The corresponding colony masks computed by segmenting the stitched phase contrast images
(3) The classification labels assigned manually by experts

We opted to conduct the study with measured images rather than synthetic images because we had no mathematical models for generating synthetic images that span a wide range of image features, and we found the measured images to be a good initial approximation of the range for most of the image features. Figs. 7.6 and 7.7 illustrate the ranges

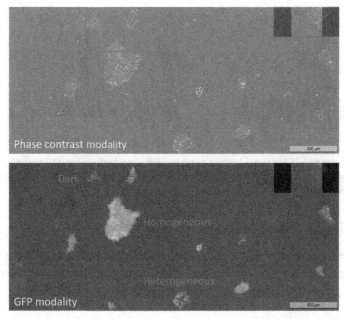

Fig. 7.5 Cell colony classification into three classes: homogeneous (bright intensities), heterogeneous (mixed bright and dark intensities), and dark intensity (indistinguishable dark intensities from background). The classification is based on gray-level image intensities of fluorescently stained cells with Oct4 pluripotency marker.

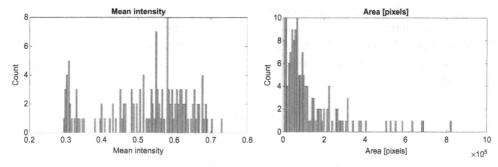

Fig. 7.6 Histograms of mean intensity (left) and area (right) features from the objects defined by test images and their masks.

of image features extracted from the selected measured images (140 colonies). Fig. 7.6 shows the histograms of intensity (mean) and shape (area) features. Fig. 7.7 displays two textural gray-level cooccurrence matrix (GLCM)-based features. According to the figure, the textural feature values cover $(\max(\text{Data}) - \min(\text{Data}))/\max(\text{Theory}) = (3.8 - 2.1)/7 = 24.3\%$ (texture contrast) and $(0.067 - 0.025)/1 = 4.2\%$ (second angular moment) of the possible feature value range.

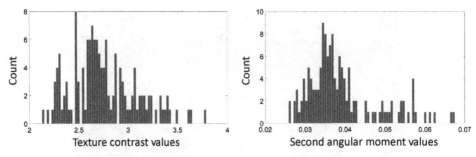

Fig. 7.7 Histograms of GLCM-based texture contrast (left) and texture second angular moment (right) features. Both were computed by using a Python library with parameters set to offset=3, angle=0 degrees, and the number of GLCM bins=8.

6. Variability of image features

We define the evaluation metrics for feature variability in Section 6.1, present analyses of intensity, shape, and textural feature variability across five libraries in Section 6.2, and discuss the sources of differences in Sections 6.3 and 6.4.

6.1 Feature variability metric

For any two feature extractors containing the implementations of the same feature, we compute two numerical values per ROI. When the computation is applied to a set of ROIs, then it results in two vectors of numerical feature values, $\vec{V}_1 = (V_{1i})$ and $\vec{V}_2 = (V_{2i})$, where i is the index of the ROI. To compare the two vectors, we first calculate a vector of relative errors, $\vec{E}^{1,2} = (E_i^{1,2})$, that correspond to differences normalized by the average of V_{1i} and V_{2i}. Next, we count the elements of the relative error vector for which the error values exceed a specified threshold T in order to define the dissimilarity metric **SF**:

$$E_i^{1,2} = |V_{1i} - V_{2i}|/(0.5*(V_{1i} + V_{2i}))\tag{7.1}$$

$$SF = \sum_{i=1}^{n} f_i \quad f_i = \begin{cases} 1 & \text{if}\left(E_i^{1,2} > T\right) \\ 0 & \text{otherwise} \end{cases}\tag{7.2}$$

where n is the number of ROIs, T is the user-defined error threshold, and the **F** in **SF** stands for "feature." In our work, T is set to 0.01, which can be interpreted as a 1% deviation from the average. The purpose of T is to include only significant feature value differences. The error is normalized by the minimum value, which represents the worst-case error scenario. In this example, the dissimilarity metric (SF) is the number of colonies where the relative error was larger than 1%.

Table 7.3 Summary of a pair-wise comparison of feature extraction libraries (rows) in terms of the number of common (overlapping) features (CF) and the number of features with relative error larger than 1% (*SF*)

Feature extraction library pair	Intensity		Shape		Texture	
	SF	CF	*SF*	CF	*SF*	CF
Python versus CellProfiler	2	3	6	11	12	12
Python versus MaZda	0	1	0	3	12	12
Python versus ImageJ/Fiji	0	3	9	12	0	0
Python versus Java	0	1	0	11	0	0
CellProfiler versus MaZda	0	2	2	3	36	44
CellProfiler versus ImageJ/Fiji	0	5	8	8	0	0
CellProfiler versus Java	0	3	4	7	0	0
MaZda versus ImageJ/Fiji	2	4	3	3	0	0
MaZda versus Java	0	4	0	3	0	0
ImageJ/Fiji versus Java	1	6	2	10	0	0
Sum	5	32	34	71	60	68

6.2 Image feature variability analysis

Table 7.3 shows the results of image feature variability evaluation using the metric defined in Section 6.1. The rows report pairwise comparisons of feature extraction libraries. The columns are organized based on the three types of features (i.e., intensity, shape, and texture). The tabular entries document the values from the metric *SF* ($T = 1\%$, $n = 140$ cell colonies per feature) and the total number of common features in a pair of feature extraction libraries based on their definition.

For instance, out of 44 common textural features between MaZda and CellProfiler, 36 show a significant difference in values. Python and CellProfiler have 12 common textural features whose values show significant differences for all the features, which is similar to the evaluation results for Python and MaZda. For the five open-source feature extraction libraries (Python, CellProfiler, MaZda, ImageJ/Fiji, and Java), we found 5 out of 32 intensity features, 34 out of 71 shape features, and 60 out of 68 textural features to differ in their pairwise comparisons. These findings correspond to 15.6%, 47.9%, and 88.2% of intensity, shape, and textural features that differ in values, respectively.

6.3 Sources of image feature variations

To illustrate feature variability, we plotted the difference values between the feature value V_{ji} (*j*, feature extractor library index; *i*, ROI index) and the average of all feature values over all feature extractors containing the implementation of that feature. Figs. 7.8–7.10 provide such visualizations for one of the intensity, shape, and textural features, respectively. In Fig. 7.8, CellProfiler deviates from most feature extractors for mean intensity.

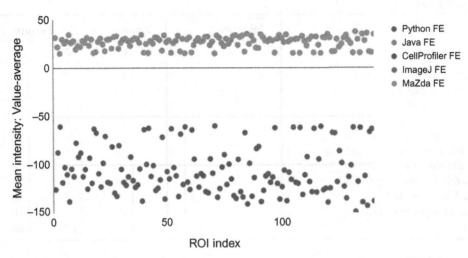

Fig. 7.8 Mean intensity feature (ID = 24) differences over multiple regions of interest (ROIs) from cell colony images [20].

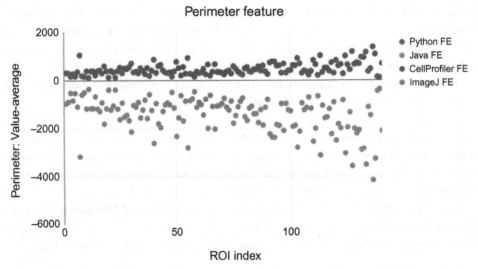

Fig. 7.9 Perimeter feature (ID = 8) differences over multiple regions of interest (ROIs) from cell colony images [20]. The unit is image pixels.

In Fig. 7.9, ImageJ/Fiji reports different values from the rest of feature extractors for the perimeter (shape feature). Fig. 7.10 shows gray-level cooccurrence matrix (GLCM)-based texture contrast difference values for the MaZda, Python, and CellProfiler libraries. In this illustration, CellProfiler and MaZda agree in values but disagree with the values from Python.

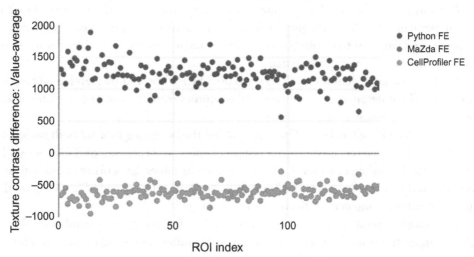

Fig. 7.10 Texture contrast difference feature (ID=28) over 140 ROIs. The values are plotted as the difference between the computed feature and the average of all three values from MaZda, CellProfiler, and Python.

Next, we have analyzed some of the sources of variation for the features referred to in the Appendix. The sources of feature variations included theoretical formulas for the same image feature, the physical units used to represent pixel-based measurements, the definitions of objects in images (called regions of interest or ROIs), algorithmic implementations, and the number of exposed parameters to a user in multiple feature extractors. Our analysis also includes features requiring special attention because they are prone to variation.

6.3.1 Intensity features

Kurtosis and Skewness: The kurtosis disagreement in values between software packages depends on whether the excess kurtosis or kurtosis is implemented (fixed, offset by 3). Similarly, one has to be aware of multiple definitions of skewness (e.g., sample versus population skewness).

Histogram bins for intensities represented by more than 8 bits per pixel (special attention): ImageJ/Fiji uses the max value +1 as the upper value of the last bin. It assumes that the lower value of the first bin is always zero.

Python and its numpy library provide two definitions: B=histogram(X, N) uses N equally spaced bins within the appropriate range for the given image data type. The returned image B has no more than N discrete levels. B=histogram(X, edges) sorts X into bins with the bin edges specified by the vector, edges. Each bin includes the left edge but does not include the right one. The last bin is an exception because it includes both edges.

6.3.2 Shape features

Perimeter and Circularity: The perimeter variability comes from the fact that algorithmic implementations differ in counting interior or exterior pixels, use 4 or 8 connectivity of pixels, and might interpolate between the boundary points. Circularity is inversely proportional to the perimeter squared.

Solidity: The same definition of solidity is used by Python and ImageJ/Fiji (area/convex area). The difference between these values comes from the convex area differences because the implementations vary.

Centroid (and Bounding Box): The centroid and the bounding box are both subject to the choice of the reference coordinate system (+col ~ x; +row ~ y or +row ~ −y). In addition, the bounding box of a ROI is defined by its upper-left-corner coordinate and its width and height. However, the bounding coordinates might vary depending on the choice of values as integers or floats in a raster image.

Euler number (special attention): The Euler number definition is the number of objects (ROIs) minus the number of holes. The value might differ depending on the assumptions about the number of ROIs (Python assumes #ROIs = 1).

Orientation (special attention): The orientation is the angle between the major axis of a given ROI and the x-axis. It can be computed using two mathematical formulas: (1) $\theta = \operatorname{atan}\left(\frac{V_y}{V_x}\right)$, where atan is the arctangent function and V_x and V_y are the x- and y-decompositions of the major axis of the ROI; and (2) $\theta = \frac{1}{2}\operatorname{atan2}\left(\frac{2I_{xy}}{I_{xx}-I_{yy}}\right)$, where I_{xx} and I_{yy} are the second moment of area along the x- and y-axes and I_{xy} is the product moment of area. These two formulas are equivalent if the first one is computed in the range of $[-\pi/2, \pi/2]$ using atan, and the second one in the range of $[-\pi, \pi]$ using atan2. The variations are observed if different value ranges or angular units would be reported by selected software packages. The range can be either $[-\pi/2, \pi/2]$ or $[-\pi, \pi]$, and the unit can be expressed either in radians or degrees. In addition, the sign of the output angle depends on the coordinate system (image coordinate or graph coordinate system with clockwise or counterclockwise axes).

6.3.3 Textural Features

In comparison to intensity and shape feature variability evaluations, the evaluation of textural features is more challenging due to a large space of possible multistep computations. The reason for this lies in the difficulty of describing image texture. According to Ref. [38], textures are complex visual patterns composed of entities that have characteristic brightness, color, slope, size, and other traits. To capture the textural complexity, we decomposed the process of extracting textural features into four algorithmic steps:

(1) Pixel selection based on regions of interest (ROIs)

(2) Normalization of intensities

Table 7.4 Parameters associated with each textural feature extraction step

Algorithmic steps	Parameters
Selection of pixels	ROI image mask
Normalization	Type (none, min-max, mean $\pm$ standard deviation)
Transformation	Spatial scale, spectral bins
Computation of statistics	Mathematical formula

(3) Spatiospectral transformation of pixels
(4) Computation of statistics from transformed pixels
Table 7.4 provides a high-level summary of all parameters associated with each textural feature extraction step.

Because objects of interest can take arbitrary shapes, selection of pixels via a ROI mask allows us to extract textural features over only the ROI area. The purpose of normalization is to adjust for various image-acquisition settings (e.g., dynamic ranges of images) to enable the comparison of extracted textural features. The goal of spatiospectral image transformations is to capture the structure of texture in a new coordinate space, such as by applying Fourier, Gabor, wavelet, run length coding (RLC), or gray-level cooccurrence matrix (GLCM) transforms. Finally, the objective of computations of statistics is to reduce the dimensionality of the resulting textural feature.

To narrow down the number of textural features and their parameters, we chose GLCM [39] as the transformation of interest because it has been implemented in many software libraries and is used frequently in biological publications [8, 40]. For the GLCM transform, spatial scale is defined by offset and angle parameters. Spectral bins map the acquired dynamic range in bits per pixels (BPP) to a smaller range and define the GLCM size, denoted by N (i.e., N corresponds to the number of distinct gray levels). In addition to defining the spectral bins, the cooccurrence in GLCM can be computed by considering black-white and white-black transitions as the same (both transition counts are added and the GLCM matrix is symmetric) or different (each transition is unique and the GLCM matrix is asymmetric). Finally, when computing statistics from GLCMs, the indexing of bins can vary between 0 and $(N-1)$ or between 1 and N, which affects numerical values derived using GLCM indices. This can be seen from the equations for the texture difference average:

$$F^{(1)} = \sum_{i=0}^{N-1} i\, p_{x-y}(i) \tag{7.3}$$

$$F^{(2)} = \sum_{i=1}^{N} i\, p_{x-y}(i), \tag{7.4}$$

where i is the index of the GLCM matrix, $p(i, j)$ are the entries in the GLCM, and

$$p_{x-y}(i) = \sum_{|x-y|=i} p(i,j). \tag{7.5}$$

The challenge of setting up the algorithmic parameters of multiple libraries lies in the lack of access to some of these parameters (and their supported ranges). Thus, a user is left with the option of only approximating parameter settings. We summarized the key parameter differences among the Python, CellProfiler, and MaZda libraries in Table 7.5. With the limited access to parameters listed in this table, we approximated the selection of pixels by zeroing pixels outside of ROIs and left others intact. All other parameters were set to the same values.

A detailed list of GLCM-based features is provided in the Appendix. It is important to note that in order to extract statistically robust GLCM-based feature values, hundreds of pixels in ROI are needed.

These complex sequences of computations and their algorithmic parameters needed for extracting GLCM-based textural features become the sources of textural feature variability. The variability originates not only from the inconsistent settings of many parameters, but also from the fact that they are inaccessible. After a careful inspection of the software, we identified additional sources of variabilities, such as naming discrepancies (e.g., GLCM angular second moment versus GLCM energy), limited support of image data types (e.g., larger than 8 BPP), and limited ranges of input parameters (e.g., GLCM angles constrained to 0, 45, 90, and 135 degrees).

6.4 Discussion

The evaluation of feature variability across image feature extraction libraries depends on the chosen metric and its parameters. The metric used in our analysis is based on a relative error and depends on a user-specified threshold that was set empirically to 1% of the relative error. Feature variation evaluations also depend on a unit of feature measurement. Our analysis uses pixel units. Note that ImageJ/Fiji reports all measurements in physical units (i.e., μm), and therefore, the ImageJ/Fiji settings must be modified. In our study, we set the units in ImageJ/Fiji to be in pixels.

To compare the magnitude of feature variability across intensity, shape, and textural feature types, we plotted the evaluation results in Fig. 7.11 for 8 intensity features,

Table 7.5 Key parameter differences in GLCM-based features extracted by Python, CellProfiler, and MaZda

| Library | ROI Support | Norm. Type | Transformation | | Statistics |
			GLCM size N	Sym.	GLCM indexing
Python	No	Min-max	256×256	A	$0 - (N-1)$
CellProfiler	Yes	Min-max	8×8	A	$0 - (N-1)$
MaZda	Yes	None	8×8	S	$1 - N$

Sym. is for symmetry, A is asymmetric, and S is symmetric. Norm. stands for normalization.

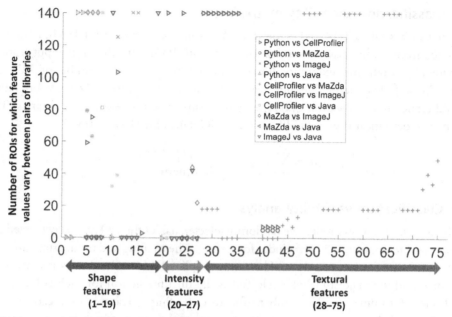

Fig. 7.11 Image feature variability based on the metric **SF**, evaluated over three pairs of feature extraction libraries. Feature categories are indicated on the x-axis and index-to-feature name mapping is provided in the Appendix.

19 shape features, and 48 textural features that are unique and common between pairs of feature extraction libraries. The image shows a total of 75 unique features on the x-axis (the mapping of a feature index to its feature name is in the Appendix) and the metric **SF** on the y-axis [the count of ROIs (cell colonies) for which a given feature value varies more than 1% between two feature extraction libraries (see the inset in Fig. 7.11)].

7. Feature-based classification

In order to evaluate the effect of image feature variability on feature-based classification, we used the manually assigned labels (homogeneous, heterogeneous, and dark) in 140 colonies. The labels are assigned based on the distribution of the Oct4 marker in each colony. From images of the Oct4 marker, we extracted 170 textural features per cell colony using Python, CellProfiler, and MaZda libraries. Out of 170 features, we identified 68 common features between pairs of feature extractors. For these 68 features and the colony labels, we built a classification model to assign each colony to one of the categories based on its feature values. The classification outcomes were evaluated based on the classification variability metric, presented in the next section.

7.1 Classification variability metric

Given the ith ROI (cell colony) in the set of ROIs and two classification labels, L_i^1 and L_i^2, obtained from feature-based classifications of the ith ROI with the same input features provided by two feature extraction libraries, the metric reports the number of ROIs for which $L_i^1 \neq L_i^2$. The metric does not measure the actual classification accuracy, but rather the difference in classification outcomes across pairs of feature extraction libraries. The SC metric definition is presented here (C in SC stands for classification):

$$SC = \sum_{i=1}^{n} f_i \quad f_i = \begin{cases} 1 & \text{if} \left(L_i^1 \neq L_i^2 \right) \\ 0 & \text{otherwise} \end{cases} \tag{7.6}$$

7.2 Classification variability analysis

To build a classification model, we randomly selected half of the 140 manually labeled cell colonies for training and the remainder for testing. The training and testing steps are performed for one feature at a time. The random split of 140 cell colonies is performed 10 times, and the majority label is selected as the final prediction for each colony.

Table 7.6 summarizes the number of features leading to feature-based classification variability and the total number of common textural features for each pair of feature extractors (rows). For this analysis, we chose the binary classification tree because it does not include any randomness during its execution. Note that the classifier choice is not important because we are not analyzing the accuracy of the results, but rather the difference in the classification outcomes. If all classification labels were the same regardless of feature extraction libraries, then SC would be zero and nonzero SF would have zero impact on SC.

7.3 Discussion

To compare the magnitude of classification variability across intensity, shape, and textural feature types, we plotted the evaluation results as illustrated in Fig. 7.12. It shows a total of 75 unique features on the x-axis (the mapping of a feature index to its feature name is in

Table 7.6 Summary of pair-wise comparison of feature extraction libraries (rows) in terms of their common features (CF) by definition and those common features that yield different classification labels according to the classification variability metric SC

Feature extraction library pair	Intensity		Shape		Texture	
	SC	CF	SC	CF	SC	CF
Python versus CellProfiler	0	3	7	11	12	12
Python versus MaZda	0	1	0	3	12	12
CellProfiler versus MaZda	0	2	2	3	42	44
Sum	0	6	9	17	66	68

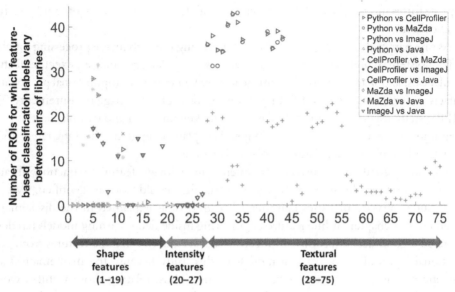

Fig. 7.12 Feature-based classification variability based on the metric *SC* evaluated over three pairs of feature extraction libraries. Feature categories are indicated on the *x*-axis, and index-to-feature name mapping is provided in the Appendix.

the Appendix) and the metric *SC* on the *y*-axis [the count of ROIs (cell colonies) for which classification labels differ between two feature extraction libraries (see the inset in Fig. 7.12)].

Based on this analysis, we concluded that the variation of intensity features had no impact on classification. However, 9 out of 17 shape features (52.9%) and 66 out of 68 textural features (97.1%) had an impact on classification outcomes.

8. Summary

This chapter focused on object measurements or features from 2D microscopy images. In the presence of many open-source and commercial image feature extraction libraries, object measurements from images were evaluated in terms of their variability across multiple open-source libraries. The impact of object feature variability was quantified by analyzing feature-based classification outcomes. By characterizing these feature variations across Python scikit-image, CellProfiler, MaZda, ImageJ/Fiji, and in-house Java libraries, we concluded 15.6% of 32 intensity features, 47.9% of 71 shape features, and 88.2% of 68 textural features differ in value. These feature variations had no impact on classification outcomes based on intensity features but had negative impact on classification based on shape features in 52.9% and based on textural features in 97.1% of single feature classifications.

As one part of this work, we are also disseminating the web image processing pipeline (WIPP) system, which integrates heterogeneous image feature libraries, executes feature calculations, and shares hyperlinked image feature values with computational provenance artifacts. Scientists can use WIPP for publishing traceable 2D image measurements. The WIPP system installation is simplified using a Docker container and is available at https://isg.nist.gov/deepzoomweb/software/wipp. We plan to upgrade the integrated image extraction libraries to their latest versions over time.

The study focused exclusively on open-source image feature extraction libraries because otherwise, the sources of feature variability could not be identified. We did not include software that uses commercial platforms, as explained in the disclaimer at the end of this chapter. While feature engineering inside deep-learning models has demonstrated a good deal of promise in recent years, we did not include features from convolutional layers of deep-learning models in this study because the mathematical and semantic meanings of those features are missing. Thus, relating those features would be almost impossible across feature extraction libraries, deep-learning architectures, parameters, and selections of training data subsets. Finally, we did not include hardware-accelerated [central processing unit (CPU)/graphics processing unit (GPU) or field-programmable gate array (FPGA)] software for image feature extraction because GPU-accelerated image feature extraction has been missing in the open-source libraries.

The overall study documented the need for standard definitions of widely used image features. In the absence of standards, there is a need for gathering provenance information to achieve transparency of image measurements and reproducible research. As of now, if a laboratory performs a complex experimental design for drug treatment or scientific discoveries, then feature-based classification results of data analyses will depend on the choice of the image feature extraction library. Thus, scientists must keep provenance information about the libraries and their parameters used for their analysis. Otherwise, the results would not be reproducible between laboratories, and the ultimate conclusions derived from the same experimental data may differ.

Standard definitions of widely used image features would also make object measurements more likely to be optimized for speed of execution and memory consumption. As reported in Ref. [37], the in-house Java package has the fastest CPU computation time for a large number of small images (8162 ROIs in 238 images of size 446 kB) with the speed-up factor of 2.81 (Python) and 36.55 (ImageJ/Fiji). However, against a large image (200 ROIs in one image with a size of 1.9 GB), Python is the most efficient, with a factor of 3.92 (ImageJ/Fiji) and 2.51 (Java), while CellProfiler would not run due to its memory consumption exceeding our 10-GB limit. In the future, these benchmarks could motivate the development of memory-efficient and hardware-accelerated implementations.

Appendix: Online information about the work

The reader can find detailed information about the work discussed in this chapter and download the metadata files from https://isg.nist.gov/deepzoomweb/resources/featureVariability/index.html.

The web pages contain information about the feature list, the feature index to feature name mapping, and all the numerical data required to plot Figs. 7.8–7.12.

The numerical feature values have been postprocessed to deliver interactive interfaces to traceable results of this image feature variability study. The set of interactive graphs and tables is publicly available from the abovementioned web page. The web pages cited in this chapter allow readers to identify interactively image features that differ across open-source feature extraction libraries and to trace the numerical feature values to the original (persistent) images used for quantification.

Acknowledgments

We would like to acknowledge Mohamed Ouladi, Antonio Cardone, Antoine Vandecreme, Julien Amelot, Philippe Dessauw, and Antoine Gerardin from the Computational Science in Metrology project at NIST, who have contributed to the code development of the web image feature extraction system. We also would like to acknowledge the following NIST colleagues for their support and input: Kiran Bhadriraju, Michael Halter, Subhash Sista, John Elliott, and Anne Plant (of the Material Measurement Laboratory at NIST) for acquiring the test image collection and creating the cell colony annotations.

Disclaimer

Commercial products are identified in this document in order to specify the experimental procedure adequately. Such identification is not intended to imply recommendation or endorsement by NIST, nor is it intended to imply that the products identified are necessarily the best ones available for this purpose.

We used the words *Python* and *Java* to refer to specific implementations of image feature extractors (the Python scikit-image and in-house developed Java libraries) written in these distinct programming languages. While we used the two words as abbreviated names for libraries, we do not intend to imply that one of the programming languages is better than the other.

References

[1] S. van der Walt, et al., scikit-image: image processing in Python, PeerJ 2 (2014) e453.
[2] M. Lamprecht, D. Sabatini, A. Carpenter, CellProfiler^{TM}: free, versatile software for automated biological image analysis, BioTechniques 42 (1) (2007) 71–75.
[3] P.M. Szczypiński, M. Strzelecki, A. Materka, A. Klepaczko, MaZda—A software package for image texture analysis, Comput. Methods Prog. Biomed. 94 (1) (2009) 66–76.
[4] J. Schindelin, et al., Fiji: an open-source platform for biological-image analysis, Nat. Methods 9 (7) (2012) 676–682.
[5] N.V. Orlov, L. Shamir, T. Macura, J. Johnston, D.M. Eckley, I.G. Goldberg, WND-CHARM: Multipurpose image classification using compound image transforms, Pattern Recogn. Lett. 29 (11) (2008) 1684–1693.

[6] Open source development, OpenCV (Open Source Computer Vision Library), *web page,* (2000). [Online]. Available: https://opencv.org/. (Accessed 19 December 2017).

[7] Oracle Java 1.7, Java ImageIO, *web page*(1993) [Online]. Available: https://docs.oracle.com/javase/7/docs/api/javax/imageio/ImageIO.html. (Accessed 19 December 2017).

[8] K. Bhadriraju, et al., Large-scale time-lapse microscopy of Oct4 expression in human embryonic stem cell colonies, Stem Cell Res. 17 (1) (2016) 122–129.

[9] P. Bajcsy, et al., Enabling Interactive Measurements from Large Coverage Microscopy, IEEE Comput. 49 (7) (2016) 70–79.

[10] A. Vandecreme, et al., From image tiles to web-based interactive measurements in one stop, Micros. Today 25 (1) (2017) 18–27.

[11] M.V. Boland, R.F. Murphy, A neural network classifier capable of recognizing the patterns of all major subcellular structures in fluorescence microscope images of HeLa cells, Bioinformatics 17 (12) (2001) 1213–1223.

[12] A.E. Carpenter, Extracting rich information from images, Methods Mol. Biol. 486 (2009) 193–211.

[13] The Mathworks Inc., MATLAB and Image Processing Toolbox Release 2015b, *MathWorks Inc.*, 2015. [Online]. Available: http://www.mathworks.com/help/images/index.html. Accessed 16 March 2016.

[14] G. David Lowe, Distinctive image features from scale-invariant keypoints, Int. J. Comput. Vis. 60 (2) (2004) 91–110.

[15] H. Bay, A. Ess, T. Tuytelaars, L. Van Gool, Speeded-Up Robust Features (SURF), Comput. Vis. Image Underst. 110 (3) (2008) 346–359.

[16] N. Dalal, W. Triggs, Histograms of Oriented Gradients for Human Detection, in: *2005 IEEE Comput. Soc. Conf. Comput. Vis. Pattern Recognit. CVPR05*, vol. 1, no. 3, 2004, pp. 886–893.

[17] J. Kannala, E. Rahtu, BSIF: Binarized statistical image features, in: *21st Int. Conf. Pattern Recognit.*, no. Icpr, 2012, pp. 1363–1366.

[18] B. Yang, S. Chen, A comparative study on local binary pattern (LBP) based face recognition: LBP histogram versus LBP image, Neurocomputing 120 (2013) 365–379.

[19] J. Ren, X. Jiang, J. Yuan, Relaxed Local Ternary Pattern for Face Recognition, in: ICIP 2013, no. 1, 2013, pp. 3680–3684.

[20] B. Julesz, A brief outline of the texton theory of human vision, Trends Neuorsci. 7 (2) (1984) 41–45.

[21] W. Liu, Z. Wang, X. Liu, N. Zeng, Y. Liu, F.E. Alsaadi, A survey of deep neural network architectures and their applications, Neurocomputing 234 (2017) 11–26.

[22] S. Bahrampour, N. Ramakrishnan, L. Schott, M. Shah, Comparative Study of Deep Learning Software Frameworks, Arxiv - a Repos. Electron. Prepr, 2016.

[23] S. Mallat, Understanding Deep Convolutional Networks, Philos. Trans. A 374 (20150203) (2016) 1–17.

[24] V. Badrinarayanan, A. Kendall, R. Cipolla, SegNet: A Deep Convolutional Encoder-Decoder Architecture for Image Segmentation, Arxiv—a Repos. Electron. Prepr, 2015, pp. 1–14.

[25] J. Heaton, An Empirical Analysis of Feature Engineering for Predictive Modeling, Arxiv - a Repos. Electron. Prepr, 1701.07852, 2017, p. 6.

[26] H.-F. Yu, et al., Feature engineering and classifier ensemble for KDD cup, in: *JMLR: Workshop and Conference Proceedings*, 2010, 2010, pp. 379–388.

[27] P. Szczypinski, M. Strzelecki, A. Materka, A. Klepaczko, Mazda software; a computer program for calculation of texture parameters (features) in digitized images, Comput. Methods Prog. Biomed. 94 (1) (2009) 66–76.

[28] M. Strzelecki, P. Szczypinski, A. Materka, A. Klepaczko, A software tool for automatic classification and segmentation of 2D/3D medical images, Nucl. Instrum. Methods Phys. Res. Sect. A Accel. Spectrom. Detect. Assoc. Equip. 702 (Feb. 2013) 137–140.

[29] A. Materka, MaZda User's Manual, Lodz, 1999.

[30] I. NIST, Image Features, *web page*. [Online]. Available: https://isg.nist.gov/deepzoomweb/stemcellfeatures, 2016. Accessed 19 December 2017.

[31] E. Deelman, et al., Pegasus a workflow management system for science automation, Futur. Gener. Comput. Syst. 46 (2015) 17–35.

[32] M.N. Gurcan, L. Boucheron, A. Can, A. Madabhushi, N. Rajpoot, B. Yener, Histopathological image analysis: a review, IEEE Rev. Biomed. Eng. 1 (2009) 147–171.

[33] J. Chalfoun, M. Majurski, K. Bhadriraju, S. Lund, P. Bajcsy, M. Brady, Background intensity correction for terabyte-sized time-lapse images, J. Microsc. 257 (3) (2015) 226–238.

[34] J. Chalfoun, M. Majurski, T. Blattner, W. Keyrouz, P. Bajcsy, M.C. Brady, MIST: Accurate and scalable microscopy image stitching method with stage modeling and error minimization, Nat. Sci. Rep. (2017).

[35] J. Chalfoun, M. Majurski, A. Peskin, C. Breen, P. Bajcsy, Empirical gradient threshold technique for automated segmentation across image modalities and cell lines, J. Microsc. 260 (1) (2014) 86–99.

[36] J. Chalfoun, M. Majurski, A. Dima, M. Halter, K. Bhadriraju, M. Brady, Lineage mapper: a versatile cell and particle tracker, Sci. Rep. 6 (2016) 36984.

[37] M. Simon, J. Chalfoun, M. Brady, P. Bajcsy, Do We Trust Image Measurements? Variability, Accuracy and Traceability of Image Features, in: IEEE International Conference on Big Data, 2016.

[38] A. Materka, M. Strzelecki, Texture Analysis Methods – A Review, Lodz, 1998.

[39] R.M. Haralick, K. Shanmugam, I. Dinstein, Textural Features for Image Classification, IEEE Trans. Syst. Man. Cybern. 3 (6) (1973) 610–621.

[40] T. Kobayashi, D. Sundaram, K. Nakata, H. Tsurui, Gray-level co-occurrence matrix analysis of several cell types in mouse brain using resolution-enhanced photothermal microscopy, J. Biomed. Opt. 22 (3) (2017), 36011.

CHAPTER 8

Deep learning-based nuclei segmentation and classification in histopathology images with application to imaging genomics

Dimitris Metaxas*, Hui Qu*, Gregory Riedlinger[†], Pengxiang Wu*, Qiaoying Huang*, Jingru Yi*, and Subhajyoti De[†]
*Rutgers University, Department of Computer Science, Piscataway, NJ, United States
[†]Rutgers Cancer Institute of New Jersey, New Brunswick, NJ, United States

Contents

1. Joint nuclei segmentation and classification in histopathology images

Histopathological assessment remains a cornerstone of the clinical diagnosis and classification of cancer. The underlying tissue architectures in histopathological images provide a wealth of information about the nature of disease, cytogenetic abnormalities, and characteristics of the microenvironment [1]. For example, malignant tumor cells can be distinguished from benign cells by the features of their nuclei [1], and the extent of lymphocyte infiltration in the microenvironment often has prognostic significance [2]. Furthermore, phenotypic variations among tumor cells, which are indicative of intratumor heterogeneity, have consequences for treatment strategies for cancer patients [3]. Therefore, the development of algorithms for refined segmentation and classification of histopathological structures, such as lymphocytes and cancer nuclei, can help improve the clinical management of cancer.

Nuclei segmentation and classification are both challenging tasks. The size of nuclei is much smaller compared to that of glands or organs, and the nuclei are often close to each

Computer Vision for Microscopy Image Analysis
https://doi.org/10.1016/B978-0-12-814972-0.00008-4

other, making it hard to segment individual nuclei accurately. The fine-grained classification of nuclei is also difficult due to the large interclass and intraclass variances in nuclear shapes and textures. Traditional methods like thresholding, watershed, clustering, and region growing [4] are not able to cope with these challenges well. Early learning-based methods learn to segment or classify nuclei using low-level handcrafted features such as color, texture, and gradients of geometric features [5–7], or learn kernel and hashing functions for classification based on handcrafted features [8–10], which have limited representation capability.

Recently, deep convolutional neural networks (CNNs) have achieved great success for image classification and segmentation [11–14]. Furthermore, many deep learning-based methods have been proposed for histopathology image analysis [15, 16], such as metastasis detection [17, 18], invasive cancer localization [19], nuclei segmentation [15, 20–22], and nuclei classification [23, 24]. Xing et al. [20] utilized CNNs to obtain an initial shape of nuclei and then to separate individual nuclei using a deformable model. In Refs. [15, 21], nuclei segmentation is performed by classifying the pixels into classes using a patch around each pixel as the input to an image classification network. The computational cost is large because each patch predicts only 1 pixel. Fully convolutional neural networks (FCNs) [13, 14], which directly output the same size of segmentation map as the input image, are more efficient and effective for image segmentation tasks and have been used in nuclei segmentation [22]. Compared to nuclei segmentation, there are fewer works about nuclei fine-grained classification using deep learning. Sirinukunwattana et al. [23] built two CNNs to detect nuclei and then classified them into subcategories. Zhou et al. [24] proposed a sibling CNN with objectiveness prior to detect and classify nuclei simultaneously.

Although the current methods have achieved good accuracy, they focus on segmentation or classification. They are not able to produce the pixelwise masks of different types of nuclei at the same time, and thus they cannot generate both nucleus features and spatial distributions, which are important for histopathology image analysis. Actually, the network structures for two tasks are similar; both need to extract feature representations from the input image.

In this chapter, we propose a framework to solve these two tasks jointly. As opposed to previous methods, our model outputs the segmentation map for every type of nuclei and the background, which can segment individual nuclei, as well as classifying them into tumor, lymphocyte, and stroma subcategories. In addition, we use one more channel to predict the contours of nuclei, aiming at separating any touching nuclei. To improve the segmentation accuracy further, we take advantage of the perceptual loss [25] that can measure small differences in two images. In addition, transfer learning is utilized to promote the training due to the small size of the annotated dataset.

1.1 Training data generation

1.1.1 Dataset

To evaluate the performance of joint nuclei segmentation and classification algorithms, we annotated a dataset that consists of 40 H&E stained tissue images from eight lung adenocarcinoma or lung squamous cell carcinoma cases, with each case having five images about 900×900 in size. There are around 24,000 annotated nuclei in the dataset, and each nucleus is marked as one of the following three types: a tumor nucleus, a lymphocyte nucleus, and a stroma (e.g., fibroblasts, macrophages, neutrophils, and endothelial cells) nucleus. For each image, we use one labeled image to encode the segmentation mask and classify the class information of each nucleus. In a ground–truth label image, pixels of value 0 are in the background. Pixels that have the same positive integer belong to an individual nucleus. Therefore, each nucleus has a unique ID, as shown in Fig. 8.1B. The integer value ID also indicates the class of the nucleus, as follows (where *mod* is the modular operation):

- Tumor nucleus: $mod(id, 3) = 0$
- Lymphocyte nucleus: $mod(id, 3) = 1$
- Stroma nucleus: $mod(id, 3) = 2$

It is easy to extract the class information from this encoding. Fig. 8.1 shows an example of an original image and its labels.

In many machine learning tasks, a dataset consists of three parts: a training set that is used to train the model, a validation set for choosing the best model during training, and a test set that aims to evaluate the performance of the trained model. Following this rule, this dataset is split into three parts: 24 images for training, 8 for validation, and the remaining 8 for testing. The training set contains three images for each case, and the other two sets have one image for each case.

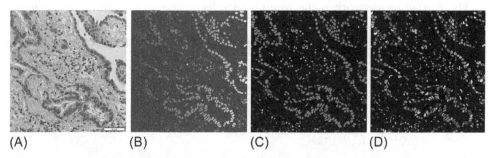

(A)   (B)   (C)   (D)

Fig. 8.1 Example of an image and its labels. (A) Original image; (B) ground-truth label; (C) classification label, red, green, and blue (dark gray, gray, and light gray) represent tumor, lymphocyte, and stroma nuclei, respectively); (D) segmentation label (distinct colors indicate different nuclei).

1.1.2 Preprocessing

As the tissue images come from different patients, there is a large variation in image colors, which has a negative effect on the segmentation results. Therefore, we use the color transfer method [26] to eliminate the color variation of these images. This method transforms the color of an image to a similar color as the referenced image in a three-step process:

1. Transform both images from the RGB color space to the $l\alpha\beta$ color space, aiming at removing the correlation of different color axes.
2. Adjust the mean and standard deviation of source image according to the referenced image.
3. Transform the corrected image from the $l\alpha\beta$ color space to the RGB color space.

This method is fast and effective to normalize all images in the dataset. Two images before and after color normalization are shown in Fig. 8.2.

Data augmentation is crucial for training deep neural networks when only a few training images are available, which is exactly the case in our task. For each large image in the training set, we extract 16 image patches with size 250×250 uniformly with overlap, resulting in 384 small image patches. For each patch, a 224×224 image is randomly cropped as the network input. Other augmentations include random scale, random horizontal and vertical flip, random affine transformation, random elastic transformation, random rotation, and normalization with mean and standard deviation by channel.

1.2 Deep learning-based segmentation and classification

1.2.1 Network structure

Our proposed framework is shown in Fig. 8.3. It consists of two parts: the prediction network, which generates the segmentation mask of each type of nuclei; and the perceptual loss network, which computes the perceptual loss between the predicted and ground-truth labels.

The prediction network is the routine encoder-decoder structure. We utilize the powerful representation ability of residual networks [12] to extract the features. The encoder is from ResNet34 [12], without the average pooling and fully connected layers,

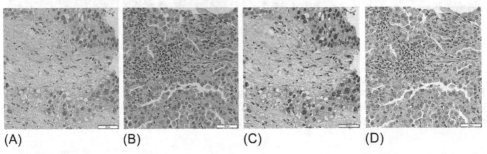

(A)   (B)   (C)   (D)

Fig. 8.2 Images before and after color normalization. (A) image 1, (B) image 2, (C) image 1 after color normalization, (D) image 2 after color normalization.

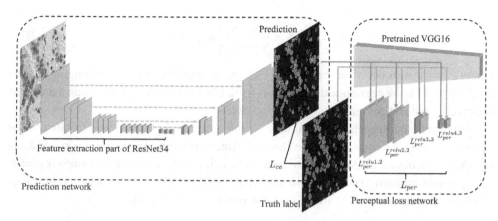

Fig. 8.3 System overview. Our framework consists of the prediction network and the perceptual loss network. The prediction network takes the feature extraction part of ResNet34 as the encoder and outputs the segmentation map of different types of nuclei. The loss network uses the fixed, pretrained VGG16 model as a feature extractor and computes the perceptual loss.

and is initialized with the pretrained parameters from image classification tasks. It extracts features of the input image layer by layer, from low level to high level. The decoder part recovers the resolution of feature maps and generates the segmentation results, with the help of the skip connections between the encoder and the decoder. This network outputs five probability maps: the background, the inner part of tumor nuclei, the inner part of lymphocyte nuclei, the inner part of stroma nuclei, and the contours of all nuclei. The contour map mainly aims to capture the contours of crowded and touching nuclei. As a result, the predicted inner parts of each nucleus are not connected, and we can obtain the instance segmentation of individual nuclei. The final nuclei mask is generated by a morphological dilation operation. In this way, we can obtain each individual nucleus without much extra effort.

The perceptual loss network is utilized to improve the segmentation accuracy of details in the image. It originates from Johnson et al. [25], in which the authors compute the loss between high-level features of the transformed image and the original image. The pretrained VGG16 model [27] is a feature extractor and is fixed during training and testing. Four levels of features are extracted using this network for the output of the prediction network and the ground-truth label (i.e., feature maps after the last ReLU layer of the first, second, third, and fourth blocks of the VGG16 model), denoted as $relu1\_2$, $relu2\_2$, $relu3\_3$, and $relu4\_3$. The mean squared loss is then computed between the feature sets of two inputs.

1.2.2 Loss function

The loss function of the method consists of two parts. The first part is the cross-entropy loss for five classes (i.e., background, inside tumor, inside lymphocyte, inside stroma, and contour). It is defined as

$$\mathcal{L}_{ce}(y, t, w) = -\frac{1}{N}\sum_{i=1}^{N}\sum_{m=1}^{5} w_i t_i^{(m)} \log y_i^{(m)} \tag{8.1}$$

where N is the number of all the pixels, $y_i^{(m)}$ is the probability of pixel i belonging to class m, $t_i^{(m)} \in \{0, 1\}$ is the corresponding ground-truth label of class m, w_i is the optional weight for pixel i, and the default value is 1 for all pixels.

When training deep-learning models, a problem is the highly skewed frequencies of various classes in the dataset (i.e., the class imbalance problem). For example, in our dataset, the frequency of nuclear contour pixels is much less than that of noncontour pixels. One possible solution to this problem is to assign different values of w_i for different classes of pixels. We set the weight using a similar method in Ref. [14]:

$$w(x_i) = 1 + w_0 \cdot \exp\left(-\frac{(d_1(x_i) + d_2(x_i))^2}{2\sigma^2}\right) \tag{8.2}$$

where d_1 and d_2 are the distances to the nearest and the second-nearest nuclei, respectively. In the experiments, we set $\sigma = 5$ pixels and $w_0 = 10$. In this setting, pixels between close or touching nuclei are assigned much larger weights because those pixels are more important to split nuclei.

The second part is the perceptual loss. Let us denote the trained VGG16 model as a function f. The features after the ReLU layer of the kth block can be written as $f_k(x)$, where x is the input of VGG16. The size of kth-level features is denoted as $C_k \times H_k \times W_k$. The perceptual loss is

$$\mathcal{L}_{per}(\hat{y}, t) = \frac{1}{4}\sum_{k=1}^{4}\mathcal{L}_{per}^{k}(\hat{y}, t)$$
$$\mathcal{L}_{per}^{k}(\hat{y}, t) = \frac{1}{C_k H_k W_k}\|f_k(\hat{y}) - f_k(t)\|_2^2 \tag{8.3}$$

where $\hat{y} = \arg\max y$ is the prediction map obtained from the output probability map y.

The loss function of the whole network is

$$\mathcal{L} = \mathcal{L}_{ce} + \beta\mathcal{L}_{per} \tag{8.4}$$

where β is a parameter that adjusts the weight of the perceptual loss and is set to 0.1 in the experiments.

1.2.3 Postprocessing

Because our model outputs the inside areas of each nucleus, we need postprocessing to get the final segmentation and classification results. The initial segmentation map is obtained by setting contour pixels as the background. Then we adopt several simple morphological operations (i.e., removal of small areas, connected component labeling, and dilation with a disk filter) to generate the final results. The dilation operation aims to recover the whole mask of nuclei from the inside mask.

1.2.4 Evaluation methods

The performance of our method is evaluated using common metrics in segmentation and classification tasks. For nuclei segmentation, we use the F1-score to measure the detection accuracy. It is defined as the harmonic mean of precision and recall, as follows:

$$F1 = \frac{2 \times precision \times recall}{precision + recall} = \frac{2TP}{2TP + FP + FN} \tag{8.5}$$

where TP, FP, and FN are the number of true positives, false positives, and false negatives, respectively. A segmented nucleus is considered as a true positive if it overlaps with at least 50% of a ground-truth nucleus. Otherwise, it is a false positive. All ground-truth nuclei that have no corresponding segmented nuclei are treated as false negatives.

The object-level Dice coefficient [28], Jaccard index [29], and Hausdorff distance are used to measure the segmentation accuracy. The Dice coefficient and Jaccard index measure how well the ground-truth object G and predicted object S overlap with each other:

$$\text{Dice}(G, S) = \frac{2|G \cap S|}{|G| + |S|}, \quad \text{Jaccard}(G, S) = \frac{|G \cap S|}{|G \cup S|} \tag{8.6}$$

where $|\cdot|$ denotes set cardinality. The higher these values are, the better the segmented results overlap with the ground-truth objects. The Hausdorff distance is utilized to measure the shape similarity between G and S, and defined as

$$\text{Haus}(G, S) = \max \left\{ \sup_{x \in G} \inf_{y \in S} d(x, y), \; \sup_{y \in S} \inf_{x \in G} d(x, y) \right\} \tag{8.7}$$

A lower Hausdorff distance indicates better shape similarity for two objects. Directly applying these metrics to the whole segmentation image results in pixel-level accuracies, which is not enough to represent the performance of instance-level segmentation. Therefore, we employ the object-level metrics defined in Ref. [30]:

$$M_{obj}(G, S) = \frac{1}{2} \left\{ \sum_{i=1}^{n_G} \gamma_i M(G_i, S_i) + \sum_{j=1}^{n_S} \sigma_j M(\widetilde{G}_j, \widetilde{S}_j) \right\} \tag{8.8}$$

$$\gamma_i = \frac{|G_i|}{\sum_{n=1}^{n_G} |G_n|}, \quad \sigma_j = \frac{|S_j|}{\sum_{n=1}^{n_G} |S_n|} \tag{8.9}$$

where M can be a Dice coefficient, Jaccard index, or Hausdorff distance; n_G and n_S are the number of objects in the ground-truth image and segmented image, respectively; G_i is a ground-truth object; S_i is its corresponding true positive segmentation; $\widetilde{S}_j$ is a segmented object; and $\widetilde{G}_j$ is its true positive ground-truth. Here, true positive has the same meaning as that in F1-score. The object-level metrics measure not only how well the segmented objects overlap with ground-truth objects, but also how well the ground-truth objects overlap with segmented ones. The area of each object is also taken into consideration by applying the weights γ_i and σ_j.

For nuclei fine-grained classification, we only consider the accuracy among true-positive segmented nuclei because they have the true class labels. For those false, positively segmented nuclei, no ground-truth labels are available. The accuracy is not sufficient to represent the performance due to the various numbers of true positives. Therefore, we list the number of correctly classified nuclei for reference.

1.3 Experimental results

Here, we test the proposed method on the lung cancer dataset mentioned in Section 1.1 and compare it to two popular approaches for segmentation. One is the fully convolutional network proposed by Long et al. [13], which is the first FCN used for segmentation tasks. The other is U-Net [14], which has been widely used in medical image segmentation. Both networks output five probability maps as ours. For all models, we trained 300 epochs with the Adam optimizer. The learning rate, batch size, and weight decay are 0.0001, 8, and 0.0001, respectively.

The nuclei segmentation and classification results using FCN-8s, U-Net and our method are shown in Tables 8.1 and 8.2. It can be observed that all three models have achieved relatively good segmentation and fine-grained classification results, showing that our idea of combining the two tasks is feasible. Compared to FCN-8s and U-Net, our method makes improvements on the segmentation of all types of nuclei, especially lymphocytes. The improvements to subcategory nuclei are larger than those to all nuclei because the classification results also affect the subclass metrics (i.e., wrongly classified nuclei have no corresponding ground-truth ones, thus reducing the F1, Dice coefficient, and Jaccard values and increasing the Hausdorff distance). For nuclei classification, our method achieves the best accuracies except for lymphocytes. However, the number of correctly classified lymphocytes is 32% and 8% more than that of FCN-8s and U-Net, respectively. Therefore, our method also outperforms FCN-8s and U-Net on the fine-grained classification.

To illustrate the effects of transfer learning and the perceptual loss, we report the results for our model without perceptual loss or the pretrained weights of the encoder part. It is evident that both techniques can promote the performance of segmentation and classification. The results without transfer learning are worse than those without the perceptual loss, showing that transfer learning is more important than the perceptual loss for this small dataset. Without transfer learning, the training images are not sufficient to train the whole network well enough.

Table 8.1 Nuclei segmentation results of various types of nuclei on the test set using FCN-8s [13], U-Net [14], our method without perceptual loss (Ours w.o. $\mathcal{L}_{per}$), our method without transfer learning (Ours w.o. TL), and our method

Method		FCN-8s [13]	U-Net [14]	Ours w.o. $\mathcal{L}_{per}$	Ours w.o. TL	Ours
All	F1	0.8630	0.8735	0.8742	0.8652	**0.8859**
	$Dice_{obj}$	0.8418	0.8651	0.8695	0.8633	**0.8759**
	$Jaccard_{obj}$	0.7696	0.8092	0.8141	0.8041	**0.8205**
	$Haus_{obj}$	5.17	4.68	4.40	4.67	**4.14**
Tumor	F1	0.7775	0.8022	0.8059	0.7970	**0.8263**
	$Dice_{obj}$	0.8072	0.8313	0.8385	0.8311	**0.8459**
	$Jaccard_{obj}$	0.7417	0.7803	0.7877	0.7764	**0.7949**
	$Haus_{obj}$	8.52	7.58	6.93	7.43	**6.66**
Lymphocyte	F1	0.5274	0.6198	0.6204	0.6346	**0.6709**
	$Dice_{obj}$	0.5653	0.6220	0.6370	0.6257	**0.6677**
	$Jaccard_{obj}$	0.5219	0.5893	0.6039	0.5924	**0.6323**
	$Haus_{obj}$	41.52	36.99	28.13	31.75	**27.26**
Stroma	F1	0.5619	0.5928	0.6186	0.5850	**0.6223**
	$Dice_{obj}$	0.5281	0.5663	**0.5986**	0.5658	0.5889
	$Jaccard_{obj}$	0.4670	0.5150	**0.5458**	0.5125	0.5361
	$Haus_{obj}$	17.88	15.93	**14.36**	15.88	14.99

Note: Bold numbers indicates the best values.

Table 8.2 Nuclei fine-grained classification accuracies (%) of different types of nuclei on the test set using FCN-8s [13], U-Net [14], our method without perceptual loss (Ours w.o. $\mathcal{L}_{per}$), our method without transfer learning (Ours w.o. TL), and our method

Method	FCN-8s [13]	U-Net [14]	Ours w.o. $\mathcal{L}_{per}$	Ours w.o. TL	Ours
All	80.96 (3448)	83.00 (3653)	83.86 (3709)	83.19 (3618)	**84.75** (3735)
Tumor	85.14 (2103)	88.72 (2139)	89.56 (2144)	**90.66** (2059)	90.29 (2139)
Lymphocyte	**81.43** (421)	75.85 (515)	80.00 (488)	72.73 (544)	75.44 (556)
Stroma	72.64 (924)	76.20 (999)	75.90 (1077)	76.32 (1015)	**79.94** (1040)

Note: Bold numbers indicates the best value. The number of correctly classified nuclei is listed in parentheses for reference.

For the subcategory results of both tasks, the performance on tumor nuclei is the best because it is easier to distinguish. The shape and size of some lymphocyte and stroma nuclei are very similar, resulting in relatively lower segmentation and classification accuracies. Actually, the segmentation and classification of subcategory nuclei affect each other. High segmentation accuracy is beneficial for classification, and high classification accuracy reduces the number of unpaired segmented and ground-truth nuclei, which can increase the segmentation metrics. Some representative image results of segmentation and classification are shown in Fig. 8.4.

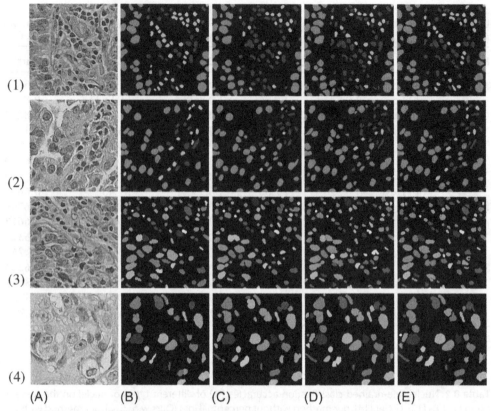

Fig. 8.4 Representative image results of FCN-8s, U-Net, and the proposed method. The top two rows (1) and (2) are the results of classification. Red, green, and blue (dark gray, gray, and light gray) represent tumor, lymphocyte, and stroma nuclei, respectively. The bottom two rows (3) and (4) are the results of instance-level segmentation. The different colors indicate individual nuclei. (A) Subimage, (B) true label, (C) FCN-8s, (D) U-net, and (E) Ours.

2. Applications to imaging genomics

Imaging genomics is an emerging field that explores the phenotype–genotype relationships (i.e., the relationships between imaging features of a disease and genomic features like genetic alternations, gene expression patterns, and other genome-related characteristics [31]). Imaging features can provide a comprehensive spatial view of the entire tumor, as well as the information on peritumoral regions [32]. Some features that seem irrelevant may have clinical significance. Genomic features, such as gene mutations, are at the molecular level and lead to the cause and development of cancer. However, it remains unclear how the genomic features affect many cancers because multiple gene mutations are often involved. Uncovering correlations between imaging and genetic features can promote the understanding of some biologic mechanisms and pathways of gene expression and lead to finding more biomarkers that are predictive of clinical outcomes, which are beneficial for cancer diagnosis and treatment.

In imaging genomics, imaging features often come from modalities like computed tomography (CT) and magnetic resonance imaging (MRI). Many studies have tried to correlate such imaging features with genomic data [32]. However, features from histopathology images are important as well. The tissue structures from those images also contain underlying molecular profiles and are related to genetic alterations and gene expression patterns. Finding the genotype-phenotype correlations for histopathology images provide a better understanding of tumor biology and further improve the precision of clinical predictions [33]. The whole slide images (WSIs) obtained by digitalization of pathologic specimens often have high image quality and contain hundreds of millions of pixels; thus, the manual feature extraction is laborious and subjective, and may not be representative of the whole image. The automatic nuclei segmentation and classification method proposed in Section 1 can be applied here for imaging feature extraction. In this section, we introduce two possible applications for the extracted features in imaging genomics.

2.1 Intratumor heterogeneity

Intratumor heterogeneity (i.e., genetic, molecular, and phenotypic differences between tumor cells within a single tumor) is a major challenge for clinical management of cancer patients, contributing to therapeutic failure, disease relapses, and drug resistance. For example, in the work [34], the authors mention that a small part of subclones within chronic myeloid leukemia (CML) is resistant to the targeted drug tyrosine kinase inhibitors that should be effective, which may result from intratumor heterogeneity. The intratumor phenotypic heterogeneity has been observed since the earliest days of cancer biology [35], and recent findings suggest that there is extensive intratumor genetic heterogeneity in all major cancer types [36]. But it remains to be understood how the genetic heterogeneity relates to intratumor heterogeneity at the pathway and cell phenotype levels.

Based on the framework in Section 1, we are able to identify the accurate locations and shapes of tumor and nontumor nuclei in histopathological slides and then compute the spatial heterogeneity according to their locations, which can be associated with genetic heterogeneity.

2.1.1 Intratumor spatial heterogeneity

The term *spatial heterogeneity* refers to the spatial difference of tumor cells in a single tumor. Such a difference may lead to a situation in which a biopsy does not provide an adequate reflection of the phenotypic composition of the whole tumor [35]. With the locations of all nuclei in a WSI, we can use some measures in ecology, such as q-statistic [37] and diversity indices, to reflect the extent of local and regional heterogeneity.

The q-statistic measures the spatial stratified heterogeneity, which may imply the existence of distinct mechanisms in strata/areas (i.e., the various tumor subclones). It ranges from 0 to 1, where 0 means the spatial stratification of heterogeneity is not significant and 1 means high significance. There are two concepts when computing a q-value, unit, and stratum. A *unit* is the smallest block that contains tumor and/or nontumor cells. A *stratum* is a relatively large area that consists of a number of units. The split of strata decides which type of heterogeneity is revealed by the q-statistic. For example, three types of strata are illustrated in Fig. 8.5. The q-values computed from the patch, row, and column strata indicate how heterogeneous the tumor is on blocks, in the vertical and horizontal directions, respectively. The steps to compute a q-statistic of that region are:

1. Divide the tumor region into different strata.
2. Remove strata that are blank or contain a small part of tissue if the ratio of tissue patches in that stratum is less than a threshold.
3. For each remaining stratum h, compute the stratum variance σ_h^2 and the stratum size N_h.
4. Compute the variance and size of the whole population, σ^2, N.
5. Compute the q-statistic of each tumor region by

$$q = 1 - \frac{\sum_{h=1}^{L} N_h \sigma_h^2}{N\sigma^2} \tag{8.10}$$

After obtaining q-statistic values for all the tumor regions, the q-statistic of the whole slide image can be calculated by a weighted average of all regions' q-values according to the regions' areas.

There are several diversity indices that can be used for spatial heterogeneity. The Simpson diversity index [38], introduced by Edward H. Simpson, measures the degree of concentration when individuals are classified into types [38]. It is defined as

$$\lambda = \sum_{i=1}^{R} p_i^2 \tag{8.11}$$

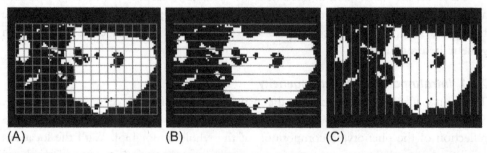

(A)   (B)   (C)

Fig. 8.5 Three types of strata. (A) Patch strata, (B) row strata, (C) column strata. White areas represent tissue regions of the whole slide image.

where R is the total number of species and p_i is the proportion of individuals belonging to the ith species. The measure equals the probability that two entities taken at random from the dataset of interest represent the same type [38]. The lower the value, the higher the diversity is. Another commonly used index is the Shannon index, proposed by Claude Shannon to measure the entropy in strings of text [39] and defined as

$$H' = -\sum_{i=1}^{R} p_i \ln p_i \tag{8.12}$$

The Shannon index measures the uncertainty in predicting the species identity of an individual that is taken at random from the dataset. A large Shannon index indicates high uncertainty in prediction, which means high diversity in the dataset; otherwise, it will be easy to predict the type of species. We can utilize these indices to compute the extent of spatial heterogeneity using the locations of tumor, lymphocyte, and stroma nuclei within a local region or for the whole image.

It is also possible to compute the q-statistic and diversity indices for various clones of tumor cells with the help of immuno-FISH and immunohistochemistry [40, 41], which can identify the known cancer gene mutation status in tumor cells on the slides, and those with similar cancer gene mutation status belong to the same subclone.

2.1.2 Intratumor genetic heterogeneity

During the formation of tumors, the driving genetic mutations are associated with the occurrence of many thousands of somatic genetic alterations [35], resulting in the genetic diversity of tumor cell populations. The clonal evolution in a branching manner may lead to clonal diversity as well [35], contributing to genetic heterogeneity within tumors.

We can use some metrics, such as clone numbers and sizes, to quantify the genetic heterogeneity. Clone numbers and sizes can be inferred using mutation and copy number data such as the following [36]:

1. Collect the somatic single-nucleotide variant (SNV) and copy number variant (CNV) data for the same tumors from TCGA.
2. Estimate the cellular prevalence of each SNV in consideration of CNVs and cluster the cellular prevalence into subpopulations using PyClone [42].
3. The inferred subpopulations are the clones, and the corresponding cellular prevalences are the clone sizes.

With measurements of both spatial and genetic heterogeneity, one can perform some analyses to explore the relationship between phenotype and genotype (e.g., the spatial heterogeneity scores and the number of clones). The relationships may help understand how genetic heterogeneity results in phenotype heterogeneity. Further, multiscale analysis integrating genetic, pathway, and phenotypic heterogeneity will provide fundamental insights into "functional" variability within and across cancers, helping to refine precise approaches to improve the clinical management of cancer patients.

2.2 Tumor-Infiltrating Lymphocytes

Tumor-infiltrating lymphocytes (TILs) are a type of immune cells that have moved from the bloodstream to a tumor. Because lymphocytes can kill tumor cells, researchers have explored the relationship between TILs and clinical outcomes and have found that the presence of high TIL density is associated with better clinical outcomes [43]. In addition, the spatial statistics of TILs correlate with cancer diagnosis and prognosis [44, 45]. Much effort have been exerted to correlate TILs with clinical outcomes, but the relationships between TILs and genetic features have not been well studied. Kochi et al. [46] have shown that genomic markers are highly associated with TIL levels in breast cancer, and TIL-associated genomic signatures can predict chemotherapy responses in several breast cancer subtypes. Therefore, it is meaningful to explore further the correlations between TILs and genomic features in various types of cancers.

The nuclei segmentation and classification method can automatically extract the pixels belonging to lymphocytes in a whole slide image with relatively high accuracy. As a result, we can efficiently compute accurate TIL density/scores instead of evaluating a rough level of TILs manually in most studies. In addition, we are able to obtain the spatial maps of TILs, which can be used to generate local and global spatial structures of lymphocytes or perform hot spot analysis like Ref. [2]. Integrated with genomic features and clinical data, these imaging features can be utilized to find possible genomic biomarkers potentially informative of novel therapeutic strategies. For example, if some imaging features about TILs are favorable for survival, genes that are associated with these features may have similar effects. The integrative analysis also may help us understand the basic biological principles in gene expressions by finding the TIL and genomics features that both have similar effects on clinical outcomes.

3. Conclusion

In this chapter, we proposed a framework that jointly segments and classifies the various types of nuclei from histopathology images. The cross-entropy and perceptual losses are combined to enhance the segmentation of details in the image. We also use transfer learning to better train the model on a small dataset. Experiments show that our method is able to achieve good segmentation and fine-grained classification results simultaneously. We then briefly introduced how to apply the framework to imaging genomics. The segmentation maps of the various types of nuclei generated by our method can be used to analyze the nuclear features and their spatial distributions. These imaging features, integrated with genetic features and clinical outcomes, can be used in analyses of intratumor heterogeneity and tumor-infiltrating lymphocytes to achieve a better understanding of the genotype-phenotype relationship, as well as improving the clinical management of cancer.

References

[1] M.N. Gurcan, L. Boucheron, A. Can, A. Madabhushi, N. Rajpoot, B. Yener, Histopathological image analysis: a review, IEEE Rev. Biomed. Eng. 2 (2009) 147.

[2] S. Nawaz, A. Heindl, K. Koelble, Y. Yuan, Beyond immune density: critical role of spatial heterogeneity in estrogen receptor-negative breast cancer, Mod. Pathol. 28 (6) (2015) 766.

[3] S. Xx, Yu Q, Intra-tumor heterogeneity of cancer cells and its implications for cancer treatment, Acta Pharmacol. Sin. 36 (10) (2015) 1219.

[4] H. Irshad, A. Veillard, L. Roux, D. Racoceanu, Methods for nuclei detection, segmentation, and classification in digital histopathology: a review-current status and future potential, IEEE Rev. Biomed. Eng. 7 (2014) 97–114.

[5] M. Wang, X. Zhou, F. Li, J. Huckins, R.W. King, S.T. Wong, Novel cell segmentation and online svm for cell cycle phase identification in automated microscopy, Bioinformatics 24 (1) (2007) 94–101.

[6] H. Kong, M. Gurcan, K. Belkacem-Boussaid, Partitioning histopathological images: an integrated framework for supervised color-texture segmentation and cell splitting, IEEE Trans. Med. Imaging 30 (9) (2011) 1661–1677.

[7] Y. Al-Kofahi, W. Lassoued, W. Lee, B. Roysam, Improved automatic detection and segmentation of cell nuclei in histopathology images, IEEE Trans. Biomed. Eng. 57 (4) (2010) 841–852.

[8] X. Zhang, F. Xing, H. Su, L. Yang, S. Zhang, High-throughput histopathological image analysis via robust cell segmentation and hashing, Med. Image Anal. 26 (1) (2015) 306–315.

[9] X. Zhang, H. Su, L. Yang, S. Zhang, Fine-grained histopathological image analysis via robust segmentation and large-scale retrieval, in: *Proceedings of the IEEE Conference on Computer Vision and Pattern Recognition*, 2015, pp. 5361–5368.

[10] M. Jiang, S. Zhang, J. Huang, L. Yang, D.N. Metaxas, Scalable histopathological image analysis via supervised hashing with multiple features, Med. Image Anal. 34 (2016) 3–12.

[11] A. Krizhevsky, I. Sutskever, G.E. Hinton, Imagenet classification with deep convolutional neural networks, in: Advances in Neural Information Processing Systems, 2012, pp. 1097–1105.

[12] K. He, X. Zhang, S. Ren, J. Sun, Deep residual learning for image recognition, in: *Proceedings of the IEEE Conference on Computer Vision and Pattern Recognition*, 2016, pp. 770–778.

[13] J. Long, E. Shelhamer, T. Darrell, Fully convolutional networks for semantic segmentation, in: Proceedings of the IEEE Conference on Computer Vision and Pattern Recognition, 2015, pp. 3431–3440.

[14] O. Ronneberger, P. Fischer, T. Brox, U-net: convolutional networks for biomedical image segmentation, in: *International Conference on Medical Image Computing and Computer-Assisted Intervention*, Springer, 2015, pp. 234–241.

[15] A. Janowczyk, A. Madabhushi, Deep learning for digital pathology image analysis: A comprehensive tutorial with selected use cases, J. Pathol. Inform. 7 (2016).

[16] Z. Li, X. Zhang, H. Müller, S. Zhang, Large-scale retrieval for medical image analytics: A comprehensive review, Med. Image Anal. 43 (2018) 66–84.

[17] Y. Liu, K. Gadepalli, M. Norouzi, G.E. Dahl, T. Kohlberger, A. Boyko, S. Venugopalan, A. Timofeev, P.Q. Nelson, G.S. Corrado, et al., Detecting cancer metastases on gigapixel pathology images, *arXiv preprint arXiv*:1703.02442, 2017.

[18] B. Kong, X. Wang, Z. Li, Q. Song, S. Zhang, Cancer metastasis detection via spatially structured deep network, in: *International Conference on Information Processing in Medical Imaging*, Springer, 2017, pp. 236–248.

[19] B. Kong, S. Sun, X. Wang, Q. Song, S. Zhang, Invasive cancer detection utilizing compressed convolutional neural network and transfer learning, in: International Conference on Medical Image Computing and Computer-Assisted Intervention, Springer, 2018, pp. 156–164.

[20] F. Xing, Y. Xie, L. Yang, An automatic learning-based framework for robust nucleus segmentation, IEEE Trans. Med. Imaging 35 (2) (2016) 550–566.

[21] N. Kumar, R. Verma, S. Sharma, S. Bhargava, A. Vahadane, A. Sethi, A dataset and a technique for generalized nuclear segmentation for computational pathology, IEEE Trans. Med. Imaging 36 (7) (2017) 1550–1560.

[22] P. Naylor, M. Laé, F. Reyal, T. Walter, Nuclei segmentation in histopathology images using deep neural networks, in: *Biomedical Imaging (ISBI 2017), 2017 IEEE 14th International Symposium on*, IEEE, 2017, pp. 933–936.

[23] K. Sirinukunwattana, S.E.A. Raza, Y.W. Tsang, D.R. Snead, I.A. Cree, N.M. Rajpoot, Locality sensitive deep learning for detection and classification of nuclei in routine colon cancer histology images, IEEE Trans. Med. Imaging 35 (5) (2016) 1196–1206.

[24] Y. Zhou, Q. Dou, H. Chen, J. Qin, P.A. Heng, Sfcn-opi: Detection and fine-grained classification of nuclei using sibling fcn with objectness prior interaction, in: *Thirty-Second AAAI Conference on Artificial Intelligence*, 2018.

[25] J. Johnson, A. Alahi, L. Fei-Fei, Perceptual losses for real-time style transfer and super-resolution, in: *European Conference on Computer Vision*, Springer, 2016, pp. 694–711.

[26] E. Reinhard, M. Adhikhmin, B. Gooch, P. Shirley, Color transfer between images, IEEE Comput. Graph. Appl. 21 (5) (2001) 34–41.

[27] K. Simonyan, A. Zisserman, Very deep convolutional networks for large-scale image recognition, *arXiv preprint arXiv*:1409.1556, 2014.

[28] L.R. Dice, Measures of the amount of ecologic association between species, Ecology 26 (3) (1945) 297–302.

[29] P. Jaccard, The distribution of the flora in the alpine zone, New Phytol. 11 (2) (1912) 37–50.

[30] K. Sirinukunwattana, D.R. Snead, N.M. Rajpoot, A stochastic polygons model for glandular structures in colon histology images, IEEE Trans. Med. Imaging 34 (11) (2015) 2366–2378.

[31] M.A. Mazurowski, Radiogenomics: what it is and why it is important, J. Am. Coll. Radiol. 12 (8) (2015) 862–866.

[32] H.X. Bai, A.M. Lee, L. Yang, P. Zhang, C. Davatzikos, J.M. Maris, S.J. Diskin, Imaging genomics in cancer research: limitations and promises, Br. J. Radiol. 89 (1061) (2016) 20151030.

[33] L.A. Cooper, J. Kong, D.A. Gutman, W.D. Dunn, M. Nalisnik, D.J. Brat, Novel genotype-phenotype associations in human cancers enabled by advanced molecular platforms and computational analysis of whole slide images, Lab. Investig. 95 (4) (2015) 366.

[34] J. Liu, H. Dang, X.W. Wang, The significance of intertumor and intratumor heterogeneity in liver cancer, Exp. Mol. Med. 50 (1) (2018) e416.

[35] A. Marusyk, V. Almendro, K. Polyak, Intra-tumour heterogeneity: a looking glass for cancer? Nat. Rev. Cancer 12 (5) (2012) 323.

[36] N. Andor, T.A. Graham, M. Jansen, L.C. Xia, C.A. Aktipis, C. Petritsch, H.P. Ji, C.C. Maley, Pan-cancer analysis of the extent and consequences of intratumor heterogeneity, Nat. Med. 22 (1) (2016) 105.

[37] J.F. Wang, T.L. Zhang, B.J. Fu, A measure of spatial stratified heterogeneity, Ecol. Indic. 67 (2016) 250–256.

[38] E.H. Simpson, Measurement of diversity, Nature 163 (1949) 688.

[39] C.E. Shannon, A mathematical theory of communication, Bell Syst. Tech. J. 27 (3) (1948) 379–423.

[40] F.C. Martins, S. De, V. Almendro, M. Gönen, S.Y. Park, J.L. Blum, W. Herlihy, G. Ethington, S.J. Schnitt, N. Tung, et al., Evolutionary pathways in brca1-associated breast tumors, Cancer Discovery (2012). CD–11.

[41] S.Y. Park, M. Gönen, H.J. Kim, F. Michor, K. Polyak, Cellular and genetic diversity in the progression of in situ human breast carcinomas to an invasive phenotype, J. Clin. Invest. 120 (2) (2010) 636–644.

[42] A. Roth, J. Khattra, D. Yap, A. Wan, E. Laks, J. Biele, G. Ha, S. Aparicio, A. Bouchard-Côté, S.P. Shah, Py-clone: statistical inference of clonal population structure in cancer, Nat. Methods 11 (4) (2014) 396.

[43] B. Mlecnik, M. Tosolini, A. Kirilovsky, A. Berger, G. Bindea, T. Meatchi, P. Bruneval, Z. Trajanoski, W.H. Fridman, F. Pagès, et al., Histopathologic-based prognostic factors of colorectal cancers are associated with the state of the local immune reaction, J. Clin. Oncol. 29 (6) (2011) 610–618.

[44] J. Galon, A. Costes, F. Sanchez-Cabo, A. Kirilovsky, B. Mlecnik, C. Lagorce-Pagès, M. Tosolini, M. Camus, A. Berger, P. Wind, et al., Type, density, and location of immune cells within human colorectal tumors predict clinical outcome, Science 313 (5795) (2006) 1960–1964.

[45] J. Saltz, R. Gupta, L. Hou, T. Kurc, P. Singh, V. Nguyen, D. Samaras, K.R. Shroyer, T. Zhao, R. Batiste, et al., Spatial organization and molecular correlation of tumor-infiltrating lymphocytes using deep learning on pathology images, Cell Rep. 23 (1) (2018) 181.

[46] M. Kochi, T. Iwamoto, N. Niikura, G. Bianchini, S. Masuda, T. Mizoo, T. Nogami, T. Shien, T. Motoki, N. Taira, et al., Tumour-infiltrating lymphocytes (tils)-related genomic signature predicts chemotherapy response in breast cancer, Breast Cancer Res. Treat. 167 (1) (2018) 39–47.

CHAPTER 9

Open data and software for microscopy image analysis

Mei Chen
Microsoft, Redmond, WA, United States

Contents

1. Data is oxygen

Working with real data has always been crucial to developing computer vision algorithms that are effective in the real world. With the advent of deep learning-based data-driven approaches, having a considerable amount of real data with ground truth has become even more critical to achieving state-of-the-art performance. In fact, the latest developments in deep learning for image classification and recognition have essentially turned into a *game of data*, that is, whoever can afford the largest-scale training on the largest-labeled dataset with the largest-parameter model tops the leaderboard [1, 2].

Unlike images captured by digital cameras, quality microscopy image data need to be acquired and annotated by trained personnel. In addition to the expense of image acquisition and labeling, there is also the nontrivial cost and labor of procuring and preparing the biology samples to be imaged. This makes it ever more challenging to obtain a substantial amount of labeled microscopy image data by individual laboratories or research groups. It would benefit and help advance the field to openly share research data and software.

Efforts to make methodologically collected and annotated data publicly available for research and benchmarking existed before the popularity of deep learning, and there have been more concerted undertaking in recent years propelled by the success and promise of deep learning.

2. Open data

Multiple research groups and laboratories have made commendable efforts over the years to make their data available to the public for research purposes. Below is a nonexhaustive list of a few large repositories—new datasets are being released time and again.

Computer Vision for Microscopy Image Analysis
https://doi.org/10.1016/B978-0-12-814972-0.00009-6

- The cell image analysis archive (https://doi.org/10.17605/OSF.IO/YSAQ2)

  This is an open source dataset [3]. It consists of 49,919 phase-contrast microscope images of myoblastic stem cells (C2C12) (TIFF format, 1392×1040 pixels, 16 Bit depth) organized into 3 sets comprising 48 image sequences. For each sequence, 5000 cells were initially seeded on a 35 mm polystyrene dish and then incubated for about 72 h at 37°C. During cell growth, microscopy images were captured every 5 min using a ZEISS Axiovert 135TV Microscope. There are four culture conditions: Control (no growth factor), 50 ng/mL FGF2, 100 ng/mL BMP2, and 50 ng/mL FGF2 + 100 ng/mL BMP2, with 12 image sequences for each culture condition. There are 48 worksheet files (CSV format) detailing the pixel intensity attributes of each image sequence and used for validating individual images.

  Perhaps the most invaluable are 48 manual cell tracking annotations (XML format) generated by a team of trained personnel and additionally curated by expert annotators with at least 5 years of cell culture experience. Along with the manual tracking results, 48 computer-aided cell tracking annotations (XML format) generated using published algorithms [4–7] are provided.

  Also included are an XML Schema file (XSD format) for validating cell tracking annotations and an Adobe Acrobat file (PDF format) containing R code that enables the visualization of image sequences and tracking annotations together or separately as well as resizing of image files. Fig. 9.1 shows a few examples from the dataset demonstrating the diversity it captures.

- Spatiotemporal mitosis detection benchmark (http://media.m2i.ac.cn/mitosisdetection/download/).

  Mitosis events in one set of 16 image sequences from the above *Cell Image Analysis Archive* (four sequences for each of the four culture conditions) have been annotated and made available to the public. The annotation is captured in MATLAB files (.mat) containing matrices of size $N \times 3$, where N denotes the number of annotated mitotic events in the corresponding sequence and each row of the matrices containing the spatio-temporal coordinates of the mitotic event (t, x, y). t, starting from 1, is the frame number of the mitotic annotation while x and y are the horizontal and vertical distance

Fig. 9.1 Example images from the cell image analysis archive to illustrate the diversity of the dataset.

(in pixels) from the top-left corner of the image. A contest using this data has been organized in conjunction with the IEEE Workshop on Computer Vision for Microscopy Image Analysis (https://cvmi2019.github.io/new.html) to drive the research on spatiotemporal mitosis detection in image sequences.

- Mitosis detection in breast cancer histological images (http://ludo17.free.fr/mitos_2012/index.html).

This is an evolving dataset [8] originally proposed for the Mitosis Detection in Breast Cancer Histological Images contest held at the International Conference on Pattern Recognition in 2012 and 2014.

The dataset consists of images of hematein and eosin (H&E) stained slides of breast cancer. The images were captured using two different slide scanners with different resolutions to produce RGB images and a multispectral microscope producing images in 10 different spectral bands. In addition, for each spectral band, digitization was performed at 17 different focus planes, with each plane being separated from the other by 500 nm. For each slide, there are two RGB images produced by the scanners and 170 grey scale images for the multispectral microscope (10 spectral bands and 17 layers Z-stack for each spectral band).

Two or three pathologists have annotated mitosis manually in each selected high power field (HPF) on the images generated by the scanners and the multispectral microscope. In each slide, the pathologists selected 10 HPF at $40 \times$ magnification. These 50 HPFs contain more than 300 mitosis in total. As there are several possible shapes for mitosis, it is necessary to have a large dataset to be able to cover all the cases.

In addition to mitosis annotation, the set also provides the confidence degree for each mitosis according to pathologist agreement or disagreement, scores for nuclear pleomorphism by two or three pathologists, and values of six criteria related to nuclear pleomorphism given by three pathologists.

- Cell tracking challenge (http://celltrackingchallenge.net/)

The Cell Tracking Challenge [9] was organized in conjunction with the IEEE International Symposium on Biomedical Imaging (ISBI) in 2013, 2014, and 2015. The goal of the challenge was to make test datasets for a broad spectrum of cell-tracking applications publicly available, introduce standardized performance measures, and facilitate objective and fair comparisons of existing cell tracking systems. In October 2018, a new "spin-off" time-lapse cell segmentation benchmark was launched and initially hosted by ISBI 2019. After this launching event, both the Cell Tracking Benchmark (CTB) and the Cell Segmentation Benchmark (CSB) continue to run online and share the same datasets.

The datasets consist of two-dimensional (2D) and three-dimensional (3D) time-lapse video sequences of fluorescent counterstained nuclei or cells moving on top or immersed in a substrate, along with 2D Bright Field, Phase Contrast, and Differential Interference Contrast (DIC) microscopy videos of cells moving on a flat substrate.

The videos cover a wide range of cell types and quality (spatial and temporal resolution, noise levels etc.). In addition, 2D and 3D videos of synthetic fluorescently stained cells and nuclei of different shapes and motion patterns are also provided.

Both the original image data and all available reference annotations can be downloaded as a single ZIP archive for each training dataset.

3. Open software

Microscopy imaging has greatly advanced with the unprecedented ability to track biological phenomena in high resolution in physiologically relevant conditions. As these imaging technologies become mainstream tools for biologists, there is a strong need for software tools that drive the information workflow from image acquisition and image analysis to visualization and dissemination. Different image processing and visualization techniques need access not only to the data, but also to each other. There needs to be compatibility not only in file format but in interoperability to preserve and communicate what processing or manipulation was done to the image. There is a great opportunity in achieving this interoperability by developing tools that work together in a seamless manner to improve efficiency and effectiveness.

As Dr. Daniel Hoeppner articulated in Chapter 1, most biologists will not learn a programming language as a prerequisite to run an image-processing algorithm. Therefore, it is prudent to consider the existing software environment used in biology before launching a tool aimed at biologists as end users. Given the complexity and heterogeneity of modern microcopy imaging, it might serve the community to have more than a single software solution. The microscopy community has been adopting open source libraries including scikit-image [10], CellProfiler [11–13], and ImageJ/Fiji [14–16], or feature extractors built in-house using open source libraries (e.g., OpenCV https://opencv. org/, Java ImageIO https://docs.oracle.com/javase/7/docs/api/javax/imageio/ ImageIO.html.

Scikit-image https://scikit-image.org/ is an image-processing toolbox written in Python. Its library supports basic image manipulation and low-level processing, typically employing traditional image-processing techniques. It is community-developed and open to contributions.

For high-throughput image processing, another widely used open source package is CellProfiler https://cellprofiler.org/ [11]. The CellProfiler project team is based in the Carpenter Lab at the Broad Institute of Harvard and MIT, and the software is actively improved and maintained. It is developed for the quantitative analysis of biological images, and no prior experience in programming or computer vision is required.

Currently, the most widely used image-processing tool for biologists is ImageJ https://imagej.net/ImageJ_1.x [14]. It is an open source Java image processing program inspired by NIH Image. It runs on any computer with a Java 1.8 or later virtual machine.

Downloadable distributions are available for Windows, Mac OS X, and Linux. ImageJ has a strong, established user base, with thousands of plugins and macros for performing a wide variety of tasks. It continues to evolve through community support of new plugin development and core feature development that respond to the evolving needs of the microscopy community as FIJI [15]. Fiji is ImageJ with extras. It is a distribution of ImageJ with many plugins useful for scientific image analysis in fields such as the life sciences. It is actively maintained, with updates released often, and is the recommended version of ImageJ.

Efforts towards interoperability and extensibility in the ImageJ consortium include contribution from partners such as Cell Profiler, FIJI, KNIME https://www.knime.com/, and Open Microscopy Environment groups https://www.openmicroscopy.org/about/. Researchers are actively developing software libraries including Bio-Formats [17], ImgLib [18], and ImageJ Ops https://imagej.net/ImageJ_Ops to facilitate the analysis and visualization of microscopy image data.

The unique characteristic of this era of deep learning-based computer vision for microscopy image analysis is that there is a strong and collective effort in making both data and trained neural network models publicly and freely available, with an intent to accelerate the research development and benchmarking efforts. Such an effort will only grow in intensity, momentum and scale.

References

[1] Anonymous submission, An Image is Worth 16X16 Words: Transformers for Image Recognition at Scale, October https://openreview.net/pdf?id=YicbFdNTTy, 2020.

[2] A. Kolesnikov, L. Beyer, X. Zhai, J. Puigcerver, J. Yung, S. Gelly, N. Houlsby, Big transfer (BiT): general visual representation learning, May 2020arXiv:1912.11370 (2020).

[3] D.F.E. Ker, S. Eom, S. Sanami, R. Bise, C. Pascale, Z. Yin, S.-i. Huh, E. Osuna-Highley, S. N. Junkers, C.J. Helfrich, P.Y. Liang, J. Pan, S. Jeong, S.S. Kang, J. Liu, R. Nicholson, M. F. Sandbothe, P.T. Van, A. Liu, M. Chen, T. Kanade, L.E. Weiss, P.G. Campbell, Phase contrast time-lapse microscopy datasets with automated and manual cell tracking annotations. Sci. Data 5 (2018) 180237, https://doi.org/10.1038/sdata.2018.237.

[4] S. Huh, D.F. Ker, R. Bise, M. Chen, T. Kanade, Automated mitosis detection of stem cell populations in phase-contrast microscopy images, IEEE Trans. Med. Imaging 30 (2011) 586–596.

[5] T. Kanade, Z. Yin, R. Bise, S. Huh, S. Eom, M.F. Sandbothe, M. Chen, Cell image analysis: algorithms, system and applications, in: IEEE Workshop on Applications of Computer Vision, 2011. https://ieeexplore.ieee.org/document/5711528/.

[6] K. Li, M. Chen, T. Kanade, Cell population tracking and lineage construction with spatiotemporal context, Med. Image Anal. 12 (2008) 546–566.

[7] Z. Yin, T. Kanade, M. Chen, Understanding the phase contrast optics to restore artifact-free microscopy images for segmentation, Med. Image Anal. 16 (5) (2012) 1047–1062.

[8] M.N. Gurcan, L.E. Boucheron, A. Can, A. Madabhushi, N.M. Rajpoot, B. Yener, Histopathological image analysis: a review, IEEE Rev. Biomed. Eng. 2 (2009) 147–171.

[9] Ulman, et al., An objective comparison of cell-tracking algorithms, Nat. Methods 14 (12) (2017).

[10] S. van der Walt, J.L. Schönberger, J. Nunez-Iglesias, F. Boulogne, J.D. Warner, N. Yager, E. Gouillart, T. Yu, the scikit-image contributors, scikit-image: image processing in Python. PeerJ 2 (e453) (2014), https://doi.org/10.7717/peerj.453.

[11] T.R. Jones, I.H. Kang, D.B. Wheeler, R.A. Lindquist, A. Papallo, D.M. Sabatini, P. Golland, A. E. Carpenter, CellProfiler analyst: data exploration and analysis software for complex image-based screens, BMC Bioinformatics 9 (1) (2008) 482, https://doi.org/10.1186/1471-2105-9-482. 19014601 PMC2614436.

[12] A.E. Carpenter, T.R. Jones, M.R. Lamprecht, C. Clarke, I.H. Kang, O. Friman, D.A. Guertin, J. H. Chang, R.A. Lindquist, J. Moffat, P. Golland, D.M. Sabatini, Cell Profiler: image analysis software for identifying and quantifying cell phenotypes, Genome Biol. 7 (10) (2006) R10.

[13] A.E. Carpenter, L. Kamentsky, K.W. Eliceiri, A call for bioimaging software usability, Nat. Methods 9 (7) (2012) 666–670.

[14] C.A. Schneider, W.S. Rasband, K.W. Eliceiri, NIH Image to ImageJ: 25 years of image analysis, Nat Methods 9 (7) (2012) 671–675.22930834.

[15] J. Schindelin, C.T. Rueden, M.C. Hiner, K.W. Eliceiri, The ImageJ ecosystem: an open platform for biomedical image analysis. Mol. Reprod. Dev. 82 (7–8) (2015) 518–529, https://doi.org/10.1002/mrd.22489 Epub 2015 Jul 7. PMID: 26153368; PMCID: PMC5428984.

[16] J. Schindelin, I. Arganda-Carreras, E. Frise, V. Kaynig, M. Longair, T. Pietzsch, S. Preibisch, C. Rueden, S. Saalfeld, B. Schmid, J.-Y. Tinevez, D.J. White, V. Hartenstein, K. Eliceiri, P. Tomancak, A. Cardona, Fiji: an open-source platform for biological-image analysis, Nat. Methods 9 (7) (2012) 676–682.

[17] M. Linkert, C.T. Rueden, C. Allan, et al., Metadata matters: access to image data in the real world, J. Cell Biol. 189 (5) (2010) 777–782.20513764.

[18] T. Pietzsch, S. Preibisch, P. Tomančák, S. Saalfeld, ImgLib2—generic image processing in Java, Bioinformatics 28 (22) (2012) 3009–3011.

Index

Note: Page numbers followed by *f* indicate figures, *t* indicate tables, and *b* indicate boxes.

Printed in the United States
By Bookmasters